DANCE OF THE SEXES

| | | ALICE MUNRO

DANCE OF THE SEXES

| | | Art and Gender in the
Fiction of Alice Munro

BEVERLY J. RASPORICH

| | | THE UNIVERSITY OF ALBERTA PRESS

First published by
The University of Alberta Press
Athabasca Hall
Edmonton, Alberta
Canada T6G 2E8

Copyright © The University of Alberta Press 1990

ISBN 0-88864-207-5 cloth
ISBN 0-88864-208-3 paper

CANADIAN CATALOGUING IN PUBLICATION DATA
Rasporich, Beverly Jean.
  Dance of the sexes

Includes bibliographical references.
ISBN 0-88864-207-5 (bound).—ISBN 0-88864-208-3 (pbk.)

  1. Munro, Alice, 1931– Criticism and
interpretation.   2. Women in literature.   3. Sex in
literature.   I. Title.
PR8576.U57Z876 1990   C813'.54   C89-091575-X
PR9199.3.M66Z876 1990

Frontispiece photograph: R.J. Nephew Photography
Cover illustration: Paul Rasporich
Typesetting by The Typeworks, Vancouver, British Columbia, Canada

Printed by Hignell Printing Ltd., Winnipeg, Manitoba, Canada

For my grandmother
Pearl Thompson Traer

Sunset and evening star,
And one clear call for thee.

CONTENTS

| | | | PREFACE

My motive in writing this book was twofold. First, I wanted to pay tribute to one of Canada's most accomplished contemporary writers, Alice Munro. I first excitedly discovered her work, just as it began to be recognized, in the short story "Postcard" published in 1968 in the Canadian literary magazine *The Tamarack Review*. Since that time Munro's reputation has grown steadily. A three time winner of the Governor General's Award for fiction, in 1968 for *Dance of the Happy Shades*, in 1978 for *Who Do You Think You Are?*, in 1986 for *The Progress of Love* and nominated in 1983 for *The Moons of Jupiter*, Munro has won many accolades both within and without the country. *Dance of the Happy Shades* won the Great Lakes Colleges Association New Writer's Award, *Lives of Girls and Women* the 1971–72 Canadian Booksellers Award, and *Who Do You Think You Are?* was nominated for the Booker Award in Britain. In 1977 Alice Munro was awarded the Canada-Australia Literary Prize and in 1986 the Marian Engel Award. A regular contributor to *The New Yorker*, her work highly coveted by magazines in Canada and the United States,

Munro has been invited to speak in several countries, and her work has been translated into various languages, including Norwegian and Russian.

If the literary critic is motivated to celebrate an author, naturally he or she writes because he or she believes that he or she can lend insight into appreciation. My aspiration is no different, excepting perhaps that the emphasis is on the she. It seemed to me, in fact, that much of the criticism of Munro's work had been written with an odd neutrality, and curiously so, since Munro is a passionate woman writing passionately about women. My second motive, then, was to investigate the feminist possibilities of her art, not in a dogmatic or exaggerated way, not by shoe-horning and squeezing her fiction into a feminist's Cinderella slipper, but by attempting an honest fit. To this end, I have focused on the gender implications of Munro's work, but not exclusively or single-mindedly. If my analyses are occasionally tentative or shift onto more neutral asexual ground, it is because I am not absolutely certain that Munro as an artist thinks and creates only in sexual terms. On the other hand, her gender does color and influence her art in dominant and dramatic ways. I hope that this book will serve primarily, then, as an introduction to Munro's female, feminine and feminist sensibilities as they affect fictional form, technique and content.

The intended audience for this text includes interested readers of Munro and those serious students who come fresh to her fiction at junior colleges and universities. This includes male readers whose masculine conditioning and male way of experiencing and interpreting the world may prevent them from reading the fiction of Alice Munro in its fullest sense. My aim has been to reach as general an audience as possible, as well as to interpret Munro's art as broadly as possible through the perspective of gender. This is reflected in my critical approach. I do rely on the exciting, rapidly developing areas of feminist critical inquiry and feminist literary theory, but my study is not meant to develop the field of this critical scholarship as such. I am primarily concerned with introducing the student of feminist literature, rather than the expert, to the imaginative female worlds of Alice Munro.

For assisting me in this endeavor, I extend my thanks to Alice Munro herself who offered me encouragement and interview time. I am also indebted to the Canada Council Explorations Programme for awarding me an initial grant to pursue this project, to Hugh Dempsey and Robert Kroetsch for their recommendations, to Dr. Hallvard Dahlie for his dialogues about Canadian literature, to Dr. Marsha Hanen and the late Dr. Charles Steele for their support, and to Doreen Nordquist and Jo-Anne Kabeary for the typing of several drafts of the manuscript. Of great assistance to me, as well, were the comments of several readers, including those from the University of Alberta Press Committee. I wish also to acknowledge the Killam Foundation and the University of Calgary for granting me a Killam Fellowship and leave time so that I might complete this text, and the University of Calgary for a grant in aid of publication. I am grateful to the staff, Special Collections Division, University of Calgary Library, who were helpful in providing access to the Alice Munro papers, and to Alice Munro for permission to publish from them. Finally, a special thanks to my husband, Anthony, my four children, my parents, and my friend Marilyn Strachan for their faith in me and this project. An earlier version of a part of Chapter Two was published as "Child Women and Primitives" in *Atlantis* 1, no. 2 (Spring, 1976).

| | | | INTRODUCTION

When I was a girl growing up in the fifties in small town Ontario, my girlfriend and I spent countless hours with the Eaton's catalogue playing a simple game which we called fathers, mothers and babies. A father was dutifully selected from the section advertising men's suits and then ignored; a beautiful young model was chosen as mother and various babies and children assigned to her; their clothes—exotic lingerie for the mother and cute, swaddling dress for the babies—were decided upon by each of us taking a turn, both of us close to religious delight. While my friend, like Naomi in Alice Munro's *Lives of Girls and Women,* went on to play out this role with a vengeance in her adult life, I, like Del Jordan, found myself dissatisfied with the limitedness of this game. The world of books, discovered somewhat haphazardly in local library and classroom, suggested other, grander possibilities. Looking backwards, I wonder now how I might have assimilated as my own the fiction of masculine conquest: the thrilling epic of Captain Ahab in *Moby Dick,* the male endurance and enterprise of Hemingway's characters, the grimy, criminal worlds of Graham Greene's soldiers of fortune. Did I notice that this action and excitement was the province of men, not women, and that I, as a woman, was outside of even its lesser thrilling possibilities both in fiction and fact? I do not know. I do know now that in most of the books I read in youth, women found no true existence as individuals and that as I matured, I wanted to complain about a literature which pictures a world in which the role of woman is minimized and her character is interpreted through the reality of a man's sexuality. The amazing wonder and, for that matter, grace of Alice Munro's fiction is that it did and does articulate what I conceived to be my own eccentric, isolated experience and its silent protest. Literary art must interpret life in some way, and it is this pursuit of the truth about women which is one of the salient features of the work of Alice Munro.

Munro has an acute social intuition which depends on her personal response to the environment she knows best. Her method is not that of the didactic social critic, but that of the literary artist who filters and refracts society through the prism of her own imagination and experience. Acknowledging in an early interview that she writes from her own roots, that of small town Ontario, Munro explains, "I don't generalize. I don't see beyond."[1] However private and unique her visions seem to be, readers of Munro are stunned by her capacity to go beyond. They consistently praise her sensitivity to social history and psychology, recorded in her precisely remembered depictions of the fading world of the universal North American town of the forties and fifties, of the childhood experiences and adolescent pains attached to this time and place, and for many female readers, in the chronicle of the realistic psychology of a central female voice, which, originating in a small town past, fights to shake free of conventional sexual roles in order to achieve independence and maturity in a modern, urban context.

The metamorphosis of this voice which informs Munro's literature, which is threaded through her stories and defines the two major heroines of her longer fictions, her modern versions of "novels," Del Jordan of *Lives of Girls and Women* and Rose of *Who Do You Think You Are?*, is a literary chapter of an ongoing feminist social history. The novel has traditionally been the looking glass of the character of society and its dominant culture and, if we are to believe Simone de Beauvoir's conviction that since primitive time society has always been male and women's place relegated outside of it, then we can expect that society's fiction has been predictably limited in its representation of the role and function of women. De Beauvoir explains how even the mythology of female power in ancient civilizations is misleading:

> the Golden Age of Woman is only a myth. To say that woman was the *Other* is to say that there did not exist between the sexes a reciprocal relation: Earth, Mother, Goddess—she was no fellow creature in man's eyes; it was *beyond* the human realm that her power was affirmed, and she was therefore *outside of* that realm. Society has always been male; political power has always been in the hands of men. "Public or simply social authority always belongs to men," declares Levi-Strauss at the end of his study of primitive societies.[2]

Certainly in the eighteenth and nineteenth centuries the novel sheltered a masculine Christian interpretation of woman, largely reaffirming for Western bourgeois society its view of her as a dependent guardian of the domestic keep, of children and morality—a sometime saint, or, conversely, as the seductive old Eve. From the prostitute Moll Flanders in Daniel Defoe's rudimentary novel of the same name to Jane Austen's struggling-to-be-recognized domestic heroines, women in pretwentieth century fiction have been essentially portrayed in the roles of outrageous, socially déclassé whore or the respectable, dependent woman of virtue, versions of Mary Magdalene or the sainted mother; sometimes there has even been the liberal exception, a more modern amalgam of both as that of Nathaniel Hawthorne's New World Eros-mother, Hester Prynne, of *The Scarlet Letter*. Whatever function or combination of functions of saint or whore women have played out in fiction, they have invariably been, to use the phrase of the narrator in Munro's short story "Material," "at the mercy."[3]

Twentieth century fiction has also been a social indicator and, as an agent and the medium of the sexual revolution, has contributed to the disintegration of the frozen sexual roles of Victorian society. Even as the mother of Munro's heroine, Del Jordan, in *Lives*, echoes the many voices of female discontent when she gravely comments, "There is a change coming I think in the lives of girls and women,"[4] we, as readers, experience the revolutionary change through a wide range of fiction, from uncomplicated stories of female alienation in popular women's magazines to angry polemical narratives written by the true daughters of the revolution. Although some writers, and Munro is not one of them, make easy claim to knowing the true female identity and understanding the necessities for the rightful liberation of women, essentially what the sexual revolution has meant for women, society at large, and its literature is an unsettling process of sexual redefinition. Many of the best writers, responding to and precipitating this process, have consequently produced a body of literature which dramatizes the uncertain, complicated psychologies and conflicts of modern women.

Yet, despite the *angst* of the modern heroine, she continues to quest self-fulfillment. Acknowledging, as Del Jordan's mother does, that: "All women has had up 'till now has been their connection with men" (*Lives*, 146), the modern heroine renounces the subordinate, nurturing role of the past in favor of independence, social authority and her own humanity. Slamming the door of her doll's house, as did Ibsen's lonely Norah a century earlier, she has adopted what psychoanalysts have called the "male principle of exploit"[5] which simply put in laymen's language is the impulse to act rather than the willingness to be acted upon.

What assuming the principle of exploit has meant for the growing number of female writers is daring to write in concert about women's concerns being at the heart of things rather than at the periphery; it has meant challenging a previous literature which defined women according to male-directed fantasies and perspectives. While an earlier writer like Virginia Woolf was ultimately uncomfortable with feminine and feminist novels, preferring instead to accommodate a masculine system by advocating a sexless art of androgynous values, contemporary writers such as Margaret Drabble, Doris Lessing and Alice Munro's Canadian counterparts, Margaret Laurence, Margaret Atwood, Adele Wiseman, Jane Rule, Audrey Thomas, Marian Engel and Aritha van Herk have striven for authentic presentations of the interior lives of girls and women. In the last two decades, feminism and art have proved not to be incompatible, and a web of authorial sisterhood has been firmly established.

Under the umbrella of feminism, feminist literary criticism has also come of age, disclosing exciting, sometimes startling new paradigms of gender related experience in art, often in conjunction with other dominant modes of literary criticism, and certainly producing a body of impressive literary scholarship in a very short period of time. One particularly influential school has been the French, language-centered critics, who, like Julia Kristeva and Hélène Cixous, have identified "*l'écriture féminine*," a practice of writing "in the feminine" as one which "undermines the linguistic, syntactical and metaphysical conventions of Western narrative"[6] and is practiced by avant-garde writers, both male and female. Influenced in their concern with language by the neo-Freudian Jacques Lacan, the deconstructionist philosopher Jacques Derrida and the structuralist critic Roland Barthes, French feminist theorists have been remarkable leaders in contemporary intellectual thought, and exercise a strong influence on many feminist critics in Britain and America.

Although there are many internal differences between Anglo-American critics, as Elaine Showalter explains, in a general way Anglo-American feminist criticism "tries to recover women's historical experiences as readers and writers."[7] Her own work has led the way. In her classic work A Literature of Their Own—British Women Writers From Bronte to Lessing, Showalter reclaims the female tradition in writing by examining the special female self-awareness that emerges through literature in every period. Hers is a revisionist literary history that includes the following largely accepted historical definition of the three stages of writing for British authors. The first Feminine Stage (historically from the appearance of the male pseudonym in the 1840s to the death of George Eliot in 1880) involves imitation of the prevailing modes of the dominant tradition and internalization of its standards of art and its view of social roles; the Feminist phase (winning of the vote—1880–1920) is one of protest against these standards and values while the Female phase (1920 to the present, with a new stage of self-awareness about 1960) is a phase of self-discovery, a search for identity.[8]

All three phases may be discernible and may even collapse into one another in the work of a single feminist author outside the British tradition, as they do in the work of Alice Munro. Munro's first fascination with the Female Gothic mode and the Gothic villain as lover,[9] particularly in Lives, is outlined in Chapter Four and illustrates both her imitation of a tradition, albeit a subgenre, and her revolt against it. Most importantly, her work belongs to that body of female writing Showalter defines as having been established from 1960 on. The search for identity, the quest for definition and place has been the central ongoing theme of Munro's fiction. And as her heroines pass hopefully through and ironically beyond the traditional passive fantasies of waiting for Prince Charming, for Darcy from Pride and Prejudice in "An Ounce of Cure,"[10] or the chivalric knight from Tennyson's "silly" poem "Mariana" (Lives, 200), they begin to take charge of their own lives and pass into social history. Liberated into action, they advance a modern quest and a new mythology which is equally as moving, profound and *heroic* in the lives of girls and women as traditional epic masculine odysseys have been.

My own critical approach in this study of the feminine, feminist and female features of Munro's art does not belong to any one school, yet it would seem not to be entirely out of the mainstream of feminist criticism. It is one that Annette Kolodny has argued for, that of a "pluralism, responsive to the possibilities of multiple critical schools and methods, but captive of none, recognizing that the many tools needed for our analysis will necessarily be largely inherited and only partly of our own making." I am in full agreement with Kolodny that "Any text we deem worthy of our critical attention is usually, after all, a locus of many and varied kinds of personal, thematic, stylistic, structural, rhetorical relationships."[11] I would argue for a further broadening, interdisciplinary approach to feminist scholarship, particularly in the interests of the general reader and novice student, for whom this particular book is intended. A literary study need not be exclusively an exercise in literary methodology, particularly if one considers that the author of the text may have sweeping intellectual interests and is the recipient of many, varied influences. Scholarship and parallels drawn from other disciplines can illuminate the literary text and I have used some sociological analysis, folklore scholarship and peripheral references to painting, in just this way. Neither is this approach out-of-step with the philosophic currents of feminist thought as it intersects with postmodern evaluation, particularly in Canada. Linda Hutcheon asserts that the liberal humanist tradition of Western culture has been a male homogenizing system which has stressed the principle of universality and which is now giving way to a more diversified concept of experience. Uniformity and unity are no longer *prima-facie* values. Borders are being broken down and merging, including those between disciplines, "to form a new theoretical frame of reference within which postmodern literature is both written and read."[12]

Also, my use of the term "feminine" should not be confused with Showalter's historical/literary labelling of a fictional stage in writing. I am using feminine in the more general sense of the word, the meaning of which is rooted in the sociology of gender. Femininity is described by Susan Brownmiller, remembering being trained into it as a young woman, as a "brilliant, subtle esthetic that was bafflingly inconsistent at the same time that it was minutely, demandingly concrete, a rigid code of appearance and behaviour defined by do's and don't-do's."[13] Femininity, then, is learned behavior and is equivalent to modes of perceiving, thinking and acting that the larger society demands of women to realize the roles assigned to them. Femininity is of major interest to Munro who questions and revolts against its imprisoning effects, but as I explain throughout the text, and particularly in Chapter Three, understands its possibilities as a "brilliant subtle esthetic."

Furthermore, Munro and her heroines do not easily, or clearly always want to, divest themselves of their femininity. The concept of love itself, the persistent concern with the sexual dance in Munro's art, is understood by feminist thinkers to be one of the primary concerns of femininity. It is a social-psychological requirement and expectation that women devote themselves to love. Brownmiller explains: "The territory of the heart is admittedly a province that is open to all, but women alone are expected to make an obsessional career of its exploration, to find whatever adventure, power, fulfillment or tragedy that life has to offer within its bounds."[14] Although Munro's adventurous heroines often angrily move beyond wearing their hearts on their sleeves, in the author's continuing concern with the territory of the heart as fictional subject, she remains, paradoxically, something of a "feminine" author.

One of the bordering concepts of my analysis of Munro as a female artist, although I certainly have not exhausted it, is that which many feminist thinkers have claimed as theory: that is, women's writing proceeds from the female body. As Susan Gubar argues about creativity, "many women experience their own bodies as the only available medium for their art, with the result that the distance between the woman artist and her art is radically diminished."[15] There is no doubt that Alice Munro does write the body in a number of ways. What is most obvious is that the *corpus* of Munro's six collected works is constructed through the physical aging of herself and her heroines. *Dance of the Happy Shades* restores childhood experience; *Lives of Girls and Women* revives adolescent discovery; *Something I've Been Meaning to Tell You* and *Who Do You Think You Are?* advance heroines into midlife and *The Moons of Jupiter* and *The Progress of Love* are menopausal progressions.

Writing the body also partly explains the several levels of reality in Munro's fiction. The body is the central metaphor of narrative structuring and beneath the skin of carefully documented social realities and physical places that have contributed to Munro's reputation as representer of her time and locale are covert, secretive, interior spaces: these are identified in my analysis as subtexts of psychological landscapes and a mythic pagan world where ordinary characters occupy another dimension as earth mothers and primitive, sisterly subdeities, substantiating the maternal principle and the author as Mother-Goddess behind the text. Throughout Munro's stories, and my own considerations of them, certain rhetorical strategies, principles and images are also highlighted as illustrative of female physicality and writing the body. The most explicit of these is the proliferation of images of severed or isolated body parts, particularly in her mature work. In *The Progress of Love*, for example, skin and genitals and head are stripped from the body in separate and separated images, disclosing a profound understanding and anxiety on Munro's part that in life, as "in art for a long time men have fragmented, distorted and cut women's bodies into pieces of false perspective."[16]

I am well aware that "writing the body" can be taken much farther through text-centered criticism, through rhetorical and syntactical analyses of Munro's texts as self-reflexive modes of the act of literary creation and that various theorists, including the following, have written extensively on the subject of the text as body. Roland Barthes has sensitized us in *The Pleasure of the Text* to the erotic pleasure of reading the "body" of texts, and radical feminist theorists have postulated that *écriture féminine* is connected to the rhythms of the female body and to sexual pleasure (*jouissance*), with female writers being particularly disposed to what amounts to subversive writing in their dislocations of text. This last argument is particularly compelling in the light of another, that there has been a longstanding sexual definition of writing with the text thought of as a blank, virginal (read female) page and the pen—penis as an active extension of the active creative artist (read male). For critics like Susan Gubar, this tradition plainly excludes women from the creation of culture, clearly also places the female author in a trying position when attempting to assume authorship, with the subject of her authorship becoming the subject of her work. Although I realize the possibility and importance of what might be an exhaustive study on the female artist as figure and text in the fiction of Alice Munro, that is another book.

Rather than limiting my study to a single theme or thesis appropriate to feminist scholarship, which for me, in any case, seems something of a phallocentric demand, I have chosen to approach Munro as a female artist, in the contemporary feminist spirit of her own work, from a number of different angles. Chapter Two focuses thematically on the feminist, or in Showalter's terms, female, quest in her six works for female independence, identity, and authority. Chapter Three looks at Munro both as folk artist and ironist, definitions which underline the feminine and feminist dimensions of her art and Chapter Four, beginning with the neutral, critical term of regionalist that has been often applied to Munro, shifts into discussions of the gender implications of place including writing the body, in all of her collected works to date. Chapter Five is a more direct consideration of some aesthetic and stylistic features that seem to me to be clearly influenced by her sex.

I have begun with a first chapter on the personal Munro because I believe as Susan Gubar does that currently, at least, the distance between the woman artist and her art is minimal. The inclusion of the subjective, personal expressions of the author may also be helpful in advancing an understanding of the female authorial "I." As Linda Hutcheon argues, historically, the Western liberal humanist tradition has defined "subjectivity" according to the masculine experience of rationality, individuality and power. Writing "women," then, "must define their subjectivity before they can question it; they must first assert the selfhood they have been denied by the dominant culture" before they can contest it.[17] I am also of the opinion that for the feminist critic, the new company of female authors has to be as interesting and as worthy of study as their heroines. Although we understand that the private expression of the romantic poet was extremely subjective, we also know that he belonged to a literary movement greater than himself and that he felt the influences of the literary company he was exposed to and kept. He felt the social winds of his macrosociety, even as he developed as the individual artist. In the same way, the feminist writers of the late twentieth century will be fully understood by future generations. It is important then, as Elaine Showalter has suggested "to see the woman novelist against the backdrop of the women of her time"[18] including other authors, and to do so it is necessary to record at every opportunity the private and public lives of today's literary women. In 1981 Alice Munro goes to China, meets the radical feminist writer Ding Ling, and gives a speech in which she addresses the female experience; quoting Jean Rhys, she claims: "I write about myself because I am the only truth I know" and later, "I work in the dark."[19] Who, then, is this lady of the dark whose connection with a Chinese author has been drawn by the international female community of her time, and what can she personally tell us about being an artist and woman of her day?

| 1 | ALICE: THE WOMAN
BEHIND THE ART

The first of my many images of Alice Munro is borrowed. I initially met her quite by accident, in January of 1980, on a crowded train between Thunder Bay and Calgary. I should say that my husband first met her for as he struggled out of a train bedroom into the narrow corridor with our young son, he recognized a dark-haired, attractive woman in passing as Alice Munro. It is his image of an upturned face, in which he saw obvious maternal delight in the presence of a child, that was passed on to me.

My second image is that of a quick helper who, used to serving, moved quickly into my kitchen to assist me in opening a difficult bottle of wine after I had invited her over to my home to interview her in February 1981. If I was tense and worried about entertaining a celebrated Canadian author, she was eager to put me at my ease by very kindly assuring me that her own good friendship with the Canadian writer, Audrey Thomas, began in such a natural, comic, bumbling moment. Audrey, she explained, had come to visit her for the first time in Vancouver and when she, Alice, had gone to the refrigerator to get her a drink, she accidently dumped its contents, relaxing and amusing them both.

My third image came later. We were both in Toronto in June 1982, and although she had come into town from Clinton, where she lives, to a hectic schedule which included a CBC interview, she agreed to dinner together, and a taped interview back at an apartment in a seedy section of town, that she claimed was on loan from an artist friend. Here she was vivacious, friendly and unguarded, treating me like an old friend and female confidante. One of the first things she shared with me was that she had recently bought a blouse, with real lace, cheaply, at one of the nearby secondhand stores and later, as we walked together through a street of derelicts and down-and-outers, that once she had been somewhat frightened when she was followed by a man here, but he was harmless and she shooed him off "poor thing, like a dog." A few weeks earlier I had seen her photograph in a Toronto newspaper: stylishly, appropriately gowned, she and Maureen Forrester were cutting a huge birthday cake in an official Ottawa celebration of the arts in Canada. My final image of her, however, is that of an adventurous, somewhat down-at-heel country woman in slacks and rumpled blouse, suddenly remembering to take off a string of cheap colored beads as we left her city friend's apartment, explaining that she had been invited to use whatever was there that pleased her.

In light of these three meetings, I am tempted, as most critic-admirers of a particular author are, to characterize the real Alice Munro, and by so doing capture for her reading audience the essence of the personality behind the art. The temptation is to simplify, to ask which of these faces—maternalist, serving member of the sisterhood, bohemian artist, Canadian celebrity, country cousin—is the truest? Ultimately, however, this attempt to "catch" her person is to fall into the same trap that she alerts her reader to in her fiction, that is, to think twice about judging a female author by her cover. Munro may personally fulfill all of these roles; she may even be the sum total of such "parts." Yet, despite her extraordinary emotional honesty, she is a complicated woman of many poses, one who willingly admits that it is very possible to "feel yourself somehow the same person in different disguises at different periods in your life." Aspiring women understand well enough this posture of disguise, the female role playing which does not necessarily correspond with who or what they think they really are. They understand, too, that this tension can be most acutely felt by the female artist, particularly if she has known, as Munro has, the conflicts and tensions between the conventional, passive role of woman and that of the active female author, a lifestyle which until very recently has been isolating and difficult in a male-sponsored world.

On the one hand, then, Munro has been, and still is, the traditional woman, used to nurturing, devoted to her children, her second husband and domestic routine. She is a woman who lived a fairly conventional married life until the age of forty when she wrote the final draft of *Lives of Girls and Women* and discovered that combining marriage, motherhood and authorship was close to impossible. Caring and cooking for her three children and a friend's as well, she worked regularly from nine to two A.M., sleeping on the average four hours a night. Finding herself overworked with her first marriage over, she admits that it took her two years to recover physically from the cumulative strain. In 1981 she insists,

> I'm much more aware of people and human relationships than when I was younger, and I want my children to be happy and I want my marriage to be good. I probably want these things in a far more conscious way, in a deeper way, than I did when I was a young woman. The dutiful, young mother was a mask for a very strong drive—a kind of monomania about being a writer.

Munro's accommodating femininity and aspirations to a "normal" life, however, can be misleading, prompting the kind of critical response offered in an offhand, pejorative way to me by one male English professor, a few years ago that she was merely a "housewife writer."

Actually, while Munro is mother, wife and homemaker who is seemingly unimpressed with her own success, she is neither the naive intellectual nor casual artist she sometimes pretends to be. She is an extremely sophisticated, literate and literary woman, an obsessively dedicated writer who has served a long apprenticeship, writing continuously since she was fourteen years old, a woman with an exacting mind when it comes to a discussion of her work and the literary process, and however careful she is of other's feelings, quietly does not suffer either imprecise thinkers or pretentious people gladly.

Her lack of pretension and sympathy for the socially déclassé probably derive from a childhood that was characterized by extreme poverty and a feeling of dead-endedness. All of her early years were spent in Wingham, Ontario, where her father was a fox farmer during the Depression and after he went bankrupt in the postwar years, a foundry worker and then a turkey farmer. Her early memories are those of living in a kind of limbo, in a physical setting outside of town:

> at the end of a dead-end road that didn't lead out to the country because the river curved around and cut us off, and it was sort of the last reaches of the town, and the road was like the Flats Road. I've used this same community in *Who Do You Think You Are?* A rural slum wouldn't quite describe it. It wasn't part of the town and there were a lot of boot-leggers. And also this was the tail end of the Depression. So there were a lot of people who were just out of work, but a lot of pretty marginal type people tended to live in this area—so that it was a very different commu-nity from the town or the surrounding farming community.

The family home, an old red brick Ontario building, fairly recently sold out of the family, is also vividly recalled by Munro. Cold, inconvenient, hardly modernized except for a bathroom put in during a brief period of prosperity when she was twelve, it showed, by the end of her teens, "ter-rific effects of poverty both in and out" despite her mother's shrewdness in "trading off" for some Victorian antiques to give it elegance. Nonetheless, Munro's artistic sensibility seemed to be encouraged by the house's loca-tion and view, for, "West of us was nothing but fields and the river and hills... in the farming country, it's rare to find this kind of view. It was like a world view to me as a child, and it was like the scene for the end of the world when the sun went down... you could always see the sunsets."

Munro acquired another kind of world view in the Lower Town School which she attended for three years before her mother, worried about the kind of ungenteel education she was getting, scraped together the extra fees to send her to the Wingham Public School. A sensitive and protected child, she was shocked by her first exposure to school, by the terrific violence and vulgarity of its elementary life: "the impact was enormous—of a very frightening and unintelligible but interesting world, and in the first six months there I probably learned more than I ever have at any other time in my life." Because she was going to be the only child in grade two, the teacher pushed her ahead. As a result, she was not only younger than those in her grade in Wingham Public School, she had "embarrassing gaps," like subtraction, in her education. Most of her memories of public school are of awkward and humiliating moments, of her own extreme physical clumsiness, of social dislocation, unsympathetic teachers and unjust punishments; and such traumatic incidents are often painfully reworked in her fiction.

Her family life was somewhat more secure, and extended from her younger brother Bill and sister Sheila, to her father Robert Laidlaw, and her mother Anne Clarke Chamney, who were third cousins, to her paternal grandmother Sarah Jane Code, and Sara Jane's sister, Munro's great aunt; these two women were important and close to the immediate family. While Munro's paternal grandfather was Scottish, his wife was of Irish descent, as were her mother's parents who came from the Ottawa Valley. As a child, she visited the Ottawa Valley relatives several times. Protestant Irish, they were different from her father's controlled and pragmatic Scottish side. Colorful and of somewhat belligerent attitudes towards the French and Catholics, they liked to celebrate, to sing, to dance, and to take a drink. Munro sees herself as being brought up amongst these relatives "in the conventional Protestant way" through the United Church and its societies such as C.G.I.T. (Canadian Girls in Training). Like her heroine, Del Jordan, however, she began to question and distance herself from this society at an early age, losing her religious faith, for example, when she was twelve or thirteen. In fact, Munro displays the disquiet and questioning apprehension of the natural poet in her earliest first memory of life's mystery, one which she embarrassedly recounts because it is "so ridiculous, so rural, so very Canadian." As a memory of impending female death, it would also seem to be a telling beginning in the development of Munro's female consciousness and authorial psyche:

It's an Ottawa Valley memory because I suppose being there on a visit there with my mother, things were more noticeable. And I know when it was, I was two and one half. And I was leaning over the rails of the pigpen watching my Uncle Joe, my mother's brother, slosh food into the pigs I mean that's just a pictorial memory . . . I can't remember how I felt about the pigs but I can remember some slight feeling about my grandmother who was dying at that time, and I was put to have my nap with her. But just a feeling of age and some mystery or some kind of queasy feeling.

Although Munro claims that there was no active support of the arts in her family and that "I wouldn't have had the idea that it was an activity for ordinary people," there was at least one example of a genteel, Anglo-Saxon maiden aunt who liked to draw and more importantly, at least in retrospective discovery for Munro herself, the tradition of a writer in the family. Through genealogical research, Munro has drawn the Laidlaw line back to the eighteenth century writer James Hogg, whose mother was a Laidlaw. With obvious pride in both creative, oral, and female source, Munro speculates that "I think they were a family of shepherds where there had been a long preservation of ballads and stories spoken, the spoken word, not written down. But the mother was a noted storyteller, and no doubt some of the stories Hogg used were from her." Munro's own father, Robert Laidlaw, began to write when he was seventy. Perhaps stimulated by his daughter's success, he began writing little things for a local monthly, *The Village Squire*, out of Blyth. His first and only full-length work, *The McGregors*, was written when he was seventy-four in the last year of his life, and has been published posthumously.

Munro is proud of her father's facility for storytelling, if somewhat saddened that it was a latent, stillborn talent for most of his life:

[The McGregors] came from a short story. He had written a story which was about the old man's death, which is the way the book ends, and then he began expanding it. As he got nearer the end, he became... I've never known a writer more obsessed with his work. I remember visiting him in the hospital in March, I guess it was... All this time his heart condition was worsening. . . . And he immediately sat on the side of the hospital bed in his pajamas and wanted to know what I thought of the latest draft of the book.

After Munro offered him "a reader's criticism, not a very technical criticism," Munro's father wrote steadily in the two weeks before an operation and his death, "grasping all kinds of complicated things [fictional techniques] right at the end." A master of charming and comic letters sent to his daughter over the years, Munro's obviously loving conviction is "that he had all those things you can't teach people, like a feeling for rhythm in prose. He really had this gift all his life."

Munro's father, whom she sees to have been much like herself, may have shared his literary disposition, but it is her mother, stricken with Parkinson's disease when Munro was a young girl, who seems the stronger figure out of memory and a certain recurring presence in her fiction. Anne Clarke Chamney was ambitious, a career woman, even a businesswoman by inclination, who, in her youth, went west to Alberta as a public school teacher and did not marry Robert Laidlaw until she was thirty. A forceful and charming personality, she was not inclined to accept a life of poverty easily. At one period when Munro's father was failing economically at fox farming, she took the initiative, had the fox skins made into the then fashionable fox-head scarfs, and easily sold them door-to-door with a "high class demeanour" and a sales pitch that began, "I've heard from so and so that you are interested..." According to her daughter she was an "organizing force" and "theatrical personality" who channeled her energies, as was expected of a conventional woman of the times, into domestic life such as the making of her children's clothing which were very often of an elaborate and pretty costume type for Alice. Her tragedy was the slow, degenerative illness which gradually killed her, a situation which not only forced her daughter into early household responsibilities, but left her with the conforming desire, when she herself became a mother, to provide a normal, conventional life for her children, to be dutiful and average for them so that "they wouldn't have any kind of problem from having a weird mother."

Although Munro is affectionate about both her parents, there is a melancholy note in her evaluation of the traditional sexual roles society forced them to play out in their marriage, and in their relationship with their children. Her mother she believes was terribly frustrated as a woman:

> Not that she resented housework in any particular way or anything like that, but she just had all that energy that couldn't be properly used. And the fact, too, that we were poor. I think if she had married a leading citizen she could have used that energy to be a big organizing force as there always were women in small towns who were and that's what she could have been quite happily. I've really often wondered about diseases like Parkinson's and how they happen...

Munro herself always got along well with her father, and however shocked he may have been at how personal some of her fictional material was, he never conveyed any dismay to her. As he became older, she suggests, he was a terribly good father who recognized his children as separate individuals. Nonetheless, during her childhood there was a strong division between male and female roles, with a gradual distance developing between father and daughter.

> At first he [her father] took quite a bit of interest in me and I used to help him (this is in one of the stories). I used to help him with the foxes and I was very proud of this. I don't know why, but it was the first work I felt good about doing. And then my brother got old enough to do it and my mother was getting sick, so I had to go in and do housework which I always hated. It seemed tedious, and the kitchen was dark and there was endless potato peeling and that sort of thing, and outside was all adventure and meaning to life. I remember resenting it somewhat but being so convinced of what the roles were that it wasn't a big resentment. And later on when I was a teenager my mother became so helpless and out of things that I rather enjoyed housework because I was in charge. So my father, from then on, was not close; he was a man and his roles were different.

Despite, or perhaps because of, the restrictions of her environment, Munro became very competitive in high school; on graduating, she obtained a scholarship and in 1949 left for the University of Western Ontario where she enrolled in journalism. Discovering that she was "too lazy" to cope with a required economics course, she switched into English literature as a major in her second year. Even with a two-year scholarship which paid her tuition, "the money situation was very tight" and she was forced to take other jobs and compete for small academic prizes to see her through. While she waitressed at a Muskoka lodge between her first and second year and worked in the university and public libraries, she still found time to write. By the time she married Jim Munro, son of an established Oakville family, in 1951 and left for the "adventure" of Vancouver at the age of twenty and at the end of her second university year, she had published three short stories, "The Dimensions of a Shadow," (April 1950), "Story for Sunday" (December 1950) and "The Widower" (April 1951) in the university's literary magazine *Folio* and had sold another.[1] Written in 1951, "The Liberation," about a woman she had worked with rolling bandages in a hospital, was the first of several short stories, including "The Strangers" to be sold to Robert Weaver at CBC radio. Her first commercial story, "A Basket of Strawberries," was published in the Canadian magazine *Mayfair* in November 1953.

Of her twenty some years of married life in British Columbia, which included the birth of four daughters, Sheila, Jenny, one who died shortly after birth, and Andrea, and the coestablishment of a bookstore in Victoria in 1963 after her husband left his job at Eaton's in Vancouver, Munro has no regrets. Although she published only a few short stories of quality during this period, later collected in *Dance of the Happy Shades*, she feels that the time was necessary, not so much to learn the "technical craft of writing" but to "find your subject, to find your real subject, and to face it." She explains, "I've got a wonderful quotation by Sam Shepard, the playwright, which says that all writing. . . succeeds or fails to the extent that the writer is able to face himself. And I think that this was that period. . . the long, long struggle."

Despite the psychological necessity of this period for her, she did acquiesce to the conventions of the young housewife during the fifties which included "socializing in a particularly trivial way" at neighbourhood coffee parties. She acknowledges that she wasn't brave enough to define herself out of it. In fact, what she remembers most fondly are those other, few disgruntled housewives like herself, who found some intellectual consolation and self-education together:

> I had a very good friend in West Vancouver and we used to spend every Tuesday afternoon together, drinking coffee and smoking until we were dizzy. And we were dizzy with the excitement of talking, and we would talk about our husbands and families as women do, but we would also talk about books. We read all the books by and about D.H. Lawrence, Katherine Mansfield, the Bloomsbury group, and then we'd get together and we'd talk with incredible excitement. . . I think with another friend we discovered Salinger in *The New Yorker*, the Franny and Zooey stories. . . I didn't like them and she did, so we had great conflicting conversations about this. . . I was seduced by the style and enjoyed it, but I found a terrible, cloying preference for Franny and Zooey and I found that I was identifying more and more with the crass, terrible people who annoyed their sensibilities rather than with them as I expect that I was supposed to.

Even if this period of Munro's life left her very unsure of herself as a writer, drained of her early youthful confidence, forced to mark writing time by children's naps and playpen periods, her final assessment is positive: "Probably had I been out earning my living as an academic, or an advertising writer or a librarian or whatever I would have done, it might indeed have made me less of a writer. I think being a housewife, in spite of all the intrusion, left me really more time, more time in my own head."

Even though by 1968 Munro had published *Dance of the Happy Shades* and won the Governor-General's Award for this book and by 1971–72 was receiving rave reviews for *Lives of Girls and Women* (1971), when her marriage ended in 1972 (she was formally divorced in 1976), she found herself economically and emotionally distressed. Never having learned how to handle money in her married life, she was the feminine equivalent of Stephen Leacock's little man in "My Financial Career," with little experience in opening bank accounts or providing for herself. The first job she got was that of teaching summer school in 1972 at Notre Dame in Nelson, British Columbia: "I remember that I was so elated that I was getting paid. And the woman who was the head of the department picked me up at the bus depot and said, 'Do you mind telling me why you came. We didn't think anybody would for this little money.' I didn't even know that this was a little money. For me it was great." Frightened, with her three children living with her, Munro developed some confidence by handling this job. Later, in September, while she was living in a motel in Victoria trying to decide what to do next, she was offered a job at York University teaching one day a week; this she gladly took, the small salary "sounding marvellous to someone who never earned money." Commuting to Toronto from a London apartment ("There must have been something weird about going back to London where I lived right before the marriage"), she managed to survive, with two of her daughters living with her. In 1974–75 she went on to be writer-in-residence at the University of Western Ontario where she remet Gerald Fremlin, a former friend, a government geographer, editor of the *National Atlas*, a Huron County man, and later, Munro's second husband. In 1974 she published her third volume, *Something I've Been Meaning to Tell You*; in the summer of 1975 she went up to Clinton to live with Gerry, who was then retired, to help him with his ailing mother: "It was obvious that someone had to look after her. And since we could live and do our work anywhere, we decided to live with her and we did for two years until she became very ill and went into a home. And then we stayed in Clinton so that we could visit her." Since remarrying in 1976, Munro has become the country wife, a role she happily reveals is, at least, in 1982, dictated primarily by her husband's preference for country living, for gardening, cross country skiing and long walks:

> I do it because my husband likes this kind of life, and I probably feel it's good for me and like it if someone else gives me a push. But I think perhaps left to my own devices, I'd own an apartment in the city... go to restaurants every night. I love Montreal. And I also like bookstores and plays and new clothes and looking at things. So probably I'm not a country person if I was only given the choice, although I love the landscape... I'm not a very strong-willed person. As long as people will let me write, I'm pretty adaptable.

"As long as people will let me write." Alice Munro, the artist, is the "same person" who outlasts all of her "disguises," all of those womanly roles and functions she has fulfilled, or discarded with painful decision, or left behind through the course of natural time. If the woman behind the work seems somewhat inaccessible, slippery, and difficult to catch, it is because Munro, with stubborn pride, insists on being her art.

| | | —

By now, Virginia Woolf's argument that the female author has the uphill battle of resisting the conventional female role, which is obviously historically and socially determined, is a familiar one.[2] Munro has not taken the route of the single-minded artist in bohemian protest against what society expected her to be as a woman. She did not give up the conventional responsibilities of daughter, mother, wife. In some basic ways, her lived experiences have conformed to the social-sexual history of upwardly mobile females of her Canadian generation: she moved from rural roots through education to middle class marriage, to motherhood, divorce, economic displacement and remarriage. Her solution to the problem of artist-as-female was quite naturally and bravely to become the female-as-artist, and as an interpreter and puzzling critic of the roles of women and codes of sexual conduct she knew and witnessed, a quiet revolutionary.

Munro has travelled beyond Woolf who consciously fought the constraints of Victorian respectability and domestic duty, a specter that Woolf named the Angel in the House. Despite her revolt, as Elaine Showalter has argued, Woolf capitulated mightily.

> Virginia Woolf developed a literary theory which had the effect of neutralizing her own conflict between the desire to present a woman's whole experience, and the fear of such revelation. It is a theory of the androgynous mind and spirit; a fusion of masculine and feminine elements, calm, stable, subtle, unimpeded by consciousness of sex or individuality. . . . Whatever else one may say of androgyny, it represents an escape from the confrontation with femininity.[3]

If, as Showalter observes, Woolf was pressed to neutralize her femininity, to consciously refrain from writing about her own sexuality and to renounce female passion, Munro works closely to the core of her own feminine consciousness and through the authority of her own fragmented and transformational experience. In a letter to Joyce Johnson of McGraw Hill Book Co., dated 8 February 1973, Showalter praises Munro's effort:

> Thank you for sending me Alice Munro's *Lives of Girls and Women;* I had seen some enthusiastic reviews. Reading such a strong novel of the female consciousness makes me feel rather like an astronomer who had predicted the existence of a comet, and then watching it appear—it's very exciting to read beyond androgyny.[4]

Munro's life has been that of meeting the challenge of shifting roles for herself, and her fiction has been, and continues to be, that of a cathartic feminism, moving beyond androgyny. Unlike a Mary Wollstonecraft, a Virginia Woolf or a Sylvia Plath, she is, as a female author of feminine persuasion, a survivor.

| | | —

Survival, as Margaret Atwood's thesis about the Canadian identity implies, is very close to the Canadian female authorial imagination. In fiction by modern Canadian female writers, their protagonists, like the gothic heroines of old, struggle to escape imprisonment and drowning, and attempt, in a modern, constructive way to manage space, to achieve room and office. The tone of the novels and short stories of these contemporary women is often confessional, ironically, stridently, sometimes, not unlike earlier writers like Woolf, even apologetically so—unconsciously directed to a male audience who will finally understand, and perhaps even forgive the serpentine bite of the thankless child. I am not really Goneril, the female author often seems to say, but your own Cordelia. Because for literary antecedents the female author has to draw on images of women created out of a feudal, paternal imagination, she very often finds herself hopelessly confused by them and the values attached to them (which is she to ad-mire—Goneril the Vicious or Cordelia the Victim? Both? Neither?). As a result, she very often writes what has been categorized as highly autobio-graphical fiction, depending on the honesty of her own experience and so-cial observation to shape and define her female characters. This is the first stage in the development of not one, but many new heroines, and a new reality for women, a stage which can be brought to its greatest fruition through a collective understanding of female writers and their life experi-ences. To this end, the dialogue between female writers, critics and their readers must be an ongoing one.

The feminist thinker, Susan Brownmiller, understands well the princi-ples of female dialogue and discourse. In her discussions of woman's voice, she describes in detail what it means to speak "in feminine," in that mode of communication "which is determined by one's female gender" and which, as an imitative process, "begins early in life."[5] One of the first prin-ciples of feminine speech is that of "self-centred interest in personal experi-ence and feelings," a verbal strategy, indeed a writing strategy favored by Munro herself in fiction of indeterminate biographical-autobiographical boundaries. While speaking and writing feminine is often disparaged by men who have been trained to avoid the confessional mode with its risk of personal admissions that may reveal weaknesses and failure, dependence and vulnerability, Brownmiller insists that the personalized female voice is not intrinsically negative.[6]

Certainly, self-disclosure is music to the ears of a female audience. It is concert, even, for Munro substantiates here, in dialogue, Brownmiller's point that women prefer equality and community in discussion, rather than the hierarchy of leader and led discourse. In the following, selected com-ments from informal discussions with Munro, the author and the critic shift into speaking "the subjective and communal feminine." The author's comments which tell of personal and literary influence, life tensions, the authorial process, and her response to early critics anticipate and document themes and stylistic features discussed in the text.

| | | —

Commenting on her early dream of writing a novel of "powerful archetypal things," Munro explains that she gave this up at about twenty-two. For the author, personal experience and maternal influence are quite clearly connected and important in her art.

> The idea of using experience came to me with "The Peace of Utrecht" which was after my mother's death when I went home. . . I went to my grandmother's house and she showed me my mother's clothes. And then the story was shaped and I had to write it, and from that time on I had this new thing about writing. . . had I not got to that point I would not have had enough power to work as a writer.
>> *How do you remember your grandmother?*
> Very much as I describe her. I've used her (my father's mother) an awful lot. She's in "Winter Wind." I'm very much like her physically. . . I'm not really like my mother, although you might think so because she was frustrated. My grandmother was a handsome, energetic, intelligent woman who was entirely conforming, conforming with a vengeance. . . . She was three-quarters Irish Protestant, strongly conventional, but with this funny depth that was never allowed to show.
>> *She sounds very much like my Irish grandmother who, in*
>> *retrospect, seems to have been part of an Irish matriarchy.*
>> *Do you think this is true of yours?*
> Yes.
>> *My grandmother was also very conforming, and sympathetic*
>> *towards me, but I always sensed that she felt she had to*
>> *keep me in check.*
> That's exactly what I felt. She knew the same forces were struggling in me and her answer was to put them down. . . . And yet, you know, I feel that my mother was not actually an unconventional woman. She wanted an unconventional role, but there was a value system which she could easily have accepted. But I feel that my grandmother was actually more questioning. For instance, I feel that her Christian beliefs were probably maintained with a great deal of effort, whereas with my

mother, they would be maintained effortlessly, because she was not intellectually curious. But I feel that my grandmother was.

| | | —

Munro comments on her relationships with men:

> *Relationships with men are probably as important as those with grandmothers. When you look back at your first marriage now, do you feel any resentment? Do you think that it made you less a writer having had to be a housewife?*

No... I think being a housewife left me more time, although it made me very unsure of myself. I didn't know, until I left my husband, what you did in a bank. I didn't know how to open an account. I could write cheques on a joint account. Terrible!

> *Your roles were very divided then; he looked after everything, including the finances, while you stayed home and tended house and raised the children.*

Yes... our roles were very divided as to work... though he was very sympathetic to the idea of my being a writer, he didn't take on any chores at home, nor did I think that he ought to. I'm still not sure that a man ought to. That's a very antifeminist thing to say, but he was working hard already.

> *Do you think that a man of your generation married to a writer, confronted by his wife's success, would find such a situation difficult?*

Yes. And even if he isn't finding it difficult, other people may not be slow to let him know that they think he ought to be finding it difficult. I know when I got the Governor-General's Award, other people actually would come up to Jim at parties and say, "I think you're taking this very well," as if I had been arrested for shoplifting or something. And he wasn't having problems with this at all. And I think other writers' husbands have been taken to task, too.

> *How do you find your relationships with men now as the successful artist woman?*

They are not particularly difficult. Occasionally there have been a lot of problems that sort of surprised me with men of my own age or older who are just put out by the achieving woman. I mean it doesn't matter if I'm an artist, or if I was a judge or gynecologist. They're shaky on that. . . . But I had all this early training growing up in Wingham which has been good in one way and probably not good in another in that I conceal; I defend myself constantly so my manner is never challenging.

Do you still do that? In an interview with Barbara Frum some time ago you said you wouldn't argue with men because you were afraid of being called an aggressive bitch.

I think I'm much more open than I was at that time. . . now, I would argue. But I tend to back off from arguments with anybody, not just men. I have a very protective thing—I may call it protective, it may also be cowardly but I back off from confrontation. I don't use my energy that way. My work, which is the most important thing, I will also protect. . . from mental irritation or upheaval. The only thing that is as important as my work are the few people who matter to me, and there I would defend. I would not back off. But I think that most women are like that, most women will defend their men and their kids. But, you know I don't get into theoretical arguments because most of them seem ridiculous.

Why?

Because most arguments that pretend to be about, you know, intellectual topics, seem actually sort of simple ego struggles, simple one-up-manship. And I suppose I know that I'm not good at that, but I also don't see any need to do it. And I think many women are reacting this way so that in a way we castigate ourselves for not being assertive enough but we may just be unwilling to waste the time. You know, when women talk together there's often a nice harmony that isn't agreement. You can get discussions with women where nobody's ego is pushing. You could have three or four women and no one is really pushing anyone else; that doesn't happen as often with men.

Do you think that abstract argument is somewhat frivolous?

No. . . I think it's often not really. . . about what it seems to be about, because often it's about things that are simply unprovable and people defend their own positions.

So you see rhetorical argument almost as a masculine province.

Yes, I do.

I think that you are right. Rhetorical debate, as in parliament, certainly seems a masculine world. And it is very dif-

*ficult for women to psychologically enter into it because
they have to adopt all the masculine manners and conventions that go with it; in a sense, they have to erode their
femininity in order to participate.*

| | | —

As the following excerpts highlight, of major interest to Munro is the metamorphosis of her own female body.

What period of your life would you regard as the happiest?
Now... well, it started getting better about ten years ago. In fact, I think it never was very bad. I've had periods of... being a social misfit and of being unhappy in superficial ways, but often that has coincided with being quite confident and happy in other ways. That's true of adolescence... I think probably the period between thirty-five and forty was awfully restless. That's when my first marriage was breaking up, that's a period when most women who are changing their lives do it.
Why do you think they do?
I don't know. I guess that you feel it's a last chance. Do you think it's because of hormones?
*I don't think so. I think hormonal change comes much later.
I think that it probably has to do with loss of good looks and
a desperate feeling that...*
You're becoming discardable... I must say, that's what I feel now... it's like adolescence all over again. There are superficial things that bother you, and yet underneath there seems to be a greater and greater power. I do feel a power now that I haven't felt since I was very young, probably since I was about twelve, and I do think there is this power at both ends of the sexual life.

That's interesting.
I can't be quite sure what it is because the loss of the sexual life, at least of sexual attractiveness and sexual viability, is very painful and it will probably go on being so for quite a long time before you reconcile to it. But there is something growing underneath that I didn't expect.
*You have a strong sense of self, of identity, of personal
power?*

Yes. And that pleasure you have as a child which doesn't come from recognition by other people or social role or achievement or anything at all but the moment. And I remember having that very strongly from about nine to twelve. That's the girl's period of power, really, and then the whole female thing has to be dealt with. And I guess you go on dealing with it then for about forty years in one way or another.

| | | —

Discussion on being the female artist:

> *I would like to talk about feminism and your art if we can; I am interested in how you respond to critics who evaluate your work as "female," and whether you see the female artist as having any special problems. One of the things I wondered about was your response to the critical controversy that developed over the introduction by Hugh Garner to Dance of the Happy Shades.*

I didn't know there was one.

> *Controversy is perhaps too strong a term, but at least two female critics, Beth Harvor and Audrey Thomas, took issue with the introduction.*

Do they think he is condescending?

> *Yes, and Beth Harvor said that you were damned by faint praise because Garner criticized some younger writers which made it seem as if your own work was perhaps not up to par, or that you had limitations as a writer.*

I don't think that is a feminist question; I think that's the older writer and the younger writer. . . I don't even think it's malicious.

> *You don't object, then, if critics refer to you as a feminine writer? Listen to Kildare Dobbs and see what your response is: "A friend once complained to me that Alice Munro's stories were dangerously close to the style of the fiction in women's magazines and it's true that in some of her pauses one can imagine her putting on a kettle for a pot of tea. But this is only to say that she is a very feminine writer. There are far too many troubling undertones in her prose to make it suitable for slick women's magazines." How would you respond to a comment like that?*

Well, my defense to the women's magazine thing would have been exactly the defense he makes for me. I think probably the people who say this is like stuff in women's magazines are judging it by the subject matter. Now, do you mean do I think Kildare is defending in a patronizing way?

I wonder.

No, I don't think so. I don't see how else he could defend me... and, as for the cup of tea, well that is a little bit dated because we now understand that men are capable also. My husband often makes a pot of tea in the pauses...

What about this comment on Dance? *"One is almost aware, sometimes, of the writer consciously holding herself in, too much afraid that if her voice becomes passionate, even for a moment, she will be accused of writing 'women's stories' and told to get thee to* Chatelaine *or the* Ladies Home Journal.

I think the stories in the first book do show a sense of restraint, but not because I am afraid of being passionate. It's because I was, in fact, during writing many of the stories in that book, a journeyman writer. I was learning by practice. There are only a few stories in the first book that are passionately felt. I think "The Peace of Utrecht" is passionately felt. But this has nothing to do with being afraid of being feminine. I don't think the stories in *Chatelaine* are passionate; I think they are sentimental. And I don't think I ever felt a temptation to be sentimental.

Let me try this one: "For what preoccupies her [Munro] above all else in her three... [works]... is the emotional dependence of women. She is not on record as agreeing with— but she would—Mary Wollstonecraft's impassioned observation, 'I plead for my sex... Independence I have long considered as the grand blessing of life, the basis of every virtue'."

Of course, I agree, but Mary Wollstonecraft tried to drown herself for love, so there was certainly a time in her life when love must have seemed—and I think it was the love of a fairly ordinary man—must have seemed every bit as desirable as independence. What I think is constantly interesting about a woman's situation is just that contradiction.

Between...

Between the desire for a kind of attachment to a man which has been—because of social causes, you can't tell—more intense than the attachment men feel for women. The attraction is not more intense, but the

desire to attach, not to lose, not to let go of, is. And there is this thing
on the one hand with a woman like Mary Wollstonecraft—and this was
after her intellect has fully developed and I think after she had written
Vindication of the Rights of Women. So the two are trying to coexist.

> *It's interesting though that feminist critics and writers have
> claimed that writing about female passion is itself a feminist
> statement...*

Yes. But, you know, what happens in a book... in a story or novel is
not necessarily a philosophic statement by the writer. It's what happens
in the context and you are not sure why it happens.

> *Do you think this is true of all women, though, this...*

This contradiction we are talking about? One simply doesn't know....
You are not a sociologist so you don't go out and get statistics to find
out if the situations you're showing are typical. You just... you portray
them and then you get feedback which seems to convince you that
they're not at least uncommon. But you simply don't know, and the
thing, of course, that we don't know about women at all, that I don't
know, is there a change in women? Is there a new type of woman?

> *One of the things some critics say about Del Jordan in* Lives
> *is that while she had difficulty in finding role models (that is
> a woman who combines both sexuality and intelligence), she
> quite conclusively envisions her world in female terms. How
> conscious are you, as an artist, of doing this?*

I'm not at all conscious of doing it, but it has certainly become apparent
to me that this is what I do. I simply don't know why? Perhaps (but this
is a very simplistic explanation) it could have something to do with the
kind of environment I grew up in where the world of out-of-doors belongs to men and they're out doing things, and the whole world of personal events seems to be the property of women. You know, it's the
women in the kitchen who talk about everything that's happening to
everybody and so the community's personal life would seem to be much
more strongly seen and felt by women than by the men, or at least...
that would be the interpretation a girl child would get.

> *Do you see the female artist as having any special problems
> that the male artist does not have?*

Oh yes, lots... we all know the thing about time. This is the practical.
Do you mean the kind of writing she can do?

Yes.

Well, I think that one of the problems here has been that women are trained to be reticent, to be nice, to be genteel, although they are all through their lives in contact with physical body realities like changing diapers and menstruating and all this. It is sort of perverse in most societies for them to mention or seem to be aware of these things. And I think although this is a very Victorian notion, it certainly persisted right up until my adulthood.

Do you think this may be the reason that you don't write about childbirth as a dramatic event?

No, I don't think so because I can write about a lot of other things. I mean I can write about turds in the snow and that doesn't bother me. . . . But, somehow there is a . . . you know, Virginia Woolf writes things about James Joyce that I feel are very influenced this way. Sometimes I think her femininity and her class get in the way of her marvellous gifts as a critic, and she feels that Joyce is just . . . well, she sounds a bit like the president of the Ladies' Literary Society saying, "Is all this necessary?" And I think it's very hard for women to manage the kind of exposure that they may feel has to be done in their fiction. I think all this has changed, of course. But I think that it is a problem.

. . . the other problem I feel that is related to the woman's life as a woman and her life as an artist is that writing is dangerous to the psyche. It's unbalanced. It's like a trip you take alone, all serious writing is like this. Now this is something we are accustomed to thinking of the male artist as doing. It may not be very nice for his wife and kids but it is important that he do it. And we have a picture of woman which is very strong in our minds as being the person who doesn't go on journeys, the person who is there looking after the material wants but also providing a kind of unquestioning cushion.

You remember in *Anna Karenina* Lenin has a big religious crisis and then he meets Kitty in the woods after the thunderstorm and he realizes that Kitty's simple mind never frames these questions or doubts. And I think there are some things that men have for centuries required in women which is the very opposite of what the female artist has to do. So you feel in what you do not only that you have no support (as the man has support in the woman), but that you are doing something that is against nature. And that is far more difficult than the matter of finding time to write or, you know, all these mechanical things, or will your husband be jealous if you're a success. It's far more important that you are betraying to men that this still center that they thought was there, this kind of unquestioning cushion, is not there at all, because you know that you are not a freak. You are just the artist woman as the man is the artist man.

| | | —

In the following discussion, Munro comments on literary influences and the authorial process; including her interest in the gothic, her attitudes toward her heroines, and the concepts of time, childbirth, and female landscape in her fiction.

> *Are there other writers today whose techniques of writing you particularly admire?*

Oh, there are just too many to mention because I admire quite different qualities which makes me feel I can't have jelled yet as a writer... there's an American short story writer named Elizabeth Cullinan who writes almost flat stories. The effect is so quiet, and half-way through you'll think, "Is she really going to be able to pull this off as a story?" and then the afterglow of the story is terrific. And I admire that very much. That kind of indirection that doesn't look fancy is what I'm getting more and more excited about now. But then there are periods when something quite different will get to me. I mean, there's probably a new writer every year that I've discovered that I really, really, am moved by and that I really would tend to... not to imitate, but I would strive for the quality that I admired there for that time. But I notice that what I strive for does change.

> *What are you striving for now?* [1982]

Well, there again, it changes with each story. You really strive for what the story seems to demand. Even the book that is coming out in October [*The Moons of Jupiter*] is sort of past. The last story I wrote for it was sort of florid.

> *What is that story called?*

It's called "Bardon Bus." And its... I wrote it here last summer when I was down for weekends, and I was getting a very strange feeling from Queen Street. It was of a kind of almost hysterical eroticism. It was something about women's clothes and the very, very whorish makeup that women were wearing. And all of this was sort of nightmarish. And I wanted to do this in a story and then I had an anecdotal framework that I was using as well. And now I'm writing something that is conversational, almost straight autobiography, not in fact but tone. It's the sort of story that people will read and they'll say, "Well, this really happened." So you see it does vary. Each time it's as if the story itself dictated the way you were going to tell it.

> *How real are your characters to you? How real are Del Jordan and Rose?*

Oh, very real, because they are aspects of myself.

> *You are not like Charles Dickens, then, who used to sit and imagine that he was conversing with his characters as other people?*

No. I don't think I've ever created characters in that sense; in the stories where I am quite removed from the characters... [they] will have been drawn very much from real life. I've either done that or used aspects of myself. One of the creative characters, I think, is the mother in *Lives* because she is quite a long way from my own mother and she has quite a lot of several people in her, and actually, she is about the only character I feel that I have completely created because she is quite different from anyone I've ever known.

> *The rest are all modeled on specific people?*

To a certain extent. . . . The aunts are very much modeled. They come up again and again in my fiction, and they are modeled.

> *They come up differently, though, every time.*

Yes, because I see different things about them, so they are not direct reproductions of my grandmother and my great aunt. But they don't go that far afield either, you know, the way the mother in *Lives* goes right away from my own mother and becomes another person. But they don't do that. . . . I think there are writers who create out of their imaginations but I am not one of them. I'm on the Audrey Thomas side of the fence, though I think I put them through more washes, you know, to bring them up.

> *Yet some of your stories seem far less personal than mythic.*

"The Stone in the Field" for example really struck me with a powerful sadness, and when I began to analyze it, it seemed to me to be resonating with Christian myth, with the story of Christ and the resurrection, and the rolling away of the stone.

That's one of the stories that comes from facts... though I've put them together in an odd way. There was this stone and I did go look for it about three years ago... just before writing the story. And I remember the man who was buried there, and I did find an item, or Gerry found an item about him, in the old newspapers he was looking through. And I did have a family of... they were not aunts, they were my father's cousins... who were exactly like that family. And so they were a kind of extreme statement of the qualities of that side of my family.

How do you respond to the criticism that you are limited by being an autobiographical writer, in particular by being a white, Anglo-Saxon and Protestant one. Here is one critic: "The unspoken theory behind WASP behaviour is that if you do not mention something it will go away or will never happen or will not mean anything. Do not celebrate too much and do not mourn too loudly. Try not to feel because feeling brings you trouble. Hide yourself behind layers of insensitivity. The best way to do this is to look and act as much as possible like everybody else. If there is a single moral impulse behind Mrs. Munro's work it is contained in the sentence 'I do not believe things are there to be worked through' said by Eileen in "Memorial." Reality must be confronted and felt, however painful it may be. Her narrators are frequently involved in this process. They are trying to break out of the WASP cage of slippery evasions into the clear light of the truth."

Well, I think that whole statement about WASP philosophy is true and I think the exploration of it is what I'm doing. I can't do anything else. I can hardly set myself up as a Jewish writer or an Indian writer. . . . But I think the interpretation of that statement is altogether wrong.

What I meant by "I do not believe things are there to be worked through" is I do not believe that facile intellectual theories about things are satisfactory. I think the narrator is reacting against a whole approach to life which can be seen in the more short-sighted kinds of psychotherapy—that life contains problems but if we can identify the problems and adopt a positive attitude we will manage to get through them. And so that's what the statement is taking issue with.

| | | —

> *I wonder why it is Canadian female writers are preoccupied with the Gothic, and it seems to me that they are. You acknowledge that you began to write by trying to imitate Southern Gothic stories, in the style of Carson McCullers. Marian Engel and Margaret Atwood have a penchant for the gothic; and one of your characters effectively remembers*
Wuthering Heights.

That was the biggest book of my life.

> *Are you aware that you are using the traditions, the conventions of the Gothic novel, such as the imprisoned virgin in the house or tower, in sophisticated ways in your fiction?*

No, I hadn't been aware of it. . . I've always had the Rapunzel story as a very important story, but you know I wasn't aware of using it.

> *Part of the process of being the gothic heroine is the threat of loss of virginity. How significant a topic in the 1980s is the virginal woman, or as your character Miss Leviston in one of your unpublished manuscripts puts it in "Yellow Afternoon": the "gospel of virginity."[7]*

I don't suppose it is significant at all in itself, but anything that's explored with honesty and feeling and excitement on the part of the writer remains interesting I think. You know, I can read Victorian novels, I can still read Jane Austen about people, who they are going to marry and who's going to inherit a fortune.

> *Do you admire Jane Austen?*

Yes, I like her a lot, but I don't think I'm in the stream of Jane Austen writers.

> *Several female critics have said you are. I don't think you are either.*

No, I don't think so. I mean, if you put Charlotte Brontë here and Jane Austen here, I'm on Charlotte Brontë's side of the fence. But I can read about wills and things that no longer mean anything in twentieth century terms because of the light that throws on the people, so I think that virginity can remain interesting.

| | | —

> *Let us look at your heroines a little more closely. I think that Rose in* Who Do You Think You Are? *begins to move into the Jane Austen tradition, if you like, in that she certainly has a great deal of concern with money...*

Yes, I got very interested in money when I went back to live in Huron County... that's where I wrote the book... when I went back I remembered how strong the class system based on money actually is... now this is something that people don't talk about much in all small town stories, and people don't.... it was something that suddenly I thought had been neglected and had been neglected by me, and suddenly I got very interested in it.

> *Both Del Jordan and Rose seem to me to be loving heroines in that they are both striving for love, but Rose is almost dispassionate in the end where you seem to dictate a kind of platonic ideal of universal brotherhood. I would call her a cool heroine...*

Oh, I don't think she's cool. I think she's quite passionate but there's just a lot of exploration in the latter half of the book of the way people use each other. Del Jordan is probably going to go out and use people, too, but it isn't so apparent in childhood.

> *Iris Murdoch has said that most novels are about love and power. Do you agree with her?*

Yes, I do. I think I would often write from the side of the person who loses power, but not always... in a story like "Mischief" the woman has a lot more power than the man... the whole state of being in love is one that I haven't written about nearly as much as I want to. And I see this from a sense of powerlessness. But then a man could too.... In a way, *Lives of Girls and Women* was a retreat from what I had discovered as a grown-up woman into the use of power that you have as a young woman, that you can have, because Del was a person of power, of intellectual power. She analyzed and saw through; her abdication was fairly short....

> *Lives is a very optimistic, almost triumphant book, and it's interesting*

that I wrote it at a time in my life when I had absolutely no power. And the growing-up girl is able to be very optimistic about what she can manage; writing about middle-aged women, I wouldn't have that tone. It has a jaunty tone.

> *Tell me a little bit more about Rose because I think she's an absolutely fascinating character and I insist that she has a cool quality.*

I think she is risk taking. She's introspective but she's curious. I think my heroines—the ones I'm closest to—are more curious than anything else. Maybe that's a cool quality, but it can be a pretty hot quality as well.

> *All of your heroines are adventuresses.*

That interests me in women—the adventuress who is not calculating her own advantage, who never seems to quite be able to calculate it even when she tries. The hold on life which is never there by manipulating events but is there somehow by just the effort to understand them.

> *Rose has no last name.*

No. I forgot.

> *Which reminds me. One of the things often missed in your fiction is the ironic perspectives. I enjoy your humor, not only the irony of your heroines but the exaggerated comedy of your Ontario folk types and I can't help recalling the folk world of the Quebecois writer, Roch Carrier, where the hyperbolic humor is the consequence of the way the French Canadian peasant thinks, when I read Alice Munro's similar depictions of rural Ontario life.*

Yes, and... there's sometimes an uneasy marriage of the kind of milieu I grew up in, which is the Flats Road of the lower town, where you get these folk characters. Flo is a folk character... And a later world where you get the modulated, well-educated people... I think I had to move on from the whole folk character thing. I became dissatisfied with that... I began to want to treat people who are like we are, who are complicated and deceptive, and in a sense, more interesting.

> *Is there a comic dimension to Flo that comes from the folk?*

Oh, yes. I intended her to be... I intended that whole early part of the book to be full of that kind of thing. And then one of the problems for me was how it drained off and I didn't have it for the latter part of the book because I was dealing with different people.

| | | —

> *What of your concept of time? I like the structure in your fiction because the present is superimposed on the past, except in the fourth book where in each chapter but "Wild Swans," the past and the present are also somewhat balanced in the conclusion of each episode. It would seem that you prefer an organic structure to an old-fashioned chronological sequence.*

I know I like having jumps. . . . One of the things I like working with (I've never really done a story about this but I'm intending to) is the way you meet people you've known in a past time and you haven't known them in the gap between at all, and you know them again now in an entirely different plane than you knew them before, and you each have different memories of before, and the whole thing about the way things intersect, and there is no continuity. I'm very fascinated. That's why I think I don't write a novel because. . .

> *Time is relative.*

Yes. I can't work in continuity because I don't actually feel it in life.

| | | —

> *One of the things that really interests me is that while you deal with the loss of virginity and most other physical experiences, you don't deal with childbirth in your fiction and I wonder why, because most of your fiction has to do with the education of a heroine.*

Do you know, I really don't know why. Childbirth was easy for me—that could be a reason, but that really isn't valid is it—it's a big event whether it's easy or hard, isn't it?

> *You flirt with the experience in* Who Do You Think You Are? *and you use childbirth as a metaphor. . . . When you stop to consider, birth is not often dramatized in fiction, yet it is one of the most dramatic moments in the human experience.*

Doris Lessing does it.

> *Have you consciously avoided it?*

No, I haven't consciously avoided it. I know I have a strong bias against using my children. . . . I think it is because childbirth is so dramatic and universal. You know, it's a lot easier for sex to be unique and personal. . . . I would find it easier to describe sex than to describe childbirth, which seems to me to get into such a universal area as to almost not be interesting to me, though I'm saying slightly the wrong words here. . . obviously, it isn't very interesting to me or I would have used it. And yet I remember each labor in great detail, and like most women, could fill you in for half an hour on how long the first stage lasted, etc.

> *Feminist critics argue that female authors create sexually suggestive landscapes and that they are really extensions of the female body, that is, they are never alpine; they are hilly, high lying. . . do you think this is a reliable observation?*

That's speculation. It's interesting. I know that I am very drawn to bare hills, landscapes with bare hills, like the drumlins around Peterborough, or broken hills like the kame country. . . and when I went to Scotland, to the border country where my people have lived for hundreds and hundreds of years, that is exactly the country they lived amongst. How do you know what is ancestral memory?

> *How do we know, indeed. And how do we define, assuming ancestral memory is real, its distinctively female features?*

| | | —

Alice Munro in 1989 on being the female artist, on her gender/art:

> *In 1982, you said that you were loving the country life, a choice which was, in part, dictated by your husband's preferences. Is this still true?*

It's even more true now—the countryside is very important to me, but it's very much a shared thing, with my husband, at its best a calm but intense harmony.

> *In 1981–82, we discussed your interest in the metamorphosis of the female body. In your last book to date, The Progress of Love, it seems to me that you are quite concerned with the menopausal exit. Are you very much interested in the subject now?*

Of course. I'm always interested in where I'm at.

You are certainly delineating the complexity of emotions as-
sociated with female aging. "Lichen" is a wonderful story in
this regard. How angry do you think women ought to be
about society's attitude toward them as "dead meat?"

I can't say how angry anybody "ought" to be. As angry as they like. As
angry as is useful. Recently I read a poem by Irving Layton about old
women, and I felt contempt; it seemed silly and frightened. Anyway I
think this attitude is changing—maybe. In "Lichen," the woman's techniques of survival serve her at least as well as the man's serve him, and
I think in life this is true. Aging in itself, for men and women, can be
rotten and "unfair." The way women have to face up to it may not be
all disadvantageous.

Earlier you indicated that you felt a certain amount of power
which came with the decline of sexual life. Sophie in "White
Dump" is an interesting character for a whole number of
reasons. One of the encouraging things about her is that as
the Old Norse, she has almost a goddesslike authority. Do
you consider Sophie a different kind of character from others
that you have created?

I don't know—Sophie has been a forceful lonely person always and
there's a lot she's not too smart about. But I like her. I think, though,
she's more limited than wayward Isabel, who may seem not so ad-
mirable. I like her too.

More than in any of your other works, you consider the
question of madness in The Progress of Love. *Would you*
agree with some contemporary feminist thinkers that given
Western culture, madness is almost synonymous with the
condition of being female?

Madness doesn't seem to me a gender thing—I have more madwomen
simply because I know more women and I know stories through women.

Finally, is it any easier in 1989 than it was in 1981–82 for
you, personally, to be the female artist? You said then that
it was difficult for a number of reasons.

No, it's worse if anything. A female artist is seen as a nurturing figure
by female readers—someone to hear about and help them with their
lives. The claims laid on her—to listen, to comfort—are different, I

imagine, from the straightforward demands for career help that men get. And I get those too.

Thank you, Alice, for being helpful to your readers.

| | | —

The interview material is taken from personal interviews conducted in February 1981, June 1982, and the last section from private correspondence between the interviewer and Alice Munro, September 1989.

| 2 | FEMINIST

Her Own Tribe: A Feminist Odyssey

Sons branch out, but
one woman leads to another.
Finally, I know you
through your daughters,
my mother, her sisters,
and through myself.

       MARGARET ATWOOD,
       "FIVE POEMS FOR GRANDMOTHERS"

The feminist quest in Munro's fiction is primarily undertaken by the dominant persona of an intelligent and mature narrator who questions society's expectations of her as female both in past memory and present circumstance. Both outer and inner directed, this voice speaks for a collective female experience and, at the same time, dramatizes the compelling, private lives of individuals like Del and Rose in *Lives of Girls and Women* and *Who Do You Think You Are?* In a special sense, too, the underlying voice is outside of society or inner oriented. In part autobiographical, it confronts society not only as a woman but also as a female artist. For Munro, the feminist quest includes the search for freedom of imagination and expression through the medium of art. When, for example, the mature writer-narrator of "The Office" in the first volume, *Dance of the Happy Shades*, finds herself prevented by the bullying, small-minded Mr. Malley from writing without disturbance in the office she has rented from him, she is not only thwarted by his view of her as a woman but by his intolerance of her as an artist. At the heart of this story, and of much of Munro's fiction, the developing feminist consciousness is complicated by an expanding perception of the woman as artist.

In fact, Munro's strength as a feminist writer is both this extra facet of her female persona and the range of her portraits of women. Her gift to us is a variety of female characters portrayed from childhood to old age, whose hidden selves she explores beneath their artificial, disguised or misinterpreted social faces. Very often a part of the retrospective memory of Munro's dominant persona, they attest to the fact that unlike her character Gabe of "Material," Munro cannot erase the "language of [her] childhood."[1] Many of her characters belong to a dying or defunct Faulkneresque world of southwestern rural Ontario, a world made immediate through remembrances of time past.

Her recurrent characterizations of childish and decorous Victorian women who, subordinated by an older, patriarchal order, betray sublimated and strangled discontent, or those poor white women, the Snopses of rural Ontario, who lash out with gestures of primitive and frustrated aggression, are part of the author's contemporary urbane consciousness. A woman who is part of all that she has met, Munro is the sympathetic repository of their images and conditions. Many of her contemporary heroines, too, with their internalized conflicts and existential quests for self-knowledge, are caught in the old value systems to which these women belong. The male-centeredness of the two "modern" women in "The Spanish Lady," for example, from *Something I've Been Meaning to Tell You*, is revealed in the narrator's melancholy admission "we were attracted to each other because of the man, or to the man because of each other" (143).

Ultimately, however, many of these other women, in particular the domestic aunties, grandmothers and spinsters who inhabit the gothic milieu of the Victorian small town and their primitive sisters on the edge of civilization, provide a means of self-understanding for Munro and her questing persona. A central concept of Munro's work is that personal memory allows one to become one's own savior. She knows this as the psychological clue to identity and, like Arthur Miller and Henrik Ibsen, understands that the artistic validity of psychological drama depends on the influences of the past: that its tension proceeds from "within the person who is drawn back to the past in order to orient himself to the future."[2] In the end, it is the child-women and primitives who are standards of measurement; they are female models for the author and her reader to judge, to reject and even, paradoxically, to be inspired by.

| | | —

The inspirational nature of Munro's women signals a psychological journey that is also mythical and of feminist design. The artist-heroine is in
search of female muses in art and life; in order to authorize female experience, she reaches back into time, associates several of her characters with
primal energy, shades them with pagan and mythic features, and creates an
underground text of female goddess figures, suggestive of the pantheistic
religions of the ancient world. Retreating from the masculine Christian
mythology that has provided her identity, Munro is drawn to that pagan
religious context of Astarte and Isis where the life-giving powers of women
and the earth were joined and acknowledged.

By championing the power of primitive and pagan woman, Munro par-
ticipates in a feminist struggle against the male authority established by
Christianity, when the God-head became male, and, as Susan Brownmiller
summarizes, "monotheistic belief turned away from the concept of primor-
dial birth and superimposed the divine will of a male deity on the act of
procreation. Motherhood plays no part in the Genesis myth of creation.
Adam is not born of woman; he is fashioned directly by the hand of God."[3]
If the maternal principle was retained by Christianity in a secondary way,
that is, as it was sanctioned by marriage, maternity was desexualized and
erotic woman was conceptualized through Eve, as a danger. As Mary Magdalene and the vampish archetype of the Romantic poets, the woman of
sexual passion became the pagan seductress, the prostitute outside of moral
order and patriarchal familial structures. Christianity revoked woman's
fertility, her eroticism, her power, all that was accorded to her mythically
in the ancient world.

Munro seeks to redress this mythos and restore female genesis. The Eve
and Lilith figures of Christian and Semitic mythology for example, function as pagan archetypes in the likes of characters like Nile in *Lives* and
Beryl of *The Progress of Love*. These women are perfect artifices of femininity, prostitutelike in their affairs with pimpish men. They offer to
Munro's young heroines interesting possibilities as models of behavior, al-
ternatives to sexless maternity. As a daylight character, Beryl, Munro hu-
morously declares, is not about to have her teat pulled in the manner she
observes being applied to the milk cow;[4] she is shamelessly outside of conventional marriage and maternal definition. Like her lover, Mr. Florence,
the conventional church isn't her kind of religion. Mythically, Beryl is

seductive glamor, a hymn to femininity and its power to move men. In this capacity, Beryl, like Fern, is one of Munro's minor goddesses.

She is also a critical inquiry into the myth itself of the female as errant seductress. In "Women's Desire/Women's Power: *The Moons of Jupiter*," Lorna Irvine argues that the female as *desirer* is a particular problem for female writers, and, quoting Hélène Cixous, that "a patriarchal society has made 'female desire a meaningless term by situating women objectively.'"[5] Beryl is the mirror of this reality. As a desirable object of male invention, she is empty dress and an emotional puzzle: "She was so noisy and shiny, so glamorously got up, that it was hard to tell whether she was good-looking, or happy, or anything" (16). Beryl's power and desire is sadly limited by her single preordained role to be the object of desire and desiring object of men.

Irvine also suggests that women writers, in attempting to combine desire with power, develop certain narrative strategies, the most overt being "positing a desiring female subject, conscious of her gender, who acts in response to her own needs." (93) This is true of the voice behind the fiction, often realized as first person narrator, in all of Munro's work. Women writers also develop protective narrative and structural strategies such as "living underground in a subtext." (95) The mythic quest is such an underground strategy, a sub/version of the ordinary lives of Munro's seemingly ordinary women and her authorial sensorium. The heroine-artist is herself, mythically, the Mother-Goddess living the body, creating a panoply of minor pagan female deities who together function as a goddesslike group. They are shades, fractured by their daylight existence, but powerfully seeded in the text.

In the progress of Munro's fiction, those characters with an extra primitive, mythic dimension are most strongly pictured in the earlier fiction *Dance of the Happy Shades*, *Lives of Girls and Women* and the later *The Progress of Love*. As the artist as earth mother becomes fertile, and as she begins to wither, her condition is informed by the chorus of the subdeities she creates. In the course of the feminist odyssey as mythic subtext, the author does not finalize the quest for a new religious or social order for women, but she does realize a truly potent and inspirational female muse in her sixth work.

In the portrait of the Venus-like Sophie of "White Dump" in *The Progress of Love*, Munro becomes a resolute mythogizer. As Susan Brownmiller has pointed out the tyranny of Venus "is felt... whenever a man thinks and tells a woman—that her hips are too wide, her thighs are too large, her breasts are too small... to meet the current erotic standard." The ideal feminine shape has most often gone under the name of Venus, says Brownmiller, "For Venus is the goddess of love, and as the poet Byron expressed it for his sex, 'Man's love is of man's life a thing apart;/'Tis woman's whole existence."[6] The aged Sophie who, as a Venus figure, rises naked out of the water to flaunt her shrinking body is an ironic reversal of the male interpretation of the goddess of love and of woman created in her image. At the same time, she is Munro's symbolic reinstatement and reinvestiture of the principle of the Mother-Goddess, of fertility, sexuality and power. As Sophie surfaces into the clear light of the day, she is shaded and deified as the Roman goddess of love and fertility who was reborn from the sea and severed genitals. In Alice Munro's last story in her sixth fictional work, she enacts a female genesis myth with astonishing self-assurance.

| | | —

In her first collected volume of short stories, *Dance of the Happy Shades* (1967), Munro begins with a questioning exploration of the dependency of women. In this volume, the order of the writing of the stories is not particularly useful in identifying the dominant persona whose centrality is evoked by any arrangement. The sense of voice is cumulative, kaleidoscopic; its effect is like that of viewing a random selection of private photographs. What is significant is that all but three of the fifteen stories are told from the perspective of childhood and adolescence, and that six of these are related from the first person female point of view in retrospect. These stories effectively collapse the boundaries between past and present, suggesting emotional and psychological growth and establishing the process of feminist self-discovery which is at the heart of the volume. Significantly, the stories here were mostly written during the fifties and sixties when Munro herself was just emerging from that period of her life as a young mother and dependent wife, a period she characterizes as a "kind of sleep" imposed by the "ceaseless activity of the care of small children."[7] It would seem, then, that she addresses herself in the childhood and adolescent character of her fiction which she admits becomes more meaningful to her as it becomes more autobiographical, as in such later first person pieces as "Boys and Girls," "Walker Brothers Cowboy," "Images" and "Red Dress—1946."[8]

Of the first person reminiscences about childhood and adolescence, the three which are seminal to the feminist theme because they make the most explicit statements about society's expectations of girls are "Day of the Butterfly," "Boys and Girls" and "Red Dress—1946." The first to be published, "Day of the Butterfly," is a slight story about a dying child in the narrator's grade six class and a poetic glimpse of a child's first experience with death. Reminiscent in mood and theme of W.O. Mitchell's story of the Chinese children's birthday party in *Who Has Seen the Wind?*, it expresses the same elementary outrage towards the social authority of the small town, towards those who make the unjust "rules and conditions of our lives" (107). What is of greater interest is its early feminist drama. Not only are the Boys' side and the Girls' side of the school firmly established, but the narrator comes to see that the social standing of girls and women is dependent on that of their fathers and husbands in the community. Psychologically, the author begins to unravel "the immense, complicated bows of fine satin ribbon" (108) which are made by the mothers for Myra's last birthday party in hospital, and which symbolize the artificial, decorative function of women. In the gift-giving of herself, the other girls in the class and the teacher, appropriately named Miss Darling, she senses the well-packaged sensibility of women and their consumer relationships. When she reveals that she will let her little brother pull apart Myra's gift of a leatherette case with a mirror and cosmetics, she expresses her anger at what society expects her to become, that is dressed up and on display. She further rebels against becoming a manager of the small purse of twenty-five cents "guilt-tinged offerings" (110) given over to a girl who can safely slip into memory and respectable myth as a "saint."

In this story, Munro begins to consider the relationship between the female writer and her material. The authorial voice is unmistakably that of the artist who wonders at her own power of myth-making, at the right to create the legend of Myra and her little brother as "small figures carved of wood, for worship or magic, with faces smooth and aged" (101). Recognizing as well that in presenting us with Myra as a fascinating object, she has possibly created only a dressed-up doll and perpetuated the artificial, masquerading psychology of women, Munro is conscious that her artistic process may betray her by its very feminine nature.

In "Boys and Girls" and "Red Dress—1946," Munro further contests the female definition. In "Boys and Girls" she records the humiliated and anguished psychology of a child who is being conditioned by society to become a "definition"—a girl, a "joke on me" (119). The child finds herself no longer free to help her fox-farmer father outdoors but is forced instead to take possession of her person in the conventional way by taking possession of the home through housework. The climax of the story occurs when the girl frees a horse who is about to be shot and by so doing demonstrates that she is "only a girl" (127). In this fiction, Munro is true to social psychology, expertly dramatizing Simone de Beauvoir's analysis of the psychology of young girls in western society:

> But for the young woman... there is a contradiction between her status as a real human being and her vocation as a female. And just here is to be found the reason why adolescence is for the woman so difficult and decisive a moment. Up to this time she has been an autonomous individual: now she must renounce her sovereignty. Not only is she torn... between the past and the future, but in addition conflict breaks out between her original claim to be subject, active, free, and, on the other hand, her erotic urges and the social pressure to accept herself as a passive object. Her spontaneous tendency is to regard herself as the essential: how can she make up her mind to become the inessential: But if I can accomplish my destiny only as the Other, how shall I give up my Ego? Such is the painful dilemma with which the woman-to-be must struggle. (336)

The conflict between regarding herself as the essential ("I continued to slam the doors and sit as awkwardly as possible, thinking that by such measures I kept myself free," (119)), and the social pressure to accept herself as passive object is exactly the situation of Munro's heroine who finds herself objectified by the passing feed salesman's casual reference to her, "I thought it was only a girl" (116). Although there is no real resolution to this situation in "Boys and Girls" and it seems that the girl is conforming to social rules by adjusting her fantasies, "for a while I might rescue people; then things would change around, and instead, somebody would be rescuing me" (126), she is partly victorious when she opens the gate in an attempt to rescue the fated horse. If her final tears, identified by de Beauvoir as "woman's supreme alibi, allowing her to founder in defeat" (608), suggest compliance, we are at least left wondering in the conclusion if her positive gesture is not better than her young brother's masculine boasting at having "shot old Flora and cut her up in fifty pieces" (127).

"Red Dress—1946" concludes with the same thoughtful irresolution as "Boys and Girls." Told with ironic distance, the story is a comic recreation of a thirteen-year-old girl's first dance. Munro's humorous approach to this initiation rite, where the girl, with a stiff new brassiere, red velvet dress, elaborately curled hair, deodorant and cologne, is forced to leave the safe "boundaries of childhood" (151) to become a sexually alluring object, implies authorial resignation to the dance of the sexes. But, at the same time, the heroine psychologically steps outside herself as the object choice of males. This dual perspective is accomplished by her meeting with the hopefully-named Mary Fortune, the girl in the washroom who is athletic, an organizer, and is not chosen by any boys. She discovers with amazement this other alternative, a plan for independence, and while she chooses to be chosen by a boy who asks her to dance rather than escaping with Mary to a restaurant, she arrives home "socially adjusted" but oppressed by the female obligation she has to her mother to be happy in this "ordinary" rescued circumstance. She simply isn't, and acknowledges to herself that she is doomed to fail at it.

In his article "The Fiction of Alice Munro," Hallvard Dahlie explains that "though emanating from a recognizable sociological reality, the situations that are characteristically depicted in her fiction frequently transcend the literal bounds of our conscious realization, and leave us with a residual uncertainty, puzzlement, or even despair."[9] As these last three stories demonstrate, Munro certainly is not offering solutions to women. And while her feminism appears to be loosely grounded in a melancholy social determinism, even this approach is not absolute. In an interview with Barbara Frum in 1973, she reveals her own uncertainty about social conditioning and what constitutes being female: "This emotional dependency I feel in myself. I don't know where it comes from. I don't know if it is a conditioned thing in women and I don't think we'll know for another generation. I think you have to be open to all possibilities."[10] Certainly, in *Dance* Munro is exploring these other possibilities when she presents to her readers a number of unmarried, unchosen women as solitary dancers luminated in a variety of interesting and ambivalent poses.

In two stories of childhood experience "Walker Brothers Cowboy" and "Images," Nora Cronin and Mary McQuade are unmarried women, and unfortunately so, but vividly evoked through the child's eye and afforded the protection of memory, they become potent, totemic even in their single authorities. They are instrumental in shaping what seems to be the author's rejection of the status quo. In the first story, the narrator as child witnesses a social visit made by her father, Ben Jordan, a travelling salesman, to his old girlfriend Nora, who, now middle-aged, crude and coarse, survives alone on a poor farm with her blind mother. When the restrained flirtation which follows culminates in Ben's rejection of Nora's invitation to dance, the narrator observes the sad implications of having to dance alone. In contrast to the girl's sick and decorous mother, however, and the grey, naturalistic despondency of the scene, Nora is a vibrant flash of color in her "soft brilliant" (17) dress and a hearty woman capable of uproarious behavior and active invitation. Similarly, Mary McQuade of "Images," the spinster cousin who makes her way by moving from house to house nursing the family sick, may be gloomy and complaining and momentary mistress only of the house she briefly inhabits, but she is a figure to be reckoned with. Big and blousey like Nora, she lets her virginal "power" (32) loose in the house and remains, within the community of the father's family, "reckless, even proud" of being an old maid (35). There is a felt privilege in the status of these women who, despite the limitations of their cutoff circumstances, seem emotionally free—at the very least, they do not have to conform to the rules for married women.

As figures out of memory, Nora and Mary are touched, enlarged by the author's conception of them as a primitive, ancestral source. To the child's eye, they are mythopoeic figures who loom like Great Goddesses, big breasted Nora "all warmth and bulk" (17), Mary, ferocious, with a closeness to animal life. If the girl in both stories is attracted, repulsed and even frightened by these earthy women and their vestal order, they clearly are arresting characters who belong to a web of sisterhood more obviously championed by Munro through Mrs. Fullerton, an earth-mother type in "The Shining Houses."

In contrast to the mature, suburban narrator of "The Shining Houses" whose own lifestyle is as blank as the molded jellies she makes for her young children's birthday parties, Mrs. Fullerton rightfully belongs to the "old wilderness city" (24) under the new subdivision they both live in, and is to be admired. While the new community interprets Mrs. Fullerton's shacks, garden and animals as *a filthy eyesore* bringing down property values, the narrator supports the old lady; she admires her unaccommodating nature, her self-sufficiency, her independent attachment to her own place after the death of one husband and abandonment by another. Like Nora and Mary, Mrs. Fullerton is for the Munro persona a female deity.

As natural inhabitant of the "wound of the earth" (23), she suggests the chaotic powers of nature, of precivilization when nature seemed to man fertile and magically female. In the mind of the narrator there is a longing for the primacy of some earlier, victorious first state which she feels Mrs. Fullerton to represent and which the "well-proportioned magic" (29) of modern community denies. While the narrator cannot win and knows herself sacrificed to masculine gods, served up as a "conversational delight for the next cocktail party," (28) her defeat, sounded by putting her hands in her pocket and keeping a "disaffected heart," (29) seems temporary. Mrs. Fullerton has been tucked into memory and translated as an inspiration.

As Munro attempts to orient herself to the present and the future, she is engaged in drawing out the strengths of women and shading them with mythic tones. Influenced by her own rural upbringing, she apprehends the agrarian earth-mother myth, and assigns a semblance of divinity or mystical power to some of her remembered rural types. Out of the mists of memory, she creates, too, a living parade of women whose primitiveness is their refuge and their authority. Alone, poverty-stricken and ferocious, these women are not without pathetic illusions, but when, in their various defeats, they respond like trapped animals, they exercise for Munro a base and primal dignity.

In "A Trip to the Coast" and "The Time of Death," two of these women are typically distanced, here by the third person point of view, as lonely defenders of female territory. They are no doubt viewed externally because, as Munro explains, with this kind of character "there are limits to what you can get at and the ways that you can express it."[11] The grandmother in "A Trip to the Coast" is for the child May a kind of priestess of their home whose power, diminishing as she approaches death, is possibly being transferred to her:

> Ever since her grandmother had followed her into the back yard she had felt as if something had changed, something had cracked; yes, it was that new light she saw in the world. And she felt something about herself—like power, like the unsuspected still unexplored power of her own hostility, and she meant to hold it for a while and turn it like a cold coin in her hand. (*Dance*, 185)

The grandmother's will is the point of the story, for she does not disappoint the child who has always seen the old woman get the better of the outside world in her encounters with it. When the old lady agrees to be hypnotized by a casual male customer in the poor store she runs, she dies but, by doing so, remains victorious, with a hard ferocious expression on her face, diminishing the man who flees in terror. Leona Parry in "The Time of Death," in her obsessive, singular ambition for her child Patricia to be successful as a western singer, is of the same primitive, tough-willed maternity as the old grandmother. The child Patricia has an insistent authority and when she finally collapses in rage and fear over her part in the death of her little retarded brother, displays the same hostility bred of poverty and impotence.

In this first volume, Munro introduces us to the poor, primitive women in her fiction who dissent with rage, who are immature and even impotent in their defiance, but who are less emotionally dependent on men than the central persona. Economically dispossessed, their hostility isolates and sustains them. The girl in "Thanks for the Ride," one of the few Munro stories told by a male narrator, is a factory worker whose father has been beheaded and who is at the mercy of middle-class men. Yet Lois "shows those guys" who take sexual and class advantage of her when she calls out with abusive irony "Thanks for the ride" to the middle-class narrator after a night of cold passion and homemade liquor. While women like Lois and Leona are jagged, verging on hysteria, they refuse to completely acquiesce emotionally. This is also true of Helen, the department store clerk in "Postcard," who tells her own story of how she was jilted through the unexpected marriage of her lover, Clare MacQuarrie, a man she cared little for but whose status in the small town, whose gifts and company, were not unpleasant diversions for the price she paid of sexual compliance. Helen is a more intelligent, better off version of Leona Parry and Lois, her relationship with her mother of that genteel and constrictive kind we see in Rachel Cameron and her mother in Margaret Laurence's *A Jest of God*. Nonetheless, she resorts to the same kind of emotional release, the noisy protest of honking her car horn in ironic chivaree outside the newlywed's home. While Helen is left with an acute understanding of something missed, her gesture is a moment of female triumph in the narrative.

In *Dance*, like the earth-mothers and primitives, Munro's decorous spinsters are viewed from the outside, but playing "stylized and simplified roles"[12] dictated by the Calvinist order of the small town. In "The Peace of Utrecht," an autobiographical story, the mature narrator introduces the unmarried aunties who will recur in her fiction and who represent a way of life for women which Munro looks back on with some despair. Childish and unfulfilled, these women live ordered lives of intricate domestic and private ritual, of teasing polished conversation and discreet circumlocution. For the protagonist there is no real possibility of communication with Aunt Annie and Auntie Lou who, thrown back on a tidy, virginal "web of sisterhood" (203), have become aged and dry mannequins of little substance and much artifice. At first glance, the two Miss Marsalles in "Dance of the Happy Shades" seem even more grotesque. Childish, sexless, wild and gentle creatures, bizarre yet domestic, living in their house in Rosedale outside the complications of time, they belong to a passing world, their lives "wholly unrealistic" (215), diminished by spinsterhood and, now, history. Munro, prone to adjusting her reader's angle of vision, does not, however, let us dismiss the central Miss Marsalles as easily as some of her other town spinsters. In her rouge and hairdo and brocaded dress she is hardly real, like a figure from a masquerade, "like the feverish, fancied-up courtesan of an unpleasant Puritan imagination" (217), but, like the courtesan, Miss Marsalles belongs to no man, and thus suggests independence and an untamed feminine magic. Like some ancient divinity, she has worked a "miracle" with the retarded child she has taught to play the piano. Thus the narrator can ask: "why is it that we are unable to say—as we must have expected to say—*poor Miss Marsalles?*" (224).

The male narrator of "Thanks for the Ride" considers *omne animal* and as Munro begins to investigate her own psyche and its many female voices, she uncovers this same primitive dimension. In *Dance of the Happy Shades*, her portraits of isolated women, betrayed by the absence of men, are often tinted by the ancient mythology which equated women with nature and its primal power; these primal women help create an impression of female tribe which Munro projects in this first volume as the source of an independent female imagination. All of her women, the earth-mothers, the primitives, the Victorian spinsters, are literally figures in relief. They remain the *Other*, outside of society, but in this condition they are like the goddesses of old, avatars to the childish imagination which permeates *Dance of the Happy Shades*. Even the spinsters suggest, as the fierce old grandmother does to the undressed May in "A Trip to the Coast," notice of naked, ancient authority, the possibility of being "one of them Queens of Egypt" (178). They advance such a possibility because of the obviousness and awful studiedness of their disguises. "Even behind my aunt's soft familiar face is another, more primitive old woman" discovers the narrator of "The Peace of Utrecht" (208).

In fact, it is with "The Peace of Utrecht," an acknowledged milestone by Munro in her authorial development, that the masquerade of being female is most acutely felt. Munro herself explains that the story came after her mother's death: ". . . the incident that is at the heart of that story is the clothes. I went to my grandmother's house and she showed me my mother's clothes. . . . and from that time on I had this new thing about writing."[13] The clothes which are central in the story are those of the dead mother, the "peach-colored bed-jacket," the "brocades and flowered silks" (*Dance*, 205); these are sad, even beautiful tokens of a life, but important talismans too of the materialism out of which the old aunts in their web of sisterhood weave their lives. Munro can be critical of this, particularly because of the material-mindedness of a Calvinist society which leaves women as empty dress, forcing them to play denigrated, stylized rôles. It is in part this recognition which causes her to consider the false fronts, to want to strip them away and research the elemental truth about the nature of women.

| | | —

The process of becoming a woman which is investigated in its early stages in the stories about childhood and adolescence in *Dance* is repeated, fleshed out and brought to greater maturity in *Lives of Girls and Women* (1971). The novel of how Del Jordan advances to the edge of adulthood is both a truthful psychological and social analysis of North American adolescence— a long overdue female equivalent to J.D. Salinger's *Catcher in the Rye*— and a modern Künstlerroman: the novel of the artist as heroine. Tracing Del Jordan's interest in fiction from her thrilling preoccupation as a child with Uncle Benny's gothic tabloids to her final artistic vision in the final chapter, "Epilogue: The Photographer," Munro gives us a sense of Del as a developing artist. Moreover, the echo of Munro's own voice can be heard in Del's double perspective as the narrator of her own fiction, as child and adolescent seen through mature memory. John Moss explains, "Del is going to be the writer that Alice Munro becomes. . . . What is being offered is the authentic version of all the phases passed through and things encountered that have gone into the making of one particular creative sensibility which now records them."[14]

The story of Del Jordan begs to be read first, however, as a feminist quest for identity and freedom, and like the frogs in the first few lines of the novel struggling to avoid the hook, Del passes through several stages in the

narrative in which she learns to cope, to wriggle free of destructive social
dicta in order to possess herself. In the early chapters, too, are depicted
some formative female influences, in particular the primitive and spinster
types introduced by Munro earlier in *Dance.*

As a child living on the Flats Road, Del is close to nature and the primitive imagination of its inhabitants. Her concept of womanhood is influenced by one of Munro's most striking models of female savagery, Madeleine of the Flats Road. Madeleine, the eccentric Uncle Benny's mail-order
bride, is a fascinating character of uncontrollable fury who, raging against
her unchosen status of wife of Uncle Benny and mother of the illegitimate
child Diane, refuses to conform to even the minimal social expectations of
the Flats Road. "You're a dirty little bugger. Dirty little spy-bugger. Dirty
little spy-bugger, aren't you?" is her amazing first greeting to the child Del
(15). Madeleine, as part of the animal world of ferrets and furred creatures
and swamp, is ready to beat, maim, perhaps even to kill to escape her captivity. Despite the awful fact that Madeleine violently straps Diane, Del is
impressed by her triumph, her raging acts against all and sundry, including
men. Cutting up Uncle Benny's good green suit, or throwing a Kotex box
at Charlie Buckle in temper, Madeline is a mad independent and equated in
Del's mature mind with animal maternity. She is like the female foxes who
"were not like domestic animals... had lived only a very few generations
in captivity," who might decide to kill their pups and

Nobody knew whether they did this out of blind irritation, or out of
roused and terrified maternal feeling—could they be wanting to take
their pups, who still had not opened their eyes, out of the dangerous situation they might sense they had brought them into, in these pens?
(*Lives,* 18)

A castrating figure, Madeleine, "her long legs going like scissors" (14), is
victorious for Del Jordan, at least in comparison to the Calvinist women,
her aunts, who practice the proper domestic rituals, accept the division between women's work and important male enterprise, who center their lives
about a man and deny the jurisdiction of the flesh.

The motif of captivity is strong in *Lives,* and when death becomes a Calvinist ritual in the Irish family's funeral for her Uncle Craig of Jenkin's
Bend, Del understands that despite the pretense of being in control at the
funeral, the spinster aunts, Elspeth and Grace, with their ordered and intri-

cately formal world displayed through preparation of enormous quantities of food and fluttering femininity, have in no sense contained death. Instead, they are the captives of the artificial male code of the Fathers of Confederation which keeps them out of touch with nature, including their own. By biting her cousin Mary Oliphant to avoid viewing the decked-out corpse of Uncle Craig, Del reverts back to the psychology and practice of the likes of Madeleine of the Flats Road. Her taste of blood is a satisfying animal connection in the presence of death. A gesture of "pure freedom" (46), *barbaric* according to the aunts and the family code, it also effectively separates her from the absolute "womb-tomb" (45) condition of the female lives of the aunts whose identities shrivel as they age, become predictably dried out, brittle with use, empty and unfulfilled when "they no longer had a man with them, to nourish and admire..." (50).

The major influence in Del's life is not these other women, however, but her mother; in "Age of Faith" Del will embrace religion, in part because her mother doesn't and in "Princess Ida" and subsequent chapters we come to understand the strong presence of the mother and the degree to which she makes Del. Only recently has the relationship between mother and daughter become central in any fiction, and while Munro does not focus on this relationship exclusively, she insightfully investigates the connection in the growth of her heroine. Renting a house in the town of Jubilee, taking Del with her and spending only the summers with the father on the Flats Road, Del's mother tirelessly writes editorials to local newspapers, sells encyclopedias door-to-door and makes speeches on birth control; thus she offers to Del a very different face of woman from either Madeline or the aunts. The world of intellect, reason and the arts is her muse, and because she doesn't conform to any acceptable ideal of motherhood in a small town is a chronic embarrassment and a social humiliation to a conforming Del. While Del remains unconvinced about her mother's denial of romantic love and her somewhat prudish attitude towards sex, she is inspired by her despite herself. Del vacillates between a conception of her as a goddess of sorts, a "priestess" (67) and a comic calamity, but it is the former interpretation which wins out. Like the Egyptian deity Isis, whose name her mother chastises her for remembering as a god, rather than as a goddess (76), the mother is the essence of mysterious, powerful female first beginnings as well as a model of intellectual womanhood.

Despite the ordinariness of the surface lives of girls and women, the novel is not without its telling mythic moments and female characters of archetypal cast. When the child Del catches the beauty of the dead cow and stands hesitating mistress over it in "Heirs of the Living Body," she recreates the attitude and power of Isis, the teacher of agriculture and goddess of fertility whose sacred symbol was the cow. The line of power between mother and daughter is thus affirmed by Munro through this symbol which is submerged in the fiction. The Egyptian motif is extended, too, in the character of Nile who comes to visit as Uncle Bill's second wife in "Princess Ida." Nile, with her calculated sensuality, her green clothes and matching green nail polish, is the epitome of the femme fatale, a model of "some extreme of feminine decorativeness, perfect artificiality" (72) and compelling beauty. Cleopatra-like, she is a striking example of the siren and a tempting invitation to Del to the female life of sexual desirability and possible conquest, which is outside of her mother's morality and motivation. Nile's pose portends further investigation for Del, for as a fatally alluring object, she anticipates the forthcoming eroticism of Del's own virginal female psyche.

The sexual urge is confounded with religiosity in "Age of Faith" where we view Del exchanging her role of wondering observer of the faces and manners of other women for that of active explorer of her own possible faith and rituals. Her examination of conventional religion is vaguely sexual, stirred by Del's positive longing for Him, and is accomplished by frequenting in somewhat comic succession the United and Anglican churches in Jubilee. But her hope for uncovering the design and designer of the universe fails and initially, while she protests her mother's agnostic point of view that "God was made by *man*. Man at a lower and bloodthirstier stage of his development than he is at now, we hope. Man made God in his own image" (89), she assumes her mother's alienation from conventional religion. She edges closer to her mother's rational intellectualism and away from the naturalism of the Flats Road (and such characters as Madeleine) when the family dog is executed, an act Del feels to be connected in some vague way with religious sacrifice.

Del's struggle towards the authority of the intellectual life occupies Munro for the rest of the novel. And while the conflict between reason and passion is an old theme in literature, rarely has woman been the protagonist of this drama. Man has traditionally been interpreted as the controlling head, woman the submissive and seductive heart; he, the I, the person; she, the sexual It. Del's problem is special because, while Man can either reject or incorporate Woman into his private odyssey, Woman is forced by conventional society to choose between sexual union, which objectifies and diminishes her and cuts off her creative potential, and the single state of the artistic or intellectual life through which she can express her selfness. "Once you make that mistake, of being—distracted, over a man, your life will never be your own. You will get the burden, a woman always does" (147) is the ominous warning of Del's mother. Del is a girl who is Munro's living portrait of the social and psychological tensions of this female condition and its choices.

In "Changes and Ceremonies" and "Lives of Girls and Women" sexual relations as a distraction and an invitation to "the burden" are at the center of the narrative. While in her obsession for books, Del is no longer "normal" in Jubilee, she is careful of preserving her relationship with her conventionally-minded friend, Naomi. As shield and sister consort, Naomi is Del's defense against the increasing social authority of boys whose humiliating sexual taunts are later remembered as that which "stripped away freedom to be what you wanted, reduced you to what it was they saw, and that, plainly, was enough to make them gag" (98). Later, Naomi is Del's confidante in culling sexual information as she anticipates the seemingly indecent mysteries of sex. Del absorbs from her small town puritan environment that absolute moral division between the prostitute and the saint, a standard which manifests itself in Del's experience in either the apparent sexlessness of her mother's life or the shocking, titillating obscenity of the three prostitutes on the edge of town, one of whom Naomi insists with prurient exhilaration "had been persuaded to serve a line-up, standing up" at the Gay-la Dance Hall (128). Given this choice, Del momentarily decides on the "condition of perfect depravity" (128), the thought of whoredom having a greater appeal because it arrests the tension of the struggle for her own person—it was a "restful, alluring thought, because it was so final, and did away with ambition and anxiety" (128).

Her opportunity to become a sexually fascinating, sensual thing, like Uncle Bill's Nile or the prostitute Peggy, is afforded through the middle-aged boyfriend of her mother's boarder, Fern Dogherty, who, lazy and sensual, seems to Del quite the opposite of her mother and "those qualities my mother had developed for her assault on life—sharpness, smartness, determination, selectiveness" (120). As a kind of Calvinist Lolita, who idealizes and objectifies lust, Del encourages the sexual advances of Mr. Chamberlain, whose secret pinches, rubs and even slaps are accomplished quickly out of adult vision on his visits to Fern, and whose assaults Del explains "was what I expected sexual communication to be—a flash of insanity, a dreamlike ruthlessness, contemptuous breakthrough in a world of decent appearances" (135). Del allows herself to become the ultimate sexual It of masculine and puritan invention when she accompanies Mr. Chamberlain to an isolated field where he masturbates at her expense, leaving her disappointed and depressed; at the same time she arrives at the mature sexual and potentially liberating knowledge that lust is not nearly so clear nor so absolute as she had assumed.

After this first sexual experience and the shedding of her Calvinist skin, Del retreats with open-mindedness into books and while they are no substitute for sex, they are an imaginative means out of the narrow, circumscribed lives of the girls and women in Jubilee. And, if, at this point in time, she does not quite understand her mother's practical solutions, her admonitions to use her brains, not to be distracted by men and to maintain her self-respect, it doesn't matter. She has matured in a more fundamental way beyond her mother's defensive female psychology and maternal custodianship:

> I felt that it was not so different from all the other advice handed out to women, to girls, advice that assumed being female made you damageable, that a certain amount of carefulness and solemn fuss and self-protection were called for, whereas men were supposed to be able to go out and take on all kinds of experiences and shuck off what they didn't want and come back proud. Without even thinking about it, I had decided to do the same. (*Lives*, 147)

Despite her resolve, Del comes under increased pressure to conform to the prevailing sexual roles of the community, and, with an expert, socially analytical eye, Munro details the conventions assumed by Naomi, who quits school for an office job in the creamery, leaving Del momentarily in abject misery and isolation. Naomi has joined the small legion of trousseau-saving women who, depilated and deodorized, adopt a whole set of pots on payment and equally steely conventions of baby-showers, dress and hairstyles. Del makes one last concession to Naomi by going to the Gay-la Dance Hall with her and getting preposterously drunk to escape the obligation she feels to be something other than she is, "somebody small, snappy, bright, flirtatious," (156) for the wise-cracking, foxy Clive of the foursome which develops. However, she finally cannot accept this abrogation of self required by such a social role. The social injunction to be decorative and passive is an upsetting revelation, one she also uncovers in a magazine article which claims that the distinction between masculine and feminine modes of thought can be illustrated by a boy and girl sitting on a park bench looking at the moon: "The boy thinks of the universe, its immensity and mystery; the girl thinks, 'I must wash my hair'" (150). Del chooses with defiance to be abnormal, to want both men to love her *and* to think of the universe, and thus sets her course without Naomi, to experience her own rites of passage into adult sexuality.

The clash between the head and the heart, intellect and sexual passion, is an archetypal theme in literature and Del's experience is not unlike, for one, that of Hardy's protagonist of *Jude the Obscure* who lusts after and marries the carnal farm girl Arabella, only to be later attracted by Sue Bridehead and her purity of intellect. Munro's approach is much less symbolic than Hardy's, much less "intellectual" in figure and allusion, but Del's relationship with the male "brain" of her grade thirteen class, Jerry Storey, and Garnet French, the uneducated lumber worker, exjailbird and converted Baptist from the backwoods, are reminiscent of this age-old problematic split, and her experiences with these two men are arranged in a recognizable counterpoint. Jerry Storey, as a potential scholarship winner like Del herself, is sympathetic intellectual company, but with Garnet French, met at a Baptist revival meeting, Del realizes what she can't with Jerry, pure physical passion, the loss of her virginity and the collapse of her scholarship hopes when she neglects her studies for love, or, at least, its sexual expression. Del comes closest to losing herself with Garnet French from whom she parts in pain when he expects her to marry him, become a Baptist and have his babies. She has never seriously entertained this choice, but the beauty and the pleasure of her romantic passion is not easy to relinquish. Del knows her own power—and deceit—in their final physical struggle in the water as Garnet tries to assert his will over her with a mock baptism into his religion:

> I felt amazement, not that I was fighting with Garnet but that anybody could have made such a mistake, to think he had real power over me. I was too amazed to be angry, I forgot to be frightened, it seemed to me impossible that he should not understand that all the powers I granted him were in play, that he himself was—in play, that I meant to keep him sewed up in his golden lover's skin forever... (*Lives*, 197)

When Garnet does not return for her, as she knows he won't, Del feels herself both relieved and desolate. The die has been cast, however, and she knows her own possibilities when cut off from the "mistakes and confusion of the past"; she feels free to adventurously get on with her own "real life" (201).

Del Jordan is faithfully drawn from life, the feminist heroine of a fiction mirroring the modern realities of rites of passage. This social and psychological realism of *Lives* is, however, only one level of the fiction. Munro is the author of mythopoeic moment and character who considers her own aesthetic through Del Jordan; Del chooses to become an author and cannot repress her own aspiration towards magic authorship in "Epilogue: The Photographer." The gothic novel that she carries with her in her head is a fantastic illusion, its photographer a powerful, if threatening, supernatural image-maker. We know that Del will become what Munro is herself, a startling executioner of the image—of marvellous portraits frozen in time and space. Most importantly, the "Epilogue" is the final statement of the artistic facet of Del's personality which develops as a shadow narrative throughout the novel and which prevents her from being an ordinary, single-faceted character. From childhood through adolescence, Del is perennially in a state of heightened imagination. Her psychology is composed of visionary states: at Uncle Craig's funeral "caught in a vision . . . of confusion and obscenity—of helplessness, which was revealed as the most obscene thing there could be . . . [a vision] . . . which collapsed of its own intensity" (48); of varying perspectives and angles, as with her brother Owen who from one vantage point seems "frail and young" (87). In short, Del becomes in the course of the narrative not only a female adolescent heroine, but the developing artist and, as other critics have observed, a female version of Joyce's Stephen Dedalus in *A Portrait of the Artist as a Young Man*.[15]

| | | —

In the collection of thirteen short stories *Something I've Been Meaning to Tell You* (1974), we are in familiar Munro country with the characters of repressed spinsters, well-bred aunts, and fierce, poor women; here are stories about remembered adolescence and childhood sexuality, grandmothers and their granddaughters, kinship in the Ottawa Valley, and the art of fiction-making itself, stories which individually hold out the promise of decoding the private language of each who comes under Alice Munro's looking glass. Here, the voice of the decoder is more mature and the techniques of the storyteller more involved than in the previous volume, the characters and their situations enticingly darkened with circle upon circle of complex ambiguity. The search for identity is here, too, but not as we might expect after the optimistic conclusion of *Lives*—realized—delivered in some happy framework; rather, it remains shrouded with unresolve. It would seem that in travelling forward from *Lives,* for the sensibility of this volume is that of a middle-aged narrator, Munro is moving backwards because the expected control, the certain and clear answers to the feminist odyssey do not materialize; instead, there is further amazement in human relationships, and a new complicating theme of the generation gap, of older women (and one man in "Walking on Water") confronting contemporary and far from satisfying or correct fashions of human behavior.

For Munro the feminist quest cannot be over, particularly as the range of the experience of her maturing persona increases; female identity becomes ever more complicated by the relative, special, often modern conditions of individual lives and situations. But despite the general ambience of something more to be seen and explored and said beyond all literal surfaces, this volume has a marked tone of female alienation which, since Munro's first volume, has become increasingly more vocal. In the stories "Material" and "The Spanish Lady" the emotions of the mature, middle-class narrators, provoked by unsatisfactory relationships with men, are blatantly threatening and hostile, in aggressive continuum with the author-narrator of "The Office" from *Dance* who fights to keep herself in control, although she really wants to "murder" Mr. Malley. Revenge, which skirted Munro's previous fiction, has become a strong and threatening declaration as the emotional lives of several women are laid bare, let loose in a string of black, murderous visions and savage cries of protest.

"The Executioners" is the most menacing and libidinous in its expression of secret female fury. While we hardly notice the young girl's malevolent intention in dangerously tricking her little brother onto a rafter in "Boys and Girls" of *Dance*, we cannot here overlook the child Helena's vicious interior monologue when she is humiliated, like Del Jordan, by the sexual taunts of a boy, Howard Troy, in her class:

Punishments. I thought of myself walking on Howard Troy's eyes. Driving spikes into his eyes. The spikes would be on the soles of my

shoes, they would be long and sharp. His eyeballs would bulge out, un-
protected, as big as overturned basins, and I would walk on them, punc-
turing, flattening, bloodying, at a calm pace. . . . I would have liked his
head torn from his body, flesh pulpy and dripping like watermelon,
limbs wrenched away; axes, saws, knives and hammers applied to him.
(*Something*, 120)

Helena's hatred is nourished by the hired girl from the bush, the one-
armed Robina who, as Munro's characteristic *omne animal* type, seems to
the child "a chief" (117), and Robina's brothers, Jimmy and Duval. The
child is exposed to their similar hatred for the taunting boy's father, Stump
Troy, and her fantasy about Howard Troy is fulfilled when she becomes a
psychological accomplice in the murder of both the bootlegger father and
the son.

Murder is also close to the surface of the female psychology of the lead
story, "Something I've Been Meaning to Tell You," as Munro adjusts her
angle of vision towards her constant small town "ladies" of a passing generation. While she tends not to explore the inner life of the Victorian spinsters in *Dance*, in *Lives* she begins to scratch the surface illusions of their
personalities. Beneath the facade of Grace's and Espeth's girlish innocence
in *Lives*, Del Jordan discovered an undercurrent of hostile emotion. The
spinsters seemingly accept their civilized and subordinate positions, but in
their jokes and conversation they betray "tiny razor cuts" (31) of malice
and potentially murderous dispositions, but not until the thoroughly chill-
ing tale of "Something I've Been Meaning to Tell You" is this kind of
woman unmasked for the reader.

In this story, the Victorian web of sisterhood has turned in upon itself
with ghastly repercussions. The old maid, Et, who has always lived an ordered, watchful life on the fringes of her sister Char's is overcome by her
desire to have and to hold as her own, her sister's husband. In Et, who begins to suspect Char of slowly poisoning the husband, Arthur, Munro suggests the roots of a primal, immature female imagination: "She did think
maybe she was going a little strange, as old maids did; this fear of hers was
like the absurd and harmless fears young girls sometimes have, that they
will jump out a window, or strangle a baby, sitting in its buggy" (11).
When Et, through intimate knowledge of her sister's psychology, occa-
sions, or, at the least, thinks she has occasioned, her sister's suicide, the
reader is left with a grotesque insight into the confused, aggressive and

hysterical spirit of an old woman, whose emotional identity is frozen in her childish past. That easy transition from a girl turning cartwheels to a respectable town fixture has only been a superficial one, for Et's desire to annihilate Char partly arises from a vengeful childhood jealousy of her sister's ability to captivate men. The awful irony in this tale is that the town's joking interpretation of Et as a "terror" is, in reality, a serious indicator of a potent hostility.

The romantic triangle of this last story is a characteristic pattern in the volume, played out in varying ways, but in "The Spanish Lady" with similar psychological and social implications as in "Something I've Been Meaning to Tell You." The narrator, compared to Et, is mature, modern and sophisticated, but after her best friend and her husband have deceived her by having an affair, left in the same condition of aggressive and angry alienation. In both past and present, the active competition of women for a man is a social design which Munro unravels as self-destructive, with female pitted against female in an elemental way to hapless and helpless ends. Here the situation is complicated by the intellectualism and the modern mores of the narrator, who may have had affairs herself and who thinks that she can gain control of the situation in the modern way by rational, civilized understanding and psychological self-counselling. This trust in reasonableness is what has victimized her, however, and ultimately her only active defense is that of an emotional response at its most basic, irrational level. The betrayed wife imagines her expression of hatred as that of the wife in *God's Little Acre*, kicking, screaming and slapping the bare bodies of her husband and friend. Finally, she is able to release her rage by howling "in amazing protest" and biting her arm: "I put my arm across my open mouth and to stop the pain, I bite it, I bite my arm..." (145).

For the mature and modern voice in this volume, sexual attitudes and language may have seemingly altered and taken on new liberated colors; the word "fuck" is no longer a dangerous word as it was for the child in "The Executioners" when it was then a "word thrown against you, that could bring you to an absolute stop" (115), but the "vulnerability which is itself a shame" remains. The narrator of "Material" is liberated, has had two husbands, but her first, a writer, has demonstrated through his fiction a greater control over their shared experience by turning it, without the distraction of sentiment, into Art. He has not been, as she has been, *at the mercy* of her own sisterly sympathetic feeling for Dotty, the woman whose apartment he purposely let flood to suit his own convenience and pocket-book, yet later could write a moving story about. Angrily, the narrator surveys her own life and her two husbands, concluding,

> looking at my husband Gabriel, I decided that he and Hugo are not really so unalike. Both of them have managed something. Both of them have decided what to do about everything they run across in this world, what attitude to take, how to ignore or use things. In their limited and precarious ways they both have authority. . . . I do blame them. I envy and despise. (*Something*, 36)

In this third volume, women do not only hate, they wait. "How I Met My Husband" is a light story about the girl Edie who, as the hired summer girl to the Peebles, experiences first love with a transient pilot who offers airplane rides for a price on a nearby fairgrounds. The humiliation anticipated in "Sunday Afternoon" from *Dance* by the girl Alva, a similar hired girl who has had a pass made at her by a male guest, is actually experienced by Edie, although remembered and related by her with comic nostalgia. When the pilot promises to write to her, after their brief fling, Edie believes him and takes up the traditional posture of a woman waiting,

> Till it came to me one day there were women doing this with their lives, all over. There were women just waiting and waiting by mailboxes for one letter or another. I imagined me making this journey day after day and year after year, and my hair starting to go gray, and I thought, I was never made to go on like that. So I stopped meeting the mail. (*Something*, 53)

While Munro solves this dilemma with the tongue-in-cheek resolution of having Edie marry the postman, she has made a pregnant point about the dilemma of waiting women which is expanded into a much more melancholy fiction in "Tell Me Yes or No."

The love letter is central in this story, too; the narrator is middle-aged, of an older generation and psychology than the modern young girls with hair to the waist who float easily between lovers. Her love affair with a married man is prompted, not of the moment, but unfashionably, by his connection to her past self; she had had a brief flirtation with him when she was a young mother. Their love affair is kept alive by a series of letters, and when his no longer arrive, she experiences the pain of waiting, relieved only by the unexpected discovery of his death; this causes her to travel to the city where he lived, to the bookstore he kept with his wife.

The real irony of the narrative is the complicated deceit of the man, for what the narrator-mistress uncovers is a series of letters written to the dead man by another woman called Patricia. These letters are given to the narrator by the man's wife who assumes the narrator to be Patricia. Imagining the suffering of this other, waiting woman, the narrator shatters and dispenses with this older standard of love which she reckons must be expendable for men, even as it claims women as perennial victims: "She [Patricia] suffers according to rules we all know, which are meaningless and absolute. When I think of her I see all this sort of love as you [the man] must have seen, or see it, as something going on at a distance; a strange, not even pitiable, expenditure; unintelligible ceremony in an unknown faith" (100).

The female faith in romantic love as total commitment is an absolute fiction and Munro underlines the point with the narrator's final admission of having invented the man and the entire situation. While Munro's fictional construct is devious, her protest is explicit, levelled squarely at that "requirement of femininity... that a woman devote her life to love—to mother love, to romantic love, to religious love, to amorphous, undifferentiating caring,"[16] while the male of the species as romantic lover moves successfully from woman to woman or maintains multiple relationships.

Something I've Been Meaning to Tell You is a volume of dramatic contrasts with Munro's authorial persona rising as a kind of Janus mask of committed romantic love or its obverse, unparalleled hate. This dual face of woman is not, of course, a modern attitude, but the expression of the sexual psychology of an older generation, at eccentric odds with the likes of the bohemian Calla who, in "Walking on Water," thinks nothing, indeed, enjoys being discovered having sexual intercourse in the rooming house hallway. A central female dilemma in Munro's fiction is that of being caught in the grip of past memory and past values and thus of feeling unable to seize the present. And this is understandably so. There is some security in the old ideal which interprets such a character as the elderly Aunt Madge of "Winter Wind" who "could have been held up as an example, an ideal wife, except that she gave no impression of sacrifice, of resignation, of doing one's duty, such as is looked for in ideals" (160).

The old role is comfortable, or has been, because it disallows the risk of coming to know oneself as a woman. It provides order to life. And without order and limits, women embark on a hazardous and lonely route. In this third volume, however, it is not enough; order and comfort pall, even for the Victorian ladies. Munro has old Et finally embrace the chaos of her own imagination, and the middle-aged urbanite of "Tell Me Yes or No" who understands, in retrospect, that her unquestioning domestic life of the fifties was rooted in a "love of limits" (107) has already begun her quest.

Yet freedom is no simple matter. There is a contemporary complication, for Munro can see that in some ways the promise of freedom has devolved into the same static designs of the past. Somewhat morosely, she dramatizes female characters who, apparently liberated, have really only adopted a new set of unnatural rituals and disguises. The mother June in "Memorial" with her sense of social obligation at her son's memorial service is no less bizarre than the old aunts at Uncle Craig's funeral in *Lives*. In her desire to fend off chaos by imposing order, June has simply substituted new fashions and ideology for old. Garments of "exotic poverty" (214) have replaced the carefully constructed dress of the older generation; a mechanical Freudian psychology operates in lieu of the Calvinist code, and the "morality of consumerism" (169) has replaced the old Protestant materialism. Even the knowing older sister Eileen, who welcomes disorder and natural expression, is gravely impaired in her search for the authentic life:

> She discovered in herself these days an unattractive finickiness about some things, about clothes, for instance, and decoration. A wish to avoid fraud, not to appropriate serious things for trivial uses, not to mock things by making them into fashions. A doomed wish. She herself offended. (*Something*, 169)

One of Munro's most damning portraits of the modern woman is that of the career type, Jeanette, in "Marrakesh." As she juxtaposes the old school teacher, the grandmother Dorothy, with her granddaughter, the college professor, Munro addresses the old feminine pattern of immaturity and posturing. With the virtue of experience and the older virtue of common sense, Dorothy attempts to decipher the "hieroglyph" of her granddaughter's identity, the identity of the new woman:

> Dorothy had seen pictures in magazines of this new type of adult who appeared to have discarded adulthood. Jeanette was the first one she had seen close up and in the flesh. It used to be that young boys and girls would try to look like grown men and women, often with ridiculous re-

sults. Now there were grown men and women who tried to look like teen-agers until, presumably, they woke up on the brink of old age. It was a strange thing to see the child already meeting the old woman in Jeanette's face. . . . with a change of light or mood or body chemistry this same face showed itself bruised, bluish, sharp, skin more than a little shriveled under the eyes. A great deal had been simply skipped out. (*Something*, 129)

Jeanette, a thirtyish woman in childish dress who relates with suppressed hysteria the fiction of "Marrakesh," is an immature horror equal to Munro's most unfulfilled Victorian child-women. And certainly her masquerade is far more insidious than that of her grandmother who, puritanical and convention-ridden, at least has a sense of self-preservation.

"Where is the feminist quest leading?" is one of the underlying problematic questions of *Something I've Been Meaning to Tell You*. The battle of the sexes is blatantly here, but it cannot be won by Munro's narrators; in fact, it seems destined to a futile repetition of a longstanding feminine mode of behavior: to posturing and deceit. The young girls who in the conclusion to "The Found Boat" are learning to lie to escape their sense of helplessness and humiliation are the psychological precursors of the modern fashionable June of "Memorial" and Jeanette of "Marrakesh."

In this volume, too, Munro points out that "making up" is not exclusive to women, that contemporary men are claiming this feminine disposition to fraudulently label or disguise themselves. The young boys of "The Found Boat," in contrast to the girls, do not need to name the boat to know it as an extension of themselves, as superior and omnipotent. Cam of "Forgiveness in Families" exists in a later time frame and is unlike them. He is a man of many tried on, fleeting faces, including the one central to the story, that of nightgowned religious cultist. And Ewart of "Memorial," consort houseboy-husband to the seemingly certain and bossy June, gives an impression of androgyny as he blends into rather than initiates his wife's world of shawls and caftans, Indian children and Indian art. Thus the conflict between boys and girls, men and women, begins to diverge, to take a new twist in this third volume as Munro studies the contrast between generations. Men are still exploitative; women still nurture. Cam remains center-of-the-universe to his mother and Ewart takes the age-old "brief restorative dip" (180) in quick, secret intercourse with June's sister, Eileen; yet Ewart, a member of the contemporary upper-middle class, also expresses a lack of purpose and a new male vulnerability in Munro's fiction that makes him more the enemy of himself than of Eileen.

As Munro's fiction of private lives develops, she demonstrates that she is quietly but deftly in touch with the pulse of the greater social climate. A dimension of this volume is that of the shifting sexual relationships and definitions, of male femininity and sexually liberated, educated women of the urban middle class in the late sixties. With a mood close to anthropological amazement, she presents the children of sexual liberation through the eyes of an older generation, like the grandmother Dorothy of "Marrakesh" who wonders at the brave new sexual modes of behavior in this tribe whose members, her granddaughter and the man next door, caught in the act of sex, seem, fittingly, "like figures in a museum" (140). For Dorothy they are figures at sea, lost, both to be pitied, and it is an understanding that Munro means her readers to take to heart. The female imitation of the male pursuit of Ego is isolating, inhumane, a self-deceit that one is more than human and beyond the dictates of nature and natural emotions. Part of the something that Munro is meaning to tell us is that for both sexes, by believing that one can walk on water, one inevitably drowns.

| | | —

With all the complexities of historical time, of class, or rural or urban place which shape women and male-female relationships in Munro's fiction, she does not let go of the feminist odyssey in her fourth volume, *Who Do You Think You Are?* (1978); but because the narrative is reported from the third person point of view, Rose is somewhat objectified for the reader. Lacking the personal, underground quality of Del's voice in *Lives*, the fiction asks for less sympathy towards its protagonist—towards her essential rightness—invites, at the very least, the reader to observe the cracks and spaces in her psyche.

The voice of female protest is still active in this fourth volume. Indeed, the story of Rose is familiar Munro in the childhood situation of the poor country girl struggling towards the intellectual life, of trying to escape the male-female order and social expectations of small town Ontario and its narrow-mindedness. There is, nonetheless, a new sense of mature resolve in the interpretation of these situations, of evaluating being placed in some abeyance, of finding fault in the interest of women receding, of anger and hatred diminishing, of love of memory of past life and its people increasing.

Protest against the social conditioning and the injustices of being female in *Who Do You Think You Are?* is sheltered and muted by Rose's increasing understanding in the course of the narrative that the past is the only one she has; to accept it with compassion is to do the same for self.

Interestingly, the motif of the missing or the inconsequential father which has characterized much of Munro's earlier work vanishes with the introduction of "King" of the royal beatings in the first episode. Absent father is restored by a somewhat repressive one whose duty is to reprimand and who functions in the larger social world of poverty-stricken West Hanratty as part of a primitive, patriarchal order. Imaginatively and with shocking honesty, Munro records the ritualized drama of the child-beating of the young Rose, when she encourages the frustration of her stepmother, Flo, as she is dutifully engaged in the Saturday afternoon routine of scrubbing the kitchen floor. Female punishes female for a dimly understood sense of humiliation as Flo calls in the father to do his paternal duty by beating Rose. What follows is no dutiful reprimand but a passionate beating with the father out of control, significantly seen by Rose as an actor who means it, realized by her emotionlessly as experiencing both a rejuvenating hatred and pleasure in this special role. Munro is quick to point out the sexual implications of this situation through Rose's younger brother Brian who escapes, "runs away, out the woodshed door, to do as he likes. Being a boy, free to help or not, involve himself or not."[17]

It is not, however, so much the sexual implications of the beating which is Munro's or her character's central interest, but the larger theater of the gothic, embracing both sexes, which is the peculiar feature of life in West Hanratty itself: a primitive and grotesque arena in which Rose's part is only marginal in the greater play of things. The savage drama of the deformed Becky Tyde, a big-headed dwarf, who has been beated by her father who in turn is beaten to his ultimate death by a group of small town vigilantes, later to become respectable male members of the community, is a much more desperate affair.

Feminist protest is muffled by this relativist point of view, by the black humor projected in these people of limited intellectual and economic resources making their own savage and exciting entertainment, by the melancholy understanding that in the end, old age and death make all, men and women alike, victims. Hat Nettleton, the horsewhipper turned centenarian, interviewed in the old age home, embodies this absurdist perception of the human condition, that Time is the great obliterator, particularly when the beating and the death he has meted out as a young man is reduced to the following ironic statement:

"You didn't have television."
Didn't have no T.V. Didn't have no radio. No picture show.
"You made your own entertainment."
That's the way we did. (Who, 22)

Furthermore, such seemingly awful beginnings as the beaten child initiate the spirit of drama and theatricality which will ultimately lead to Rose's successful career as actress-interviewer.

The reality of female as beaten and passive sexual object remains, but it is complicated by Munro's increasingly typical method of seeing characters and events from more than one perspective, and by her authorial recognition that, in effect, the comprehension of all human relationships is perilously built on the quicksands of fleeting emotions and attitudes and partially perceived realities. In "Half a Grapefruit" Rose struggles with this complexity as she considers her father's knowledge of her person, her "gaudy ambitions," her shame of his disapproval. She understands that part of her disgrace in his eyes is that "she was female but mistakenly so, would not turn out to be the right kind of woman," his idea of what a woman ought to be: "energetic, practical, clever at making and saving; she ought to be shrewd, good at bargaining and bossing and seeing through people's pretensions. At the same time she should be naive intellectually..." (46–47). Layer upon layer of conflicting attitude is peeled away by Rose as she contemplates her father's vision of her. "But there was more to it. The real problem was that she combined and carried on what he must have thought of as the worst qualities in himself. All the things he had beaten down, successfully submerged, in himself, had surfaced again in her, and she was showing no will to combat them." And the final paradox:

She knew perfectly well, too, that he had another set of feelings about her. She knew he felt pride in her as well as this nearly uncontrollable irritation and apprehension; the truth was, the final truth was, that he would not have her otherwise and willed her as she was. Or one part of him did. Naturally he had to keep denying this. Out of humility, he had to, and perversity. Perverse humility. . . .

Rose did not really think this through, or want to. She was as uneasy as he was, about the way their chords struck together. (*Who*, 47)

There is no absolute truth about relationships or identity. King of the royal beatings is but one facet of the mystery of her father's personality, a facet which is submerged for Rose (and her reader) in the later image of the loved father whom she accepts in mature memory as an integral part of self. This aspect of self is acknowledged and claimed by Rose in the final memory of the sick man who prepares to go into the Westminster Hospital to die: "She understood that he would never be with her more than at the present moment. The surprise to come was that he wouldn't be with her less" (55).

The unjust sociological reality of growing up female which preoccupies Munro in some of her early work is revived in the first four narrative segments of *Who Do You Think You Are?*, but with a stronger sense of irony than ever before and a more distanced eye directed towards the heroine. As Rose, for example, remembers the shame and outrage of schoolyard sexual antics, of the half-witted Franny perpetually sexually assaulted by various boys, including Franny's own brother, Munro explores the traditional masculine mythology which romanticizes and elevates the prostitute to a golden-haired, golden-hearted position:

Later on Rose would think of Franny when she came across the figure of an idiotic, saintly whore, in a book or a movie. Men who made books and movies seemed to have a fondness for this figure, though Rose noticed they would clean her up. They cheated, she thought, when they left out the breathing and the spit and the teeth; they were refusing to take into account the aphrodisiac prickles of disgust, in their hurry to reward themselves with the notion of a soothing blankness, undifferentiating welcome. (*Who*, 27)

Such a feminist critique begins to be modified for the reader though through the myth-making of Rose herself who is not above using this experience to impress and to gain momentary power over other people: "Rose knew a lot of people who wished they had been born poor, and hadn't been. So she would queen it over them, offering various scandals and bits of squalor from her childhood" (24). Both sexes invent to achieve advantage, to be king or queen. Rose in her own way is as culpable as the boys in using Franny; her mythology is as invidious as the male legend of the prostitute.

Similarly, later, in "Privilege," which is feminist in its authentic depiction of young girls' romantic love for one another, the treachery of another's ego is the learning experience of Rose. In love with the older, sensual, imperial schoolgirl, Cora, Rose experiences a version of "sexual love, not sure exactly what it needed to concentrate on" (34). When Rose is rewarded for her small, secret gift to Cora of stolen candy from the family store by Cora returning the candy and by so doing, enjoying her own importance, Rose understands the pitfalls of love, the awful dependence of the lover and the power of the loved. In this early scene from Rose's life, Munro depicts the naked vulnerability of a first love, and implies, as well, the universality of the condition which is not always based on the independent male in control of a love-obsessed, passive female.

While in the honest female responses and perspectives of all of her fiction, Munro disturbs the traditional masculine interpretation of women, in this fourth volume she plays fairly by beginning to examine the reverse, the female mythology of male. "Wild Swans" is just such a shrewd inquiry—in this instance, the white slave-trade myth which has persisted in oral culture, passed on from mother to daughter, is partially actualized, parodied even, in Rose's sexual experience with a man who appears in expected disguise as a United Church minister on a train to Toronto. Given Rose's fondness for theatrics, the fact or fantasy of this experience is unclear, but the perverse sexual titillation of such female mythology is demonstrated in Rose's sexual pleasure and surrender to the groping fingers of the man beside her on the train.

Even more to the point is that her victimization is in doubt. The man is as useful to her as an active object of pleasure as all those other instruments of popular legend: " A stranger's hand, or root vegetables or humble kitchen tools that people tell jokes about; the world is tumbling with innocent-seeming objects ready to declare themselves, slippery and obliging" (64). If Franny is the unwilling instrument of pleasure of the schoolyard boys in "Privilege," Ruby Carruthers, the willing, slatternly, sexual servicer of the three boys, Del Fairbridge, Horse Nicholson, Runt Chesterton under the porch in "Half a Grapefruit," roles are to a degree reversed with the minister servicing Rose in this later chapter.

Qualifications to the earlier interpretations of the sexual dance are inevitable in Munro's portrayal of Rose's mature relationships with men. As she develops into the author's first truly independent career woman, she, by virtue of exercising her own will, hurts as well as is hurt. In the next stage of her life, while she plays out the ancient scenario of beggar maid to the chivalric rescuer with Patrick, the rich university student she marries, she acknowledges her own ego satisfaction as the archetypal White Goddess. There isn't any doubt that Rose, in her marriage to Patrick, is a victim of culture, her psychological need to be overpowered by him suggesting the impotence which is due to social conditioning, but she also knows her approach to their relationship as an adventure and a test of her own authority. A social victim of being female—yes—but, in retrospect, she considers that her final decision to marry him after having once broken off their engagement was perhaps based not only on lack of plan for her own life, or economic fear, but on self-satisfaction and a sense of power: "It was really vanity, it was vanity pure and simple, to resurrect him, to bring him back his happiness. To see if she could do that. She could not resist such a test of power" (97).

The reality of their love and marriage escapes Rose in the end since it, too, like the personality of her father, belongs to shifting perspectives, to the distorting influences of immediate or past emotions. But she is no more the victim of their marriage than was Patrick, and perhaps he is even more so. His is real grief at the cruel news of her supposed affair with Clifford, a fantasy she has not even realized. And in her recognition that she meant her marriage, from its inception, to be temporary, Rose and her reader know her egocentric, silent strength of will: "She meant that she had always been planning, at the back of her mind, to do what she was doing now. Even on her wedding day she had known this time would come, and that if it didn't she might as well be dead. The betrayal was hers" (136).

In the existential search for selfness, there is little space for sentiment— to be sentimental puts one at a disadvantage and it is with a somewhat alarming credibility that Munro portrays the growth of a cool heroine towards social, economic and psychological independence. While Rose finds herself, after her divorce, rudderless without a man at least on the fringes of her life, she learns to cope with her affairs and to manage people to suit her own ends as she builds her career. The greedy sexual Rose of "Wild Swans," the wife Rose of the Patrick she had always meant to leave, is glimpsed in consistency when, by now in midlife and an independent woman, Rose revisits Clifford and Jocelyn, those friends from her married life with whom she played the romantic triangle. After a somewhat drunken experience of sexual intercourse between Clifford, Jocelyn and herself, a sober Rose feels her defenses slipping:

> The next morning Rose had to go out before Jocelyn and Clifford were awake. She had to go downtown on the subway. She found she was looking at men with that speculative hunger, that cold and hurtful need, which for a while she had been free of. She began to get very angry. She was angry at Clifford and Jocelyn. She felt that they had made a fool of her, cheated her, shown her a glaring lack, that otherwise she would not have been aware of. She resolved never to see them again. (*Who*, 134)

Such weakness is short-lived as Rose exercises her self-determination, admitting with rational candor her use of people by deciding "to go on being friends with Clifford and Jocelyn because she needed such friends occasionally, at that stage of her life" (135).

If the reader does not find Rose particularly likeable at this point in her life, it is because ambition, by its very nature, admits only selfness, and, as Rose is learning, the freedom to do, unencumbered, exacts a price. But Munro does not leave her heroine here; she moves her onward, towards a greater understanding which verges on a new humanism. While the first part of Rose's story, that of early sexuality, is played out through the children's schoolyard chant of "Too old for the cradle, too young for the bed," it is rounded out and concluded in Shakespearean fashion as "sans eyes, sans teeth, sans everything." And as both the men and women of her life are diminished by the proximity of death, individual lives with their seeming cataclysmic events become paradoxically both more and less important in Rose's understanding.

For Rose, life is inevitably theater, but gradually she begins to understand the roles chosen as mere tricked out moments in time. Rose establishes an appropriate set when, after having left Patrick, she moves into a small town in the mountains and decorates an apartment, with hanging plants, incense, dried flowers: "when all this was finished, [it] was a place which belonged quite recognizably to a woman, living alone, probably no longer young, who was connected, or hoped to be connected, with a college or the arts" (138). In middle-age the desperation of the disguise increases, the conflict between men and women abates for the real villain of the piece is death—a revelation beginning to be felt by Rose as she takes on this new role:

> The town in the mountains seemed remote from everything. But Rose liked it, partly because of that. When you come back to living in a town after having lived in cities you have the idea that everything is comprehensible and easy there, almost as if some people have got together and said "Let's play Town." You think that nobody could die there. (*Who*, 139)

And later, the sexual conflict and injury she perceives in her relationship with Simon, the man with whom she initiates an affair which he abruptly terminates, is merely imagined insult—the greater reality she will discover is Simon's incurable illness and consequent death. Rose's realization in "Simon's Luck" supersedes the daily, implicitly trivial features of male and female power struggles:

> Simon's dying. . . was preposterous, it was unfair, that such a chunk of information should have been left out, and that Rose even at this late date could have thought herself the only person who could seriously lack power. (*Who*, 177)

"The flight that concerns everybody" (208), identified by the daughter who is told of her dying mother fleeing from the hospital in the story most dear to Munro, "The Peace of Utrecht," is the real power in the final scenes of Rose's development in *Who Do You Think You Are?*; this question which reflects the social injustice and impotence of being female, which explores what constitutes personal identity, concludes as the metaphysical irony of the individual losing to time and reduced to a caricature of a human being, a diapered little old lady in the Home spelling out an absurd communication with an "air of nearly demented hilarity" (187).

The theater of the absurd life may be, but for Rose, it becomes precious under the shadow of the grim reaper. It is a new compassionate Rose who comes to put Flo in the nursing home, who is careful of Flo's individuality, of the small material possessions of Flo's life, those comic eyesores even as Flo is herself, of a poor life. By celebrating Flo and her idiosyncratic last acts of biting nurses, Rose would seem to divine that the only reality is that of the individual life lived through the subjective, psychological reality of one—and however crazy or imperfect such a life may be, the person is special in his or her own right. The question of *personality* underlies this work, intuited by Rose in the last act as not merely adopted disguise but the sum total of the people who have influenced it. Rose emerges, then, as Munro's new heroine who, by allowing herself to seriously accommodate Flo, her father and the people of her past, comes to know, to accept—to discover—herself.

Munro's nod to death in this fourth work would seem to mark her as an old-fashioned fictionalizer, one who, having fired salvos from the borders of the feminist battle in the sixties and seventies, has retreated into a simplistic age-old humanistic remedy to the modern problematic relationship between the sexes. Such is not the case. The new humanism broached by Munro in the development of Rose is, of course, the old humanism of the seven stages of man (in this case, woman), a tale full of sound and fury, told in a variety of ways by many of the world's greatest writers. But, in and by itself, it cannot satisfy the modern reader living in a new complexity, in a world where the study of man has become almost preposterously scientific. Nor does Munro intend it to. The conclusion has many inconclusive aspects, one of which, an artistic feature, is pointed to by Robert Kroetsch when, discussing parody as "a way into ending" in Canadian literature, he mentions the parodic element in *Lives of Girls and Women*.[18] And parody as a technique for concluding is certainly one investigative feminist feature of *Who Do You Think You Are?*

Language, communication, alphabet, translation—these are words which recur in the individual and collective minds of Munro's fiction and which mark the wit of her disposition. Language as trickery. Communication which fails. Alphabet only partly understood. Translation which is incomplete. The idea that language can only deceive you. Merely one layer of truth, language is equated with a kind of mischief. And if women trained in deceit and fraudulence are the natural story-tellers (mothers infect their daughters with story-telling and theatricality in both novels), the female voice in Munro's fiction striving for artistic credibility is also aware of experiencing the perpetual feminine neurosis of making up. By giving us Del in *Lives* as the beginning artist developing this self-awareness, Munro is both the self-parodying artist and witty feminist evaluator. The trick is that by proclaiming incompetence as an artist, belief in artistic competence is assured. Turning a trick. The female way.

Similarly, the transition from artist to actress as a female career, from the story of Del to that of Rose, is predictable, a joke on the Munro reader and those in Rose's life who are taken in by her. While both men and women in this work are viewed as playing roles in the little theater of life, the psychology of the posturer is much more natural to the female, to Rose, to Munro, who are taught to be objects of decoration and play. Rose's central psychology, carefully detailed by Munro throughout the narrative, is that of *real lies* and of roles and rituals determining emotions. Rose's father in "Royal Beatings," for example, seems an actor who means it, his action a catalyst in the development of the theatrical and detached psychology of the older Rose:

> She has since wondered about murders, and murderers. Does the thing have to be carried through, in the end, partly for the effect, to prove to the audience of one—who won't be able to report, only register, the lesson—that such a thing can happen, that there is nothing that can't happen, that the most dreadful antic is justified, feelings can be found to match it? (*Who*, 16–17)

Such a bloodless point of view is accented by the condition of being female, detailed by Munro in her description of the training of young girls into play-acting and making-up in "Privilege."

In Rose's case, too, the gift of mimicry is a talent which is passed on from mother to daughter, from Flo who is herself the supreme imitator and loving mocker of the woman, the substitute mother, who took her in (44). Flo's imitations of this woman in the mirror become Rose's method of survival as a rootless wanderer—without a last name to the end—who still thinks in terms of play-acting and television programming in the final line of the narrative when she feels the life of the male mimic, Ralph Gillespie, "one slot over from her own" (210). There may not be social criticism in this fiction but there certainly is a perception of the modern view of personality as conditioned role-playing, of the materialist construct on which it is based; this is a philosophy which obliterates the faith in the uniqueness of the individual in favor of the idea of personality as consumer: the nature of a person identifiable through fashion and furniture—and manners; it is a philosophy which continues to masquerade the female identity.

Thus Munro literally gives us parody as a way into ending. The author as female writer distances herself from the stagey Rose just as she herself is in alienated distance as the foremost stager. The underlying feminist question of this Munro work is not only "Who do you think you are?" then, but a mocking address to society, "What is it that you expect?"

At the source of Munro's first four major works of fiction is the question of female identity and its struggle to be. By simultaneously confirming and discarding images of women, poor rural types and small-town ladies, Munro canonizes a collective memory and establishes a female genealogy for her contemporary voice. This creation of psychological rootedness is built into the character of Rose, her mental odyssey and gypsy life another stage in the development of Munro's large authorial sensorium. Paradoxically, it is this background of female ancestry, a tribe, that allows the creation of this major heroine who, by discovering herself as a composite of both the men and women who shaped her, begins to devalue the web of sisterhood. Rose's discovery that no woman is an island could only occur after feminist territory had been mapped out. With *Who Do You Think You Are?* Alice Munro leaves her reader in thoughtful anticipation of further evolutions and adventures in the lives of girls and women.

| | | —

Neither is the reader of Munro's feminism disappointed by her fifth volume, *The Moons of Jupiter*, a collection of short stories published in 1983. Received with praise by readers and critics alike, the eleven major stories deal mainly with women, are told from a female perspective and stretch the female consciousness of her earlier work. As Urjo Kareda points out: "Read in the context of earlier stories, particularly those in *Who Do You Think You Are?* (1978), these form an emotional autobiography extended over several volumes."[19]

In *The Moons of Jupiter* female genealogy continues to provide emotional stability and strength for the contemporary woman. In "Chaddeleys and Flemings" the narrator is assured by matrilineal connections, by mother's cousins who even as old maids are powerful, full blown women who, from the narrator-as-child's point of view, knew how to get on in the real world: "they had made it take notice. They could command a classroom, a maternity ward, the public; they knew how to deal with taxi drivers and train conductors."[20] From a male perspective, these totemic women of another generation, may, like Cousin Iris, slide into a garish masquerade as they age, but they are adventurous—courageous—and mythic for women who read them. Iris, close to the pagan authority of Isis in name, and in rural associations, slides into the subtext of female goddesses that was strongly established in Munro's earlier work. Cousin Iris also provides a connection for the greater female voice of this volume which rises from the several characters of middle-aged women who are aware of themselves aging, of being in physical transition, of settling into menopause. Bronwen Wallace's perception of Munro's earlier work that "in Munro's development of character, we are never far from the persistent reality of their physical bodies"[21] is painfully true in *The Moons of Jupiter* as aging women feel forced to assess themselves through their declining physicality.

Despite the anxiety and even suppressed hysteria of their recognitions, however, the cumulative emotional stance here is one of composure, endurance and maturity; these women ultimately brave their new physical frontiers and changing sexuality with interested recognition. Lorna Irvine tells us in "Changing is the Word I Want" that change is central in Alice Munro's fiction, that transformation is an expression of the way women view themselves socially and physically.[22] Transformation and change is the condition of the female life and it is also adventure for Munro's heroines who take their leads from the mother-philosopher figure as in "The Stone in the Field": "Why not? My mother would ask, seeing life all in terms of change and possibility" (29). Munro even invests the female sensorium here with something approaching wisdom as female characters begin to accommodate their approaching metamorphoses and take pleasure in recognizing life's changing designs—or as the narrator of "Bardon Bus" muses, into "taking into account, all over again, everything that is contradictory and persistent and unaccommodating about life" (128).

Indeed, what remains most unaccommodating for woman is her male partner in the dance of the sexes; Munro's women are still engaged in exploring and defining love and their author persists in describing the traditional dance which puts women at the mercy, even more so in this last set. In "Bardon Bus," the middle-aged narrator has a short lived affair with X, a man who moves through an army of women in such relationships, seemingly without repercussions and according to social customs which allows him full advantage. As X's friend, Dennis tells the narrator with "malicious sympathy":

> Think of the way your life would be, if you were a man. The choices you
> would have. I mean sexual choices. You could start all over. Men do. It's
> in all the novels and it's in life too. Men fall in love with younger

women. Men want younger women. Men can get younger women. . . ."
A woman your age can't compete," says Dennis urgently. "You can't
compete with younger women. I used to think that was so rottenly unfair." (*Moons*, 121)

Lydia in "Dulse" and Prue of the story of the same title are similar heroines, in middle-aged transition. Lydia is recovering from an affair on a trip
to the Maritimes where she recognizes her new condition: "She hadn't got
fatter or thinner, her looks had not deteriorated in any alarming way, but
nevertheless she had stopped being one sort of woman and had become another" (36). Her lover Duncan has been as peripatetic in his several affairs
as X in "Bardon Bus" and as Lydia recounts their relationship, she shows
herself to be the dancer "on her toes, trembling delicately all over, afraid of
letting him down on the next turn" (54); she is the traditional female in
love, following not leading, love's victim to Duncan's monstrous power as
he subjects her to abuse and humiliation.

Prue, too, is in her forties, involved with an egotistical, insensitive man,
ironically a neurologist, named Gordon, who decides he loves a younger
woman and with cavalier execution informs Prue that he nonetheless in-
tends to marry her [Prue] in a few years' time. Roberta is similarly out of
control in "Labor Day Dinner." Hers is a much more routine and domestic
affair with George but she still suffers his malice about her aging: "Your
armpits are flabby." "Are they? I'll put on something with sleeves." In the
truck, now that she knows he isn't going to make up, she lets herself hear
him say that. A harsh satisfaction in his voice. The satisfaction of airing
disgust. He is disgusted by her aging body" (137).

There is incredible pain and distress in the loss of attractive sexuality for
these heroines, yet they retain their composure and resurface with some
equanimity. The narrator of "Bardon Bus" remains relatively nonplussed
in the pain of the affair's aftermath and even in the recognition that a final,
possible late-blooming female splendor shifts so easily, almost inevitably
into garish absurdity:

Even the buttercup woman I saw a few days ago on the streetcar, the
little, stout, sixtyish woman in a frilly yellow dress well above the
knees, a straw hat with yellow ribbons, yellow pumps dyed-to-match on
her little fat feet—even she doesn't aim for comedy. She sees a flower in
the mirror: the generous petals, the lovely buttery light. (*Moons*, 125)

What the narrator apprehends, however dimly, even in her physical loss, as she herself ceases to be the "fertility doll" that signifies the relationship between her younger friend Kay and Kay's new lover, are the possibilities of change and its sudden new designs. While Kay continues to invest herself in the man she takes up ("She takes up a man and his story, wholeheartedly. She learns his language, figuratively or literally" (116)), the narrator begins to reorient herself to strange new possibilities, to "new definitions of luck" (128). These new definitions of luck include life itself.

The narrator of "Bardon Bus," Lydia, Prue and Roberta are characters who are very much in limbo, aging women who are beginning to anticipate life as a spectator sport, its finality and the strange privilege of the cool distance aging and death affords—perhaps even demands. Roberta's sense of passage, of being in abeyance and especially vulnerable to an unpredictable destiny is underlined by the car that misses her, George and her daughters as it emerges out of the darkness: "They feel as strange, as flattened out and borne aloft, as unconnected with previous and future events as the ghost car was" (159). Sexual authority and power is still an issue for these women but over time they will recover from masculine ill treatment; what is more to the point, as with Roberta, is the lucky, future recovery of life itself.

At the same time, Munro suggests, that love affairs are accumulated living, complicated assertions of personality and even generation. She offers us the shrewd insight that Lydia is of that generation of woman who "has an idea of love which is ruinous but not serious in some way, not respectful" (55). Ultimately, this lack of seriousness leaves room for her to go forward. And Prue's affair with Gordon has worth for its own sake—even beauty—like the golden amber cufflink Prue takes from his house and places in her old tobacco can alongside other tokens; as a memento mori, the cufflink neatly finalizes the narrative but it is less emblematic of the death of the sexual relationship than as a talisman of one of Prue's life experiences, a rich store that she rarely thinks of but which begins to add up as past pleasure, as well as pain, and engenders a calming sense of identity.

Despite the recurrence of the motif of female as love's victim in *The Moons of Jupiter*, Munro's women have an established sensibility, a self-assuredness, a new control. Partly this is due to the way they are initially presented. In fact, seven of the stories begin with an introduction to women who are strongly defined through occupation. "Connection" begins with "Cousin Iris from Philadelphia. She was a nurse" (1). While the heroine of

"The Turkey Season" explains, "I was a turkey gutter" (60), Lydia from "Dulse" is confidently presented as an "editor, for a publisher in Toronto" (36). Frances is a teacher first in "Accident," and a lover, wife and mother secondarily and somewhat by accident; more importantly, at the narrative's conclusion her sense of self remains unshakeable: "But inside she's ticking away, all by herself, the same Frances who was there before any of it. Not altogether the same surely. The same (109). Lydia, Frances, the writer-narrator in "Bardon Bus," Prue, Roberta, the narrator in "Hard-Luck Stories" are women who have arrived; modern in their adventurousness, they can live outside the house; they are active risk-takers who have passed through changing social customs and sexual rituals, who stand midway between generations and are to be prized for their capacity to endure, recover, and find a way to live.

The relics that Prue places in her tobacco tin, the antiques the mother deals in in "Chaddeleys and Flemings," the ancient and exotic homely emblem of the trillium discovered by the narrator of "Hard-Luck Stories" in the church, bringing three middle-aged people "an unacknowledged spring of hopefulness" (197) are extensions of the dominant female psyche in *The Moons of Jupiter* which identifies itself as being of well worn value. Women who belong primarily to the past as old maids, cousins and aunts, "leftovers... belonging in another generation" are as prized as the more modern women. In "Connection" and "Stone in the Field" they begin to take the shape of polished antiques salvaged and dignified by the female narrator: splendid, massive and bold as mother's cousins; white, gleaming and as streamlined as their pine furniture as father's sisters.

Munro's familiar primitive rural women are also once again reworked with some authority. In "The Turkey Season" Marjorie and Lily, like Flo in *Who Do You Think You Are?*, are crude folk women, quick, primitive and ironic in seizing advantage and power particularly in the battle of the sexes. Marjorie and Lily refuse to take male order "lying down"; and with a black glee characteristic of Munro's folk types, Marjorie reveals to her female companions that she threatened to castrate her son when he wet his bed. All of these characters add to the credible strength of the female voice of this volume.

In Munro's previous work *Who Do You Think You Are?*, the progress of the heroine was that of the achieving woman. As Munro marked off the stages of Rose's development, she also gravely shaded in the romantic's natural, elegaic, black apprehension of human mortality and thus confirmed the relative, fleeting importance of human struggle. In *The Moons of Jupiter*, death inches even closer. "The Stone in the Field," for example, can be read as an extended obituary, a fictional epitaph to an unknown soldier-in-life resurrected by the author. And in "Visitors," Wilfred realizes in climax his brother's and his own mortality, after they soberly visit the place where their family home once stood. In "Bardon Bus" and "Hard-Luck Stories" the female narrators visit cemeteries and derive some comfort from placing themselves in a larger temporal perspective. In "Bardon Bus" Munro even hazards a philosophic challenge through the male character, Dennis, that it is perhaps women who are most often granted this privileged sensitivity and understanding beyond Ego:

> "Do you know what I think now? I think women are the lucky ones! Do you know why?"
> "Why?"
> "Because they are forced to live in the world of loss and death!.... It's my conclusion now that you won't get any happiness by playing tricks on life. It's only by natural renunciation and by accepting deprivation, that we prepare for death and therefore that we get any happiness." (*Moons*, 122)

Whatever the truth here, the awareness of death is grave, not gothic, in this fifth volume and subordinate to more philosophical questions about the enigma of human, artistic and cosmic order and of life's mysterious ambience.

"Connections" is the key word—embedding it in most of the stories, Munro slyly, and perhaps ironically, integrates the volume through the literal word. In the lead story, connections, as I have said, are ancestral, genealogical and, as mother's female cousins, they provide for the young girl "a connection with the real, and prodigal, and dangerous, world. They know how to get on in it, and they made it take notice" (7). They are exemplars of female authority. Cousin Iris, however, in relation to a later space, is altered not only by Richard's view of her but by time. Her transformation suggests the dreamlike conclusion of the piece, the final note struck by Munro being that of the vaporous fragility of human connections and our memories of them.

Touched on in "Connection" is an underlying question throughout these stories, that is, what is the relationship between our selves and others? Or between our subjective and that other external reality? Between our inner and outer lives? In *The Moons of Jupiter* characters, and artist, may invent, endorse or fail to make these connections. The narrator in "The Stone in the Field" must leave Mr. Black's stone unturned, explaining that as a younger person she "would have made a horrible, plausible connection between that silence of his, and the manner of his death. Now I no longer believe that people's secrets are defined and communicable, or their feelings full-blown and easy to recognize" (35). And Lydia in "Dulse," after her love affair, can't comprehend herself in the physical environment: "she could not make the connection between herself and things outside herself, so the getting up and leaving the car, going up the steps, going along the street, all seemed to involve a bizarre effort" (41). Similarly, the narrator of "Bardon Bus" wonders at the full meaning of extraordinary sexual connection, "the cries, pleas, brutal promises, the climactic sharp announcements and the long subsiding spasms" (124).

Munro probes further. The voice from the wings whispers—what of life itself? Is there design in it, and if so, what is its meaning? In "Accident" Frances speculates about the small part she played in the chain of events which makes Ted her husband:

> No, not a small part; an ambiguous part. There was a long chain of things, many of them hidden from her, that brought him here to propose to her in the most proper place, her mother's living room. She had been made necessary. And it was quite useless to think, would anyone else have done as well, would it have happened if the chain had not been linked exactly as it was? (*Moons*, 106–7)

While there is no resolution to Frances' question, a ray of light, a vision, is bounced off of Munro's philosopher's stone. What we see is the cosmic order of the final story "The Moons of Jupiter," where the design of the universe is "innumerable repetitions, innumerable variations" (231); Munro's universe is relative and atomic and beautiful, with humanity interpreted as light, and energy and transcendent being. In relation to the moons of Jupiter, the narrator's white dream of angelic soul, light and sweet substance in "Bardon Bus" comes clear.

> I have had a pleasant dream that seems far away from my waking state. X and I and some other people I didn't know or can't remember were

wearing innocent athletic underwear outfits, which changed at some point into gauzy bright white clothes, and these turned out to be not just clothes but our substances, our flesh and bones and in a sense our souls. Embraces took place which started out with the usual urgency but were transformed, by the lightness and sweetness of our substance, into a rare state of content. I can't describe it very well, it sounds like a movie-dream of heaven, all banality and innocence. So I suppose it was. I can't apologize for the banality of my dreams. (127)

This image of the floating white dream, which also concludes "The Turkey Season," "Labor Day Dinner" and "Connection" is Munro's antidote to what we consider, as Prue does of her first marriage, our "cosmic disasters"—those forced, missed, unhappily realized, misunderstood and often completely incomprehensible connections. In *The Moons of Jupiter* Alice Munro comes close to traditional religious vision, which she presents without apology for banality, as she reinterprets with poetic science the hopeful traditional Christian faith in eternal life and light as opposed to darkness.

Because transition is the dominant emotional milieu, superficially, this collection of short stories seems a transitional work. There is, however, a new depth in this volume, not only philosophically, but technically. While the female voice is clear, the artist as subject is less intrusive; instead, Munro concentrates on narrative innovation as spinning innumerable stories within stories. As Urjo Kareda points out, "Hard-Luck Stories... is a *tour de force* of technique and vision. There's a remarkable conglomeration of effects—two narrative frames, two months apart; three stories-within-the story, two brief, one long, all central"[23]; Furthermore, the feminist odyssey has moved half a league forward. The private hesitancies of many of Munro's earlier female characters, is dissolving. In this collection, women like Frances, Lydia, Prue, and the narrator of "Bardon Bus" may suffer the conditions of being female, but they are remembered as a rather roguish gallery of women who impress us with their survival. These are Munro's *new* heroines, answering to some degree Del Jordan's mother's hope for change in the lives of girls and women. There is some measure of victory in their composure, and their implicit right to be and to do.

| | | —

In *The Progress of Love* (1986), Munro presents a collection of eleven short stories and extends both her virtuosity and her literary reputation. In this volume, the new heroine of *The Moons of Jupiter* survives; she is here as the narrator of the lead story, "The Progress of Love," as Stella of "Lichen," the narrator of "Miles City, Montana," Trudy of "Circle of Prayer" and Isabel of "White Dump." She is overshadowed, however, by greater thematic complexities and by fictional contexts of greater historicity and expanded character relationships that are part of a new involved style for Munro. Commenting on this new technical inventiveness in Munro's work of this period, W.R. Martin observes, "Although these later stories are hardly longer than the early ones, what they give us in their complex structure, wide time-frame, and long cast of characters, is a sort of conspectus of human life."[24]

The phrase "a conspectus of human life" is especially apt. The ability of the contemporary heroine to survive as an independent is less an issue in this collection than is Munro's visionary attempt to use female experience to more fully define human experience. This means a reversal of the traditional historical approach in which a lineage of male characters are interpreted in masculine events of conquest and defeat. It also means that the quest for female identity and truths is far from over. As Ann Barr Snitow explains in "The Front Line: Notes on Sex in Novels by Women, 1969–1979," it is only very recently that women novelists had the license and desire to write about sex explicitly and seriously, and how it fits into womens' lives. Theirs has been an experimental route, with "typical productions in 1969–1979"[25] being stories of first sexual encounters and changing social manners, novels such as Munro's *Lives of Girls and Women*. As Munro reviews the progress of love in this sixth book, she demonstrates the female attitude that "sex is not one *thing*,"[26] that, for women, sexual relations and sexuality can filter into many aspects of lived experience. The broad historical revelation here is that female sexuality is the natural medium for interpreting human affairs and human existence.

This sensibility is arrived at from extending the boundaries of sexuality to include not merely the sexual dance, but a further exploration of the natural preoccupation of female writers, of living in the body. In fact, the overt dramatizations of female passage into middle-age, of exiting out of the dance in *The Moons of Jupiter* is now the implicit standard of experience behind the fiction. The perceptions in these stories evolve largely from an aging author's considerations on life as female reproductive powers die, and physical death nears.

| | | —

The historical impetus in *The Progress of Love* as the title implies, is stronger than in previous works. It is also more comprehensively feminist, as Munro seems now to be acutely aware of recording the sociological and psychological realities of womens' lives as history. In several of the stories, there is a strong sense of an encapsulated history of female generations. Given the maturity of the author, it is not surprising to discover a broader retrospective inquiry or the familiar genealogical and ancestral interest, compounded. Typically, Munro simultaneously looks backwards as she goes forwards, depicting sociological roles of women and now, delineating psychological intersections between generations. The progress of love between the sexes does not progress far in any real sense of the word for three generations of women in the lead story. The old note of feminist complaint about masculine control is struck early by Munro through the grandmother, the broken-hearted mother, the "hung" woman who has had, it seems, not an entirely happy life with a "man fond of hotel bars, barbershops, harness races, women..."[27] The emotional legacy of this first woman to her daughter Marietta is that of hatred of the father and of humiliation in the male social domain. For Marietta's daughter, Phemie, there is the further ugly legacy of "a really sickening shame" (13) over being female, and a great relief at having "two boys myself, no daughters, I felt as if something could stop now—the stories, and griefs, the old puzzles you can't resist or solve." (14).

The Original Sin of being female is partly dissipated for Marietta, however, when she assumes the authoritative posture of being the forgiver or nonforgiver of men, and there is some progress in love for Phemie who has believed in the possibility of the ideal love of perfect equality, with the freedom to act, without censure on the part of one's partner. Her vision of her father standing mutely by, accepting her mother Marietta burning her money, her paternal legacy, because it seemed "natural and necessary" may finally not be, "strictly speaking, true" (30), but it is a progressive realization that composes Phemie in her current sexual relationships. Phemie is still "making up" for and with men in the old-fashioned way of women, assuming a disguise, peeling her face off and on, like her glamorous Aunt Beryl; she is still the female repository of generations of wall papering affection, but unlike her mother and grandmother, she is a vocal protestor. The moments of "kindness and reconciliation" (30) she experiences with men, after making her positions known, seem somehow better than the buried, underground grudges of previous generations.

The question of the possibility of freedom and power in love also troubled Del Jordan as she struggled with Garnet French in *Lives*, and was initiated into womanhood. Del's passage into female sexual life is not unlike the menopausal exit which is occurring between the lines of this text, and many of the themes and motifs introduced in *Lives* are replayed here with the advantage of a mature perspective. One such theme is that of an obsessive anxiety with the female body itself. The abhorrence of the gynecological imperative that struck Del as a pubescent girl is extended in *The Progress of Love* as middle-aged melancholy and disgust projected on to the wrecked maternal body.

Despair over aging is most apparent through the character Stella of "Lichen." Stella is an old-new Munro heroine, a contemporary earthmother with all of the riotous independence of such earlier types as Nora, Mary McQuade and Mrs. Fullerton, and the contemporary survival methods of Frances, Lydia and Prue. Stella is mistress of her domain, but she, like "Nature's bounty" (34) is in danger of rotting on the vine. She remains a *riot* (53), but her body is decaying, her juices drying up, her pubic hair, like that on the fading photograph of her ex-husband's lover, turning "to gray, to the soft, dry color of a plant mysteriously nourished on the rocks" (55). Because the cult of youth is the cultural norm, Stella is discarded by men, specifically by her ex-husband, David, and both she and Munro exercise an angry, socially delinquent, sly rebuttal, in the spirit of the jilted Helen, in the earlier "Postcard."

> David thinks that Stella has done this on purpose. . . . There's the sort of woman who has to come bursting out of the female envelope at this age, flaunting fat or an indecent scrawniness, sprouting warts and facial hair, refusing to cover pasty veined legs, almost gleeful about it, as if this was what she'd wanted to do all along. (33)

This disgust and sorrow with the aging female body introduced here is emotionally echoed in other stories and while it is the male, David, who smells Stella as stale, like the dead meat she puts in the oven, it is the females who, understandably, feel it the most. Like Del Jordan, Jesse, on the brink of maturity, is thoroughly disgusted by her paired counterpart of aging maternity, the pregnant Mrs. Cryderman in "Jesse and Meribeth."

Mrs. Cryderman's "physical damage" includes "pale-brown blotches on her face and neck" like "the flesh of pears beginning to go rotten," "varicose veins. . . . Cranberry-coloured spiders, greenish lumps all over her legs" (170). In "Eskimo," the bland and silenced Mary Jo feels aversion towards both the adolescent child-woman capitulating to a first physical devotion in love, licking and kissing her lover, losing herself, and at the spectacle of maternity beyond a respectable age, at the Indian boy-child, too old by Western standards suckling at his mother's serviceable breast.

In *The Progress of Love* the juxtaposition of adolescent girls with aging maternal figures provides a retrospect on female life. It underlines, among other things, the trauma of physical passages for women, the overwhelming vulnerability of women to men during the similar conditions of sexual initiation and sexual decline, the abnegation of self that occurs for women in sexual devotion and in motherhood, and finally, the birth and death of female fertility as the central painful paradigm of human experience.

Accentuating the latter, Munro does not leave her readers in an exclusively female physical domain. She moves beyond such, to encompass both sexes in physical decline. The child, who is also the wife-mother, in "Miles City, Montana" has a more far-reaching loathing of the physical body that touches both sexes, when she views her parents at the funeral of the drowned child. "I felt a furious and sickening disgust. Children sometimes have an access of disgust concerning adults. The size, the lumpy shapes, the bloated power. The breath, the coarseness, the hairiness, the horrid secretions" (86). The disgust is based on the culpability of parents as mortal, physical agents who, by virtue of having brought one into the world, also ensure that one leaves it. It is women, suggests Munro, as she did in *The Moons of Jupiter,* who give birth and who most intuit and comprehend the progress of life, who, like Stella, are full of maternal wisdom. The experience of decaying and death is obviously not restricted to them, however.

David, for example, in "Lichen" is trapped in his own aging. Like the character of Dan in "Circle of Prayer," he is the frantic child-man lover of a succession of women. David is in desperate flight from his own decay; he manages to escape momentarily through faith in the disguises of the more youthful women he courts, the about-to-be-abandoned Catherine, and the young Dina. Like Stella's geriatric father, however, David can no more escape the ravages of time than the women can, but as a male removed from the explicit physical knowledge of declining fertility and the wreckage of childbirth, and willingly tricked out by female faces, he has an easier access to psychological escape.

Munro also suggests that David, as a middle-aged man, is more vulnerable to "romantic" love of an adolescent kind. The author continues to explore the dimensions of love and its progress through David, and what she exposes is his dependence. There is some truth in Catherine's observation, even as she intuits and rationalizes her failing relationship with David: "It can make you mean. Love can make you mean. If you feel dependent on somebody, then you can be mean to them. I understand that in David" (44). Munro also warns that there is danger for women in this kind of dependent love with its corollary, hate. Overstated, love's "murderous pleasure" (128) can culminate in violence, in the murder-suicide of the retired couple in "Fits." The violence Del encountered with Garnet in *Lives* is not restricted to youth; "not being a virgin" (127) was no guarantee of safety for the murdered Mrs. Weebles in "Fits." In any event, David's path is as lonely as Stella's; they are, as aging characters, equals. They are both lichen, living off what they manage to construct.

There are in fact, a number of sympathetic male characters in this volume, fathers and husbands and brothers who are subjects of some psychological exploration. At the conclusion of "Lichen," however, Stella significantly defines herself as an "older sister" (54) in relation to David. The web of sisterhood is an intense one in *The Progress of Love,* in the three women of "Lichen," each of whom develops a legendary stature in the fiction. The earth-mother Stella, the fey, hippielike Catherine and the close-to-pornography Queen, Dina, circle the man, and are a striking pictorial record of three different decades of women. There is a prescient sense of women's history evolving here and in other stories like "White Dump" where the three characters, Sophie, Isabel and Denise, dominate the action, forming a sisterly lineage in an architecturally complex fiction of shifting past and present relationships.

This strong sense of female history and generation is intensified by the overwhelming connection between mothers (both blood and surrogate) and daughters. *"Where are the children?"* is the mother's anguished cry in "Miles City, Montana" (99) who sees her daughter, miraculously, not drown. This cry is the passionately charged feminist desire of the aging authorial persona to know her future in daughters, to record and sustain female history, and beyond, the cry for human future in all children.

Paradoxically, there is an overwhelming retreat from maternity in the conspicuous number of absented and assumed mothers. Callie may or may not be the legitimate child of Miss Kernaghan in "The Moon in the Orange Street Skating Rink." Violet is the mother replacement to Dawn Rose, Bonnie Hope and later, to the homosexual male, Dane, in "A Queer Streak." Jesse and Meribeth are young girls without mothers and Mrs. Cryderman is a substitute mother (in "Jesse and Meribeth"). Mary Jo is the unwilling surrogate mother to Dr. Streeter's daughter but struggles to protect the Eskimo girl in "Eskimo." Besides defining the plights of individual girls and women, the status of the orphaned or adopted girl signifies the reproductive decline and the death of the mythical maternal body beyond the text. And while the mother expires, as in the fable of Callie's bloody childbirth, the child—the girls—struggle to survive in these stories. Mythically and sociologically, too, by removing the mother conspicuously from several stories, Munro is staging a tragic feminist drama. Commenting on the mythological lives of mothers and daughters in *Women and Madness*, Phyllis Chesler mourns, "Women in modern Judeo-Christian societies are motherless children. Painting after painting, sculpture after sculpture in the Christian world portray Madonnas comforting and worshipping their infant sons."[28] The psychic umbilical chord between mother and daughter is severed almost from the moment of birth and "female children are quite literally starved for matrimony: not for marriage, but for physical nurturance and a legacy of power and humanity from adults of their own sex ('mothers')" (18).

Nonetheless, survival for the children of both sexes is made possible, in part, by those who grasp hold of what is a female obligation, or has been more naturally relegated to women, of being a keeper rather than a watcher. A maternal burden, it means loss of self as in sex, and as an instinct given over to natural mothers alone, can't always be relied on, says the narrator in "Miles City, Montana" (104). Such close attention means intruding on children, constructing characters for them, being their maternal author as Munro the creative artist is herself throughout these stories. Asking them to play the parts you devise for them may be a fictional imposition but it is also a hedge against accident and the chaos of life. "Keeping" is the mechanism of human survival.

"Where are the children?" is a universal human cry of maternal voice and responsibility that fans out in these stories and seeks to control the fates and, as it does, embraces a much fuller realization and development of Del Jordan's early perception that "People's lives... were... deep caves paved with kitchen linoleum" (*Lives*, 210). In *The Progress of Love* the fiction of ordering through daily rituals and conventions keeps the hounds of chaos—the irrational both in human events and psychology—at bay. Beneath the skin of everyday events, advises Munro, lurks possible destruction and madness. Peg in "Fits" is such a controller, warding off decay by hiding a beautiful bar of soap so that "it wouldn't get cracked and moldy in the cracks" (113) and by providing Robert with a "patterned, limited, serious, and desirable life" (111). Colin is a keeper of his cracked brother, Ross, in "Monsieur les Deux Chapeaux," but it is really the two women, Sylvia and Glenna, who border the narrative and who are, respectively, the source of the irrational and of daylight order. Sylvia is an erratic, bizarre woman who lives by her own fictional constructions rather than conventional rules of conduct. Ross is her more natural offspring than Colin, who has married Glenna to take him away from his mother's confusion (80). "A problem wouldn't just thrust itself on Glenna, and throw her into doubts and agonies. Solutions were waiting like a succession of rooms" (81). The faith in Glenna as the "sane" keeper of the house is a dangerous fiction itself, although Colin isn't completely aware of it. Her penchant for order is a "design of her own" (80) taken to extremes in the sewing she does for her wedding, and in her whole-hearted enthusiasm in assisting Ross reassembling his car, without understanding of the mechanics. *Folie à deux,* an accident, is possible in this affair of car wrecking.

Because women acutely feel and are forced to confront their physical wreckage, theirs would seem to be a more difficult struggle for sanity, particularly at puberty and menopause. Stella in "Lichen" undergoes a psychotic moment when she first views the picture of the pubic hair of the young Dina as the "dark silky pelt of some unlucky rodent" (42). Dawn Rose attempts and apparently succeeds in warding off menstruation, but not madness when, employing an old Victorian folk remedy, she sits in a creek of cold water in "A Queer Streak." The question of female insanity is relentlessly pursued as a chronicle of oddness when Violet, her sister's keeper, as an old woman, approaches senile dementia. The young feminists who visit Violet have an easy solution, their own order to impose on Dawn Rose's temporary psychosis. In a letter to Violet:

Thank you a million, million times for your help and openness. You have given us a wonderful story. It is a classic story of anti-patriarchal rage. Your gift to us, can we give it to others? What is called Female

Craziness is nothing but centuries of Frustration and Oppression. The part about the creek is wonderful just by itself and how many women can identify! (248)

Munro is not so sure about this kind of simplistic dismissal of what is a central issue in this story, the history of female madness. Violet's fiancé, the young minister who breaks off his engagement with her because of her demented sister, has had the same finalizing rationale: "There is a kind of female insanity that strikes at that age," he said, "You know what I mean. She hates men. She blames them. That's obvious. She has an insane hatred of men" (230).

As the two points of view illustrate, Munro seems well aware of the long-lived cultural assumption that women are more vulnerable to insanity than men, that the exposure of "mad" women as cultural victims has challenged this view, and that for contemporary feminists, the madwoman has become an emblematic figure of freedom and struggle.[29] Munro is prepared, in part, to join the young feminists, to protest the social and psychological conditions that drive women mad. She is mad at men for what seems an easier physicality, but more importantly, for their social control. There is sympathy and authorial anger in the portrait of the agonized Violet in "crazy danger" after Trevor rejects her and she struggles to be restored to her "rightful mind," and to find a purpose for her life without a husband (232).

Despite her reticence about simplifying madness to social cause and effect, for there may even be sad, hereditary determinants that feed a queer streak, Munro's historical surveying of generational customs in social-sexual relations ultimately creates the impression of madness-in-progress. Madness *at* men and madness *by* men for women in love is a constant. Dr. Streeter is a version of the ultimate contemporary patriarch, "the Khan" in "Eskimo," who by virtue of "force of personality and financial power" and "not through hereditary right" (197) holds the modern woman, Mary Jo, as concubine. Divining her situation on her vacation trip to Tahiti, Mary Jo begins to go a little crazy. Nor is Mary Jo's situation so very different from that of previous generations, from the hung grandmother's in "The Progress of Love" or Violet's in "A Queer Streak."

Madness *at* men is a safer venue for Munro's new heroines, allowing for independence and survival, with only sporadic periods of dependence in the practice and progress of a series of love affairs. Such retrospective anger as the narrator's in "Miles City, Montana" at the "tyrannical footsteps" and the "masculine authority" (91) of her husband assists her in moving forward. Yet, one of the several paradoxes of madness, as the author and the narrator of this story know, is that love and hate, desire and anger, bridge one another, fuelling the passion that both parties feel in a sexual encounter.

Munro is even prepared to join that group of nineteenth and twentieth century female artists who have used the fictional character of the deranged woman "as the symbolic representation of the female author's anger against the rigidities of patriarchal tradition."[30] There is surely a wicked delight taken in the rage of the female child, Dawn Rose, gone mad in "A Queer Streak," refusing to be feminine and aggressively attacking the father in an obscene note:

You ought to be thrown down the toilet hole head first.
You bowlegged stupid rotten pig. You ought to have your things cut off with a razor blade. You are a liar, too. All those fights you said you won are a lie. (220)

Dawn Rose's authorship of a series of anonymous letters also suggests the figure of the artist-as-madwoman, that authorial double, who prevails in the history of women's writing and who struggles "to escape male houses and male texts."[31]

The author is not prepared, however, to codify madness as a singularly female malady or convention. In this volume, her portraits of madness include slightly disturbed men, who retain, characteristically, a typical masculine faith in themselves (the queer Ross in "Monsieur les Deux Chapeaux" dismisses the family friend, Nancy, as crazy), but who are portrayed by Munro with some affection. Here she adopts the accepting view that she did earlier through Del with Bobby Sherriff in *Lives*, that these queer men simply inhabit another world, and speak another language that is not without its own meaning. Kelvin, an inmate in the Home for Mentally Handicapped Adults in "Circle of Prayer," expresses a deep wisdom in Munro's world of relative truths and paradoxical unresolved perceptions of human affairs, with his response to Trudy's question, "Kelvin, do you pray?" "If I was smart enough to know what to pray for," he says, "then I wouldn't have to" (274).

Finally, female madness is expanded in *The Progress of Love* to become a definition of modern life. Munro hints that madness has its own validity and the supposedly sane world with its many shifting, frenetic conventions is a greater insanity. Robin's assessment of her father and his latest woman's lifestyle in "A Circle of Prayer" is a serious and ironic indictment: "Last summer, Robin went to Richmond Hill for a month's visit. She came home early. She said it was a madhouse" (260). Like Doris Lessing who, welcoming the theories of R.D. Laing and the culture of antipsychiatry, moved finally to the position that the schizophrenic was the sanest person in a mad society,[32] Munro considers the possibility, at least, of the rightness of the mad, both female and male.

| | | —

In her sixth volume, as in her others, Alice Munro proves herself to be in the good company of several contemporary female authors writing about sexual relations. Unlike male authors who tend to focus almost exclusively on sexuality as physical encounters,[33] she, like Doris Lessing and Margaret Atwood, interprets sexuality and sexual experience broadly, including the psychological and social forces that shape sexual impulses. Here, too, as in previous work, Munro insists on portraying the feminine tales of women, their customs and costumes, and seeks to strip off the skin and to penetrate to the hearts of women's lives, however painful the revelations.

Paradoxically, by this sixth volume, the juxtaposed, generational images of the skins of women, their dress, their codes, their customs are building into an evocative history of femininity. There is a growing comfort and allure in the design and artifice of women's historical pageantry. The young girls in "The Circle of Prayer," for example, dropping their jewellery in the casket of a friend may still be enacting that feminine ritual of devotion in love, which is challenged by the mother and Munro, but the religious sisterhood is one of communal beauty: "They sang, they wept, they dropped their jewellery. The sense of ritual made every one of them graceful" (263). On a mythic level, they are pagan demigoddesses, having invented their own materialistic custom, but their decorative postures and their concern and motive of undying love are inspired by their femininity.

Their beauty is also obviously their youth. The image of the stripped skin and the lost face is a disturbing metaphor in several of the stories, projecting the anxiety and melancholy of the aging narrator behind the text, who is moving beyond her physical and feminine prime. The figure who most visibly represents their condition, indeed concludes the narratives in a positive, visionary and mythic way, is that of the character, Sophie, the "Old Norse" of the final story, "White Dump."

A character who feels herself to be shrinking and unable to keep up with the rules of the charades her family plays, Sophie is viewed primarily in the last stages of her life, as ever, above social custom. A woman who has had an illegitimate child without upset, Sophie has been and continues to be a casual mother, more interested in the Icelandic literature that sustains her in her old age, *The Poetic Edda*, than domestic or parental obligation. She is colored by Munro as a singular, bold spirit of epic interest and disaffected maternity. A heroine of independence in her own right, Sophie also achieves symbolic proportions when she is trapped swimming naked, and subsequently arises out of the water to parade her nakedness with absolute assurance and shamelessness. Sophie's resurfacing is an unforgettable mythopoeic moment of renewal and a historical parallel to that of Del Jordan's in "Baptizing." In this dual surfacing, what Munro gives both her characters is a resurgence of confident identity at crucial life stages. What she gives her readers is a positive historical evolution and established saga of the female heroine and the female artist from youth to old age.

If Del Jordan was the artist that Alice Munro was becoming, Sophie is now the artist that she is. Significantly, first person narration has been greatly reduced in this volume to three stories; Munro has moved from the self-exploratory, first person "I" of earlier work in *Dance* and Del Jordan in *Lives* to arrive at a more objective sense of certain, separate voice in the authorial distance of an omniscient narrator. The mature artist is also projected here, too, through Sophie who is composed and self-directed in her intellectual pursuits.

Finally, Munro's choice of Sophie as a symbol of resurrection both for the female and the artist is deliberately pagan and feminist-inspired. Like Margaret Atwood, Munro's feminist interest throughout her fiction has been "in the use of a matriarchal goddess cult." Like other feminist writers, Munro's use of totemic figures and earth-mothers has been "of a piece with a more general move... toward reasserting the very old idea that there is magical power in the female body, in female procreativity and nurturance."[34] In Sophie, the fertility goddess is withering and dying; as the pagan divine she is "the old woman naked" with breasts "slung down like little bundles" (300). The deadening changes in the offing are not Sophie's or Munro's choice, but they are offset through Sophie's Venus-like ascent from the water. Sophie's promise, then, is a mythic one of artistic rebirth and human sexual evolution.

From *Dance of the Happy Shades* to *The Progress of Love*, Munro's own progress as a feminist writer is exceptional. She belongs to a growing tradition of female authors who are beginning to fuse the realistic, the mythological and the metaphysical. Like Doris Lessing and Margaret Atwood, among others, Alice Munro begins "with the traditional female concerns with personal relationships and the details of daily life" and expands these concerns "to include a wider and wider swath of human experience."[35] In *The Progress of Love*, the touchstone of human experience is the physical, psychological, mythic and cultural dimensions of female sexuality. By this sixth volume, the feminist odyssey has truly become a female epic.

| 3 | FOLK ARTIST AND IRONIST
Humor Comes Best to Those Who Are Down and Out

I used to be Snow White but I drifted.
MAE WEST

Humor comes best to those who are
down and out, or who have at least
discovered their own limitations and failures.
STEPHEN LEACOCK

As a mapper of feminist territory, Munro is both folk artist and humorist. In style and literary method she is clearly a priestess of High Art; her stories and novels are carefully rehearsed, almost classical in polished design; her central authorial voice is constant as the artist-woman of superior sensibilities and vision, but the medium with which she works is, to a significant degree, that of common clay, of rural life and custom, and mass popular culture.

In this dedication to the folk, Munro is a part of a new tributary of the modern mainstream of Canadian literature. From Susanna Moodie's first genteel observations in the bush to Robertson Davies's high Anglican literary imagination, the mainstream thrust of English-Canadian literature has been that of colonial Anglo-Celtic *belles lettres*. In recent years, however, a growing number of writers, concerned with the ethnic realities of a multicultural country and with regional cultures, with "real life" lived by the people (notably, *Real Life* is the title Munro first gave to *Lives of Girls and Women*), have created fictions which can be identified as being of a folk nature. Writing from either within or without folk groups, determined as such by limited geography or minority culture, or both, they embed in their fictions the particulars of folk life, often dramatizing the social, psychological or mythological realities of a small, homogeneous group of people. Gabrielle Roy, for instance, includes stories of a Chinese-Canadian immigrant mind and the collective vision of the Doukhobors on the prairies in the volume *Garden in the Wind*, and Munro in her fifth volume, *The Moons of Jupiter*, considers Finnish characters from Northwestern Ontario.

In general, these authors are motivated by a social conscience which is egalitarian and antiestablishment; and as artists, they often use informal or innovative fictional formats. While there is no mistaking a postmodernist like Robert Kroetsch as a voice of literary culture, he is clearly of folk sympathy, paying tribute to the greatest literary folk artist of them all, Chaucer, in his dedicative quotation in *The Studhorse Man* and broadening the tall tale of Western origin into a mythological tribute to the frontier in the format of this fiction. In Quebec, too, current litterateurs embrace the common weal as the oral contes and fables of village mind are recreated as a fictional dynamic in the works of such French-Canadian writers as Roch Carrier and Jacques Ferron.

In these writers and others of their ilk, humor is also paramount, proving the point of the prophetic and somewhat anarchistic American literary critic, Leslie Fiedler, that the "liberating privilege of comic sacrilege" is part of the modern antidote to what he sees as the outdated "finicky canons of the genteel tradition"[1] both in literature and literary criticism.

| | | —

For Alice Munro, as for many first-rate writers, the division between High Art and Low, between genteel, literary canons and common culture, ultimately is not such a cataclysmic and absolute choice. There is no doubt that she feels the tension, observes it even as a constant theme in her fiction in her repeated depiction of the poor country girl torn between her rustic roots and literary culture. Typical in her fiction is such an imagistic aside as that of the portrait of the poor farm girl, Beatrice, in *Lives* who, "big" and "hard-working" in her coarse, broadcloth dress, reads out slowly the incongruous, patrician question asked of her on the high-school examination: "'Englishmen in the eighteenth century valued formal elegance and social stability.' Discuss, with reference to one eighteenth-century poem" (190).

A facet of Munro the artist, Del Jordan in *Lives* struggles towards a balance between her populist attachments and her literary sensibilities, the latter born largely out of the Jubilee library and her mother's genteel aspirations. Del is the superior and mocking outsider. Watching through a window with the scholarly Jerry and discussing "like sociologists, in elegant prudish tones" the busload of country folk in town for a revival meeting, she sees them as people who "Unearthed from country kitchens... wore clothes that seemed to have grown mold," the school buses they come in like "gaudy old rickety buses that looked as if they should be rocking over some mountain road in South America, live chickens flapping out the windows" (174). But Del Jordan in her next breath becomes the lover of one of these people, of Garnet French; Munro, too, is their lover; her perspective is distanced like the pseudosociologist Del, but the images she recalls are those of the subjective textures and tones, particularized through language, of their ordinary lives.

Munro's art does not, however, stand completely outside literary tradition. Literary influence is not absent. Literary art learned from superior writers and influenced by artistic community is part of Munro's inspiration; yet, as she herself admits, her work is, to a great degree, experiential or democratically grounded in her own folk experience. A good example of her aspiration towards such balance can be seen in her script *The Newcomers*, a historical dramatization of the arrival of Irish immigrants to Canada, written as part of an immigrant series for CBC television. In the script she suggests to the producers a voice-over, that of Canada's early female writer, the British gentlewoman Susanna Moodie, as the Irish immigrants are pictured landing at Grosse-Isle.

VOICE-OVER

A crowd of many hundred Irish immigrants had been landed during the present and former day. They appeared perfectly destitute of shame, or even common decency. Many were almost naked, still more but partially clothed. We turned in disgust from the revolting scene.

Munro goes on to explain:

This is Susanna Moodie in *Roughing it in the Bush*. The two voice-over comments of outsiders that I want to use—this, and the bit from the

Elgin-Grey papers—will, of course, have to be identified as read, and this may interfere with the immediacy of the story. But they do seem useful to me. Of course, they must not be used in a way that parodies or seems to make villains of the two speakers—that would be too easy. These were two typical well-bred observers—nothing monstrous about them.[2]

While Munro meant to give the well-bred British attitude credibility in *The Newcomers*, at the same time, the script is first and foremost a sympathetic tribute, an artistic extolling even of a dispossessed and untutored people, out of whom the author-dramatist is able to recall her own Irish ancestors.

Munro is interested in and sympathetic to folk life and folk character in a broad sense, but she also projects her own gender in "writing the folk." The depiction of folk life is, in fact, a natural discourse for Munro as a feminist author, who, as suggested in Chapter One, has moved beyond the androgynous art of earlier female authors, who is confronting her own femininity, and by so doing, is laying claim to and championing the broad, primary folk group of women. While some readers may be surprised at women as a proper classification of a folk group, as Claire R. Farrar points out in *Women and Folklore*, folklore scholarship pertaining to women is a longstanding tradition.[3] In contrast, in the history of literary criticism, female folk life has not been the subject of literary analysis in the fiction of female authors; it has not influenced aesthetic and critical canons; when it has been embedded in literature, there has generally been a failure to recognize it.

As Ellen Moers explains in her classic study *Literary Women*, women writers have made an enormous contribution to the history of letters, but very often they have been assessed according to masculine or neutral standards, interpreted, in effect, through the aesthetic canons and values of patriarchal social structures. Thus, the fact that "all of Jane Austen's opening paragraphs, and the best of her first sentences, have money in them... [the] first obviously feminine thing about her novels"[4] remains undisclosed to the official literary world; such a reality is that of the secret, suppressed "folk" society of female readers who belong to a largely ignored and isolated Other culture within Culture both in sociological fact and in fiction.

As a conveyor of this Other culture, which is traditionally interpreted as female "folk" life, Munro is both conventionally feminine, particularly in her earlier work, and, at the same time, remarkably radical. The approaches and subjects—the preoccupations of her literature—are true to the conventional pattern of sociological analysis pointed out by Claire R. Farrar which is that, traditionally, among sociologists, "Women... are grouped with other women and with small children both male and female: women's hearth and home activities involve not only other women but also children of both sexes" (xiii). This is their assigned image. Within the scope of Munro's work, women come to be seen in just this way, in relation to other women, in photographic juxtaposition. In her first three volumes, men are conspicuously absent or play minimal roles. Life is often interpreted through the eyes of a child, recorded with an amazing perspicacity and authenticity. Storytelling itself is interpreted as a female talent— women telling stories to other women, in particular to their daughters, is a constant motif, included even as a kind of oral conte in *Who Do You Think You Are?*: "Here is the sort of story Flo told Rose..." (43).

Up until the final chapters of her fourth work, Munro's fictional world is, psychologically and emotively at least, a fictional world of hearth and home, of traditional female concern and female relationships, a domestic private arena which in the dance of the sexes embraces men, but which is as fundamentally divided as the boys and girls separate line-ups in the schoolyard ritual in "Day of the Butterfly" or the gathering of husbands and wives in "The Shining Houses" where the subject of real estate and bringing down house values was "one of the few on which male and female interest came together" (*Dance*, 25).

Munro is not, however, a sociologist; she is an artist who holds a rightful place in the canonized culture of Canadian, and international, literature. What is rarely acknowledged, however, is that hers is a feminine art—that the "folk" interests of domestic women: the house, furnishings, interior decoration, food, and fashion are the basic vocabulary of her art—and that such materials not only spell out celebration of womanly things, they very often spell out feminist comment and protest. This protest is clearly expressed by the narrator of "The Office" who explains with some desperation, "a house is not the same for a woman. She is not someone who walks into the house, to make use of it, and will walk out again. She is the house; there is no separation possible (*Dance*, 60). E.D. Blodgett has elaborated on this tight relationship in Munro's fiction, on the metaphorical insistence of the house which becomes even a mode of narrative organization.[5] The house is, in both senses of the word, a feminine *figure* for Alice Munro.

Munro's, then, is a literature of protest, but it is also a literature of conventional feminine mind—like that of the Lady of Shalott whose window out into the world may, from the masculine point of view, be fixed primarily on the male knight, but as other women know, becomes, if only by captive necessity, equally involved in the tower itself, in its decoration and artistic recreation and in even greater heresy, in the I itself.

Part of the appeal of Munro's fiction is her descriptions of domestic interiors and the small objects or decoration whereby women define their personalities. (Notably, however, Munro's women for the most part do not decorate the aristocratic tower; rather, they are relegated to the bargain basement.) And while Munro acknowledges with melancholy that such a preoccupation is a betrayal, that women know personality through object because they are the masculine-ordained consumers of society, she also acknowledges its value as domestic art for ordinary women. The narrator of "The Office," for example, may reject the hideous teapot covered with gilt and roses, the plant, the wastebasket with the Chinese mandarins on all eight sides given to her as a domestic imperative by her androgynous landlord, but such objects continue to exercise a delicious, poetic folk appeal throughout Munro's fiction. The Munro reader as traditional female is as much moved by the poetry of such objects as is the young, rural girl in "Day of the Butterfly" whose typical formative experience of material treasure is the gifted prize from the Cracker Jack Box, "a brooch, a little tin butterfly, painted gold with bits of coloured glass stuck onto it to look like jewels" (*Dance*, 105).

On the one hand, then, Munro's obsession with domestic interior space and her often ironic description of such are meant to invite female union and promote the escape from the doll's house and its several rooms: tattered, and obscene even, in the explicit folk objects of decoration in "Thanks for the Ride"—the glossy chesterfield with a Niagara Falls and a *To Mother* cushion on it, the china elephant planter (51); practical and neat in the "tiny sealed-off country" of cross-stitch bathroom samplers or in the neat virginal bedrooms "papered with timid flower wallpaper" (*Dance*, 204) of small town spinster aunts in *Lives* and "The Peace of Utrecht"; modern, declarative and moral in the middle-class environs of Eskimo prints and carvings, Indian wall hangings, a pair of Kwakiutl masks in June's British Columbia home in "Memorial"; neutral, thick, silent and oppressively masculine in the upper-class home of Patrick's mother with its gleaming sideboard, thick towels, rugs and knives in *Who Do You Think*

You Are? These are symbols of what women must struggle against, like the cut-glass bowl Maddy breaks as she struggles to claim her life in "The Peace of Utrecht."

However, typically, such furnishings seem at times magical in their appeal; indeed, they are often poeticized by Munro, capturing the collective imaginative eye of women, who recognize their own "folk" interest and identity elevated into artistic expression, an expression which has been too often minimized or ignored in the conventional schemata of aesthetic values. There is the beauty of domestic warmth in such a comforting and comfortable setting as that of eating a "batter pudding in the eating nook of a kitchen in a little stucco house by the bus stop, plaster pears and peaches decorating the wall, ivy curling out of the little brass pots" (156) in *Who Do You Think You Are?*; the beauty of luxurious sensuality is seen and felt in the attention to light (another age-old feminine concern since primitive times) in the "lighting-fixture over the round table" which hangs down, breastlike as "unlit flowers of thick, butterscotch glass" in "Images" (*Dance*, 31).

Besides furnishings and interior decorations, food is of extreme importance in Munro. Depictions of women nurturing by serving food serve as a feminist complaint. The girl Alva in "Sunday Afternoon" is an explicit, alarming prototype of the maid many women, particularly in the lower classes, are actually and psychically forced to become. Food given fictional prominence is not, of course, exclusive to female writers. Dickens, as a biedermeier novelist, is noted for his lavish tables of delightful Pickwickian fare. But food in Munro is charged with feminine value.

The small rewards of Munro's women, of all domestic women, have very often been that with which they are best acquainted and which, since Eve first bit the apple, has been their seduction—food. Thus the poor step-mother in *Who Do You Think You Are?*, after Saturday shopping, treats herself to a sundae, a vicarious delight to her step-children who are denied this privilege, who are "disappointed if it was only pineapple or butterscotch, pleased if it was a Tin Roof, or Black and White" (11). Rose herself will express her love to the older schoolgirl Cora by filching candy to give her and will pretend to social status with "half a grapefruit" for breakfast. The narrator's mother from "Connection" in "Chaddeleys and Flemings" in *The Moons of Jupiter* pretties up glasses of lemonade for visiting female cousins by dipping the rims in beaten egg whites and sugar; they reciprocate by making layer cakes and "marvellous molded salads which were shaped like temples and coloured like jewels" (4). If woman *is* the house in Munro's art, she *is* also food. It is a sign of her servility, her small reward, her compulsion, proof of her love, symbol of her class status (wholesome and plentiful for Munro's lower-class girls), and the medium of her artistry.

Flo will recompense Rose for her royal beating, tempt her into forgiveness with the best, the most gorgeous array of food she can muster within her limited circumstances and imagination:

> Later still a tray will appear. Flo will put it down without a word and go away. A large glass of chocolate milk on it, made with Vita-Malt from the store. Some rich streaks of Vita-Malt around the bottom of the glass. Little sandwiches, neat and appetizing. Canned salmon of the first quality and reddest color, plenty of mayonnaise. A couple of butter tarts from a bakery package, chocolate biscuits with a peppermint filling. Rose's favorites, in the sandwich, tart and cookie line. She will turn away, refuse to look, but left alone with these eatables will be miserably tempted, roused and troubled and drawn back from thoughts of suicide or flight by the smell of salmon, the anticipation of crisp chocolate, she will reach out a finger, just to run it around the edge of one of the sandwiches (crusts cut off!) to get the overflow, get a taste. Then she will decide to eat one, for strength to refuse the rest. One will not be noticed. Soon, in helpless corruption, she will eat them all. She will drink the chocolate milk, eat the tarts, eat the cookies. She will get the malty syrup out of the bottom of the glass with her finger, though she sniffles with shame. Too late. (*Who*, 19)

Food as female art is a motif not without irony, here displayed as a kind of hopeless, recurring failing of the age-old Eve, but it is also a poetic of feminine leisure and delight, as in the evocative image of the chocolate box, the gift and central emblem of the visiting female cousins for the young girl in "Connection" from *The Moons of Jupiter*,

> Long after all the chocolates were eaten, and the cousins had gone, we kept the chocolate-box in the linen-drawer in the dining-room sideboard, waiting for some ceremonial use that never presented itself. It was still full of the empty chocolate cups of dark, fluted paper. In the wintertime I would sometimes go into the cold dining room and sniff at

the cups, inhaling their smell of artifice and luxury; I would read again the descriptions on the map provided on the inside of the box-top: hazlenut, creamy nougat, Turkish delight, golden toffee, peppermint cream. (*Moons*, 3)

Food as artistic presentation of self is most clearly and positively drawn in Miss Marsalles's table in "Dance of the Happy Shades." While the food presented by Miss Marsalles, the arrangement of tiny cut sandwiches on pink and blue crepe paper and the warm punch, is puerile and symbolic of the childish, wilting character of the old lady, it is also a symbol of her strength as naive, artistic inspirer, confirming for Munro and her readers the connection between food and art. Typically, many of Munro's most effective images are those of food, which are quite appropriately generated by the feminine artistic imagination. On the first page of *Who Do You Think You Are?*, for example, Rose's mother is recorded dying with a blood clot on her lung—a "feeling" which is "like a boiled egg in my chest" (1); shortly after, Rose's nature is interpreted as "growing like a prickly pineapple" (5); here, too, much to feminist delight, the stepmother Flo is characterized in her last acts of personal defiance as an old lady in a nursing home, biting those who try to restrain her. And in *The Progress of Love*, the portrait of food, "the roast chicken and gravy and mashed potatoes laid on the plate with an ice-cream scoop and the bright diced vegetables out of a can" (23) is, in texture and imagined color, close to the visual domestic art of the Canadian painter, Mary Pratt.

Furnishings, food—and fashion—are materials "dear" to Munro. Just as dressmaking and sewing are recurring activities in her narratives, the fabric of her fiction is brilliantly texturized by descriptions of material itself and feminine dress. Often such descriptions signify social criticism of women as manipulated, decorative objects as in "Red Dress—1946" or the sorry plight, the sad cheapness of poor women aspiring to style beyond their economic grasp; such images of clothes are among Munro's most illuminating moments. Anticipated in the description of Lois' dress in "Thanks for the Ride" is her undressing, her passive and sorry unwrapping like a Christmas gift (an image women relate to as makers of the Christmas festival): "Lois came in, wearing a dress of yellow-green stuff—stiff and shiny like Christmas wrappings—high-heeled shoes, rhinestones, and a lot of dark powder over her freckles" (*Dance*, 51). Sheer crepe, satin, velvet, slub rayon, organdie, cashmere, brocade, flowered silk, pink chenille, powder-blue angora; full black taffeta skirts, short coats colored robin's egg blue, cerise, red, lime green, a soft grey dress with embroidered flowers, a dull rose hat and flowers, a dark red marino wool dress, brown and white checkered slacks and yellow top—such is the stuff of Munro's fiction. A female concern which is prominently displayed and "slipped" into Art.

The concerns and the language of Munro's literature are conventionally feminine, and her poetic narratives, the literary sociologist's record of a North American feminine tradition of Munro's own historical time and those classes of women of which she is aware. Such an awareness of recording becomes ironically explicit even in a story such as "Material" as the middle-class author-narrator explains:

> The wives of the men... are buying groceries or cleaning up messes or having a drink. Their lives are concerned with food and mess and houses and cars and money. They have to remember to get the snow tires on and go to the bank and take back the beer bottles, because their husbands are such brilliant, such talented incapable men, who must be looked after for the sake of the words that will come from them. (*Something*, 20)

Thus the broad female tribe with its values and customs and interests and the female experiences which are privately known and heard among women become fictional legend through Munro.

Besides the general subjects of furnishings, food and fashion, certain motifs in her fiction identify her as a literary folklorist of female culture. One is the association she makes between her female characters and the store. Women are, of course, as consumers, the continual frequenters of stores, and their excursions are often a means of escape from the house which *is* them, without reproof or guilt. Munro gives the store appropriate prominence. "I think of my mother sometimes in department stores" is the wistful opening line of "The Ottawa Valley" (*Something*, 182), and suitably, she makes some of her most independent women those who actually run stores. Flo is more the store than the house in *Who Do You Think You Are?* and in this capacity, Flo is able to exercise some authority. Similarly, in "A Trip to the Coast" the store-house is the female preserve of three generations of women, presided over by the old, wilful and "victorious" grandmother. Helen in "Postcard" is one of Munro's freer women, a salesgirl who runs the upstairs of the suitably named King's Department Store, predictably Children's Wear (with Toyland put in at Christmas), but with some measure of her own self-worth; Peg in "Fits" is "self-contained," the store she works in her natural active milieu. Here she smiles when she gives change—"a quick, transactional smile, nothing personal" (*Progress*, 109). Even that old spinster, Miss Marsalles, an independent of another order, is symbolically in charge of herself and others in her last move next to a house, the front part of which has been turned "into a little store; it has a sign that says: GROCERIES AND CONFECTIONERY" (*Dance*, 217).

A more expressive motif of female folklore is that of gynecological stories told between women. Aunt Moira in *Lives* is the memorable, archetypal storyteller of horrible childbirth, she herself the living embodiment of female physical ruin, with her "varicose veins, hemorrhoids, a dropped womb, cysted ovaries, inflammations, discharges, lumps and stones in various places, one of those . . . wrecked survivors of the female life, with stories to tell" (34). An earth-mother, not romantically glorified, but realistically despoiled, Moira is one of Munro's incredible folk sculptures: "She sat on the veranda in the wicker rocker, wearing, in spite of the hot weather, some stately, layered dress, dark and trembling with beads, a large hat like a turban, earth-coloured stockings which she would sometimes roll down, to let the bandages 'breathe'" (34).

Superstitions about childbirth passed down from women to girls in the rural isolation of Jubilee belong to the changes and ceremonies of Del Jordan's passage into womanhood. From Naomi's mother she learns that "babies born with cauls will turn out to be criminals, that men had copulated with sheep and produced little shriveled woolly creatures with human faces and sheep's tails, which died and were preserved in bottles somewhere, and that crazy women had injured themselves in obscene ways with coat hangers" (100). The psychological and physical apprehension of girls, all girls on the edge of female maturity, is evoked in such folkloristic detail, as well as the distaste for what they must be. Their natural physical life, at variance with the masculine ideal of them as decorative object—Aunt Moira in turban and stately dress—must, by necessity, remain secreted from men. Always, of course, there is the constant fear of disclosure, of being found out, the threat of the humiliation of the Kotex pad displayed as a joke in the trophy case of Rose's high school in *Who Do You Think You Are?* Gynecological particulars (and female attitudes towards them), such as Rose's memory of childbirth, have rarely been detailed in literary art: "She [Rose] was still dazed from the birth. Whenever she closed her eyes she saw an eclipse, a big black ball with a ring of fire. That was the baby's head, ringed with pain, the instant before she pushed it out"[6] (102). In "The Moon in the Orange Street Skating Rink" in *The Progress of Love* Miss Kernaghan's story-within-the-story of Callie's childbirth is told with graphic and naturalistic detail: "Blood was coming out of her as dark as fly poison—it was spreading across the floor. . . . Then he kicked the dog, because it was getting too interested" (*Progress*, 150). Gynecological subjects have remained the subjects of vulgar, folk life and oral female society behind closed doors; in Munro's fiction, they begin to dramatize openly the realities of "feminine" life.

In its most comprehensive sense, then, Munro's work is that of collective female mind and experience, of a cultural enclave that is largely domestic and traditionally treated as folk by both sociologists and literary critics alike. Yet, outside of her central voice, that of the maturing artist-persona who moves through childhood and adolescence from small town Ontario to urban, middle-class success, is also a society of rural or semi-rural women in Southwestern Ontario who are more specifically of a folk character and whose language and behavior are realistically authenticated through Munro's exacting ear and eye. These are the more primitive sisters and earth-mothers discussed in Chapter Two, who viewed together can only contribute to the author's reputation as a folk artist of the first order. Included in this gallery are Nora of "Walker Brothers Cowboy," Mary McQuade of "Images," Lois in "Thanks for the Ride," the grandmother in "A Trip to the Coast," Madeleine in *Lives*, Robina in "The Executioners," Flo and Becky Tyde in *Who Do You Think You Are?*, Marjorie and Lily from *The Moons of Jupiter*, Aunt Ivie and her children in *The Progress of Love*. Here, too, are Munro's more memorable men, Joe Phippen and his whiskey-drinking cat in "Images" and Uncle Benny in *Lives*. These characters are magically arresting, sculpted in memory as somewhat larger than life, reality and importance, like Joe Fafard's sculptures of super-ordinary prairie people. These people are not of the prairies, however, but are distinctly descendants of longstanding Irish-Scottish Protestant settlement in Ontario. Their customs and cultural attitudes, particularly in their Irish influence, are threaded through Munro's images and dramatizations of them, depicted, for example, in the fierce pride and independence of the grandmother who "never took the pension, never took relief" in "A Trip to the Coast" (*Dance*, 177), in the feuding imagination of Joe Phippen who believes himself persecuted by the Silases in "Images" and in the actual murderous feud, which, akin to the Black Donnelly's blood feud, is fought out between Stump Troy and Robina's brothers, Jimmy and Duval in "Executioners."

Munro's folk geography is literally and largely that of southwestern Ontario, around the Wingham area where she grew up, and her own personal experience is that of its Irish-Scottish inhabitants. Her father, Robert Laidlaw, was Scottish on his paternal side, and his mother, Munro's grandmother, was Irish and a strong influence on the family. Munro's own mother was from the Ottawa Valley Irish, a migration woven into the story "The Ottawa Valley" from *Something I've Been Meaning to Tell You* as fictional mother and daughter return to visit family, whose characteristic behavior and language Munro records with relish. Uncle James speaks with an Irish accent and is given to impulsively booming out Irish ditties: "As I was a-goen over Kil-i-kenny Mountain. . . . But I take delight in the water of the barley" (190), Aunt Dodie to folk epithets punctuated by what has come to be known as the universal, Canadian linguistic tic, "Eh?" Not on speaking terms with her sister, she replies to the possibility of her sister being too busy to see her, "Oh, busy. . . . She's busy scraping the chicken dirt off her boots. Eh?" (183). A roisterous, boisterous clan, the Irish relatives are fond of practical jokes of physical discomfort, and the mother is given to beating the children, as Aunt Lena "lays down the law." These Irish-Canadian cousins as depicted by Munro are also natural fiction-makers and politicians, "always telling and concealing, making and breaking alliances; they had the most delicate and ruthless political instincts" (186).

Like William Faulkner writing of his legendary Mississippi county, Munro communicates a mythic world of mind as much as one of manners and regional space, but it is, nonetheless, based on historical and geographic reality, for the old Irish community (in company with the Scots) was the largest ethnic group in Upper Canadian Ontario for most of the nineteenth century and quite possibly earlier, and were, and still are, settled in rural areas throughout the province as a formidable presence.[7] As their folk artist, Munro has special insight into their contradictions and contrariness preserved in a limbo of time, and she presents them as suspended in memory as if ancient, brownish and faded snapshots, like the early photographs of the young Irish grandparents as they were when they came to take up land in the newly-opened Huron tract in "Winter Wind."

While Munro's Irish descendants vary in the degree of their gentility and social success within a rural context, her more moving fictions detail those who are beyond the pale of respectability. One of Munro's most affecting and naturalistic narratives of such country folk is "The Time of Death." Feminist in its theme of a poor, trashy country woman's desperate ambition for her young daughter to escape poverty by becoming a juvenile sex symbol, by singing with the Maitland Valley Entertainers as the "Little Sweetheart of Maitland Valley, the Baby Blonde, the Pint-Sized Kiddie with the Great Big Voice" (*Dance*, 89), "The Time of Death" is a tragic cameo akin to Sherwood Anderson's haunting, pathetic, classic dramatization of the voice of the poor boy in "I'm a Fool." His aspiration towards class is hopeless, beyond his limited grasp. Similarly, Leona and Patricia Parry's hope is weighted down by the sordidness and shrunken margins of their environment and its limited possibilities.

While the folk subject of this narrative is not graphically Irish-Canadian, it seems so, especially in the convincing idiom and rhythms of Leona Parry's speech, for which Munro admits to having a self-conscious ear (in interview she mentions her step-mother from whom she says she picked up a strong Huron country idiom).[8] Whatever its precise dialect, the speech rings true in Leona Parry's pathetic aspirations for Patricia in "The Time of Death":

Never was ascared once. . . . She don't care, it could be the King of England watching her. . . . Another thing is natural blonde hair. I have to do it up in rags every night of her life, but that real natural blonde is a lot scarcer than natural curly. It don't get dark, either, there's that strain of natural blondes in my family that don't get dark. My cousin I told you about, that won the Miss St. Catherine's of 1936, she was one, and my aunt that died. (*Dance*, 90)

The pride of ordinary ancestry, in Leona's case of familial, female line, is perfectly expressed in this character who, absorbed into modern, popular culture, speaks with an appropriately muted folk expression. The colloquialism "ascared," the nonidiomatic "it don't" and "that don't" bespeak rude education and the use of "the" with a proper name, "that won the Miss St. Catherine's," and the substitution of "that" for a relative pronoun: "my cousin... that," "blondes that" suggest the Irish speech patterns which linguists have currently identified as belonging at least to the Ottawa Valley.[9]

In Munro's more contemporary stories, such use of language, however, is meant to convey felt experience, not to portray an ethnic group whose purity of custom is fading with time. Furthermore, very little of Munro's painstaking and precisely crafted fiction favors Irish-Scottish folk interest over female history, point of view and dilemma. In Leona Parry's speech, the use of "that" rather than "she" for "my cousin" can also be interpreted as a nice means of objectifying woman as the Other and of supporting the theme of the story, the possibility of Patricia Parry's social mobility as a sexual object, as the "Baby Blonde." Similarly in "Walker Brothers Cowboy," "She digs with the wrong foot," a folk expression used in Dungannon to indicate that somebody was a Catholic, is not merely folkloristic detail, but a bleak, prosaic refrain of Nora's female isolation and spinsterhood (Dance, 14); and Cousin Iris's unerasable colloquialisms "all out of puff" and "carrying the lard" in "Connection" offer points of attack for the narrator's condescending husband; they are food for his superiority (Moons, 13).

It is not only the realistic texture of such stories which accounts for the efficacy of Munro's most folklike women. One of the considerable reasons for their power is that in a poor, rural context, their functions and realities border on female folk myth. Their speech, their behavior and their functions, explicitly or suggestively primitive, often lay dramatic claim to the history of women. As keeper of the garden, of cornstalks and cabbages, tender of the fire, the custodian of the light, the maker of clothes and blankets, the preparer of food, Leona Parry is primitive woman personified. Munro establishes this female reality in the first two lines of the story which incorporate reference to the elementals of traditional female concern: "quilt," "fire," "kitchen," "light," "tea," "eat." The life of Leona Parry is not far removed from the cave and when she attempts to break the historical cycle of such feminine life through her female child, she neglects these duties, and a male child is sacrificed with terrifying effect on Patricia. The comforting women about suggest that primitive chorus of females used to serving the sick and preparing the dead from time immemorial, their voices a tragic Greek chorus of soothing lament in an archetypal female tragic drama:

> And the women in the kitchen would crowd around the couch, their big bodies indistinct in the half-light, their faces looming pale and heavy, hung with the ritual masks of mourning and compassion. Now lay down, they would say, in the stately tones of ritual soothing. Lay down, Leona, she ain't here, it's all right. (*Dance*, 91)

In "The Time of Death," the surface reality of a woman's world in Ontario folk life is a mere veneer of civilization; beyond it is the prehistory of primal woman and her functions. The artistic consequence of such mythic depth is that the story begins to assume the shape of ongoing legend—or ballad. An evocative aural story of a female balladeer becomes its own literary folk song—the ballad of Patricia Parry.

| | | —

The hidden and ignored folklore and folk life of women is the rich fabric of Munro's art. The artist is also acutely aware of the fictional uses and possibilities of traditional folkloristic genres, such as children's rhymes and fairytales. Neither is the power of contemporary urban folklore lost on Munro. Her blending of both the traditional and the modern in art is, in effect, a reflection of what professional folklorists have documented, that in a rapidly transforming industrial and technological world, traditional folklore is juxtaposed and merges with a new urban folklore transmitted as popular culture.[10] Munro is a faithful recorder of the folkloristic particulars of Marshall McLuhan's global village through such details in her art as Tastee-Freeze signs, cans of Heinz soup, waterless cooking pots, electronically communicated popular songs and Hollywood personalities. Her genius is the ability to turn the commonplace into poetic vision—into dream and magic—into extasis, and often inexplicably so. How does, for example, a tale of adolescent popular culture in North America in the 1940s built on the mundane particulars of basketball, hockey, a gymnasium dance, magazine questionnaires, a stiff new brassiere and bobby-pin cards become for the reader in what seems a magic, unfathomable moment, the framed vision, "Red Dress—1946"?

As a folk artist, Munro is not only sensitive to the interests of women as a "folk" group, she is well aware of the masculine imperative of much of both traditional and contemporary folklore. Schooled in self-expression as private, oral discussion between women, she is particularly receptive to aural forms and recreates them to express female realities.

In fact, her fiction is shot through, like the hues in taffeta, with hymns, refrains, rhymes, chants, snatches of made-up and popular songs and ballads, some unknown to the reader and some buried but revived through Munro's recollection. Some belong to the ceremonies of childhood of the Munro persona, others to the courtship rite of adolescence, which, along with the dance, are interpreted almost from an anthropological distance. The net effect of both this sociological stance and an interest in oral expression is the translation of a folk idiom into feminist art and comment. The rules of the game of life for women are spelled out in the rhymes and songs of oral culture of patriarchal society and Munro illustrates this reality as she uses them inventively to spell out the situations of her female protagonists.

Munro is very well aware of the significance and power of children's rhyme. In *Lives*, an idiot woman who lives outside the boundaries of convention is aggressive, a threat. She is rousted and attacked via a rhyme which is boldly conceived and expressed through the imagery of destruction of her female anatomy. "Irene don't come after me/Or I'll hang you by your tits in a/crab-apple tree" (6) connotes the folk expression of society towards the out-of-order woman, and Del Jordan rightly wonders at its mysterious source, "Where had that rhyme come from?" Later in *Lives*, the rhyme of Garnet French's young sisters, "This old barn is falling down, falling down" (186), becomes, through authorial invention, a psychological, Freudian integer for Del of the probability of a long-term relationship with Garnet French leading to her ruin; maternity could lead to the collapse of her person as it did for Garnet's mother. In *Lives*, again, the resonant, here extraordinarily mythic, impact of rhyme affects Munro's readers at a less conscious level in the age-old skipping chant known to many women as girls:

> On the mountain stands a lady
> Who she is I do not know.
> All she wears is gold and silver,
> All she needs is a new pair of shoes! (132)

In the history of folklore, particularly in nursery rhymes, it is well understood that there is a traditional connection between shoes and marriage: "Not only does Cinderella find her prince charming through the perfect fit between her foot and a glass slipper, but in American culture, we continue to tie old shoes on the bumpers of cars carrying newlyweds off on their honeymoon."[11] For Del Jordan, this rhyme sung by young girls "in their clear, devout voices" (132) is, in combination with the peacocks who are simultaneously crying and strutting in fantastic male color, a moment of society's seductive expectation of her to embrace her prince charming, a mythic moment in female time which has been struck over and over and over again.

As well as the rhymes of children, the songs of ordinary people are inflected with social or psychological meaning for Munro's female characters or her reader. "Nita, Juanita, softly falls the southern moon," a song of charming woman played by the youngest unmarried aunt, Edith, is a haunting, poetic refrain of a hope for love and marriage, one which underlines Mary McQuade's loss in the eyes of society in "Images" (Dance, 31). In "The Time of Death" Patricia, after the death of her little brother, selects, ironically, the sheet music May the Circle Be Unbroken, which is subtly predictive of her own failed future and a second song It Is No Secret What God Can Do which also re-establishes acceptance of the status quo, again, ironically. In "Boys and Girls," the young girl, aspiring to be more than the female which society means her to be, sings the most moving masculine ballad of them all, Danny Boy, and later she knows herself as woman-to-be as a victim, powerlessly associated with the horse about to be shot and the black man, in the mocking-sorrowful tune the hired man directs at her, "Oh, there's no more work, for poor Uncle Ned, he's gone where the good darkies go" (Dance, 120). In "Something I've Been Meaning to Tell You," the beautiful and feminine Char gaily playing the piano in the dark sings out "The flowers that bloom in the spring tra-la, Have nothing to do with the case" (3), suggesting to the reader the ironic distance between the light and dark worlds of female appearance and mind. In "Lichen" from The Progress of Love, the madrigal sung by David to Stella, his abandoned ex-wife, is a potent disclaimer of the ideal of romantic love that leaves women controlled by the will of the romantic hero:

O, Mistress mine, where are you roaming?
O, Mistress mine, where are you roaming?

> O, stay and hear, your true love's coming,
> O, stay and hear, your true love's coming, (39)

In Munro's literature, while each character may feel free to make her own private self-sustaining music, like those amassed to watch Eugene walk on water in "Walking on Water," song is most often played to the ears of women in the tune of men—like that of the popular ballad on the radio which frightens Del Jordan—"the girl that I marry will have to be, as soft and pink as a nursery" (150).

Folkloristic material and popular culture, like the previous song, are not always negatively construed for women in Munro's work. The inclusion of archetypal folklore patterns of märchen—of fairy tales—and of ancient myth, as well as popular, urban folk heroines promotes female possibility and authority. Munro clearly understands that folklore transmitted orally, or in print, or in the new electronic age, through radio, movies, cartoon strips and television, is an important element in the social life of the people and is an initiator or modifier of human behavior. Thus, such influences, at the edge of the ordinary person's consciousness, are also at the edges of her literature. Neither is it surprising that she would accommodate the fiction of childhood in her authorial imagination; many women, in their close association with children, retain such a sensibility, which for Munro as artist is genuine vision—the world of enchantment and magic recalled in such stories as "Walker Brothers Cowboy" and "Images" where the author, after an adventure with her father, concludes she is,

> like the children in fairy stories who have seen their parents make pacts with terrifying strangers, who have discovered that our fears are based on nothing but the truth, but who come back fresh from marvellous escapes and take up their knives and forks, with humility and good manners, prepared to live happily ever after—like them, dazed and powerful with secrets, I never said a word. (*Dance*, 43)

Catherine Sheldrick Ross comments astutely on the mythic substructures in Munro's art; of "Images" she explains, "The structure for "Images" is the familiar motif of the underground journey, which, in this story, ends with the heroine's meeting a figure of death in an underground house and her initiation into secret knowledge of life."[12] Another obvious ancient folkloric narrative pattern restyled to dramatic purpose is that of the evil eye. Alan Dundes explains that "The evil eye is a fairly consistent and uniform folk belief complex based upon the idea that an individual, male or female, has the power, voluntarily or involuntarily, to cause harm to another individual or his property merely by looking at or praising that person or property. The harm may consist of illness, or even death or destruction."[13] Tales of the evil eye abound in folklore and within the Indo-European and Semitic world there is hardly a more powerful folk belief.

Munro uses this ancient superstition in "A Trip to the Coast" where the primality of landscape and mind in the modern folk place of Black Horse is virtually marvellous. Amidst the mundane particulars of the setting, the Candy Apple lipstick, the bubble gum and Kleenex, the child May surveys the world with the magical and wondering eye of the first female child. And within her sensibility, Munro enacts the ancient drama of the evil eye as the wandering hypnotist is pitted against the old witchlike woman, May's grandmother. The imagery of the legend further expands the fiction to mythic proportions. In the evil eye belief complex, the power of the evil eye is transmitted through maternity, in particular through the milk of breast-feeding. The child who develops the power of the evil eye is the one who suckles greedily; weaning discourages such power. May's grandmother is painted as shrivelling maternity with the preposterous "little mound of her stomach like a four-months' pregnancy"; hers is an "undernourished look" (*Dance*, 175), and her face is the color of "curdled milk" (177). As her maternal power over her granddaughter diminishes, all her energy is drawn together for her final contest, a battle of wills through the power of the eye which she loses by dying, but by so doing vanquishes the man, the implication being that she passes her power on to her granddaughter who has been generously nurtured in an exclusively female world. In "A Trip to the Coast" Munro champions female prerogative through the folklore of the evil eye.

The folklore of the evil eye, with its complex associations, is also used as mythic symbol in the experience of Del Jordan in *Lives*. As Dundes explains, the evil eye, associated with milk and maternity, is often considered especially damaging to female animals, such as cows. The evil eye is a threat to life, to sustenance, to milk and to water, which is associated with creation. Such associations are apparent in the Egyptian funerary rite, where various offerings including food and liquid, a metaphor for life, were presented to the dead—most of them said to come from the Eye of Horus: "The Eye of Horus as a breast or other body part containing liquid is understood to refresh the deceased by offering him the necessary additional 'fluid of life' to replace the fluids lost before death or during the process of mummification.''[14]

Linked to the evil eye complex is one of the most memorable scenes in all of Munro's fiction, that of Del Jordan before the funeral of her Uncle Craig at Jenkin's Bend, wading through water, encountering the dead cow and its remarkable eye:

> The eye was wide open, dark, a smooth sightless bulge, with a sheen like silk and a reddish gleam in it, a reflection of light. An orange stuffed in a black silk stocking. Flies nestled in one corner, bunched together beautifully in an iridescent brooch. I had a great desire to poke the eye with my stick, to see if it would collapse, if it would quiver and break like a jelly... and let loose all sorts of putrid mess...—but I was not able, I could not poke it in. (*Lives*, 37)

Del's mother will later be associated with Isis, the Egyptian goddess of fertility, her uncle's wife, Nile, with Cleopatra, and in this instance as a director of the eye, Del is herself a kind of primitive goddess surrounded by the powerful ambience of maternity and life. A forewarning of the death which will occur, the eye of the cow, imagized in a feminine way through food, clothing and ornamentation, places Del Jordan in a mythic world of female importance where she exercises, symbolically, a choice between life and death.

The position of the female in the history of folk tales, legend and myth has traditionally been minimized. Hero narratives of exploit and conquest and rescue belong to men, the princess pattern of the rescued to the weaker and fairer sex. Probably the best known and most revered fairy tale of passive femininity is the Cinderella story, a folk tale pattern which Munro entertains in *Who Do You Think You Are?* This is the story of Cinderella-Rose and her ugly, monkeyish stepmother who has her beaten and who mocks her desire for and profession of love. Rose is a modern version of the Cinderella character and of her close kin, the beggar maid (*The Beggar Maid* is the American title for the book) a folk-tale heroine who does succeed by her own cleverness (if only to win a man).[15] The beggar maid is a recurring figure in Munro's fiction: in *The Progress of Love*, Callie is another version in "The Moon in the Orange Street Skating Rink." In *Who Do You Think You Are?* Munro is reworking mythology in a very basic way and by so doing, establishing new directions for women. In simple analysis, Flo the step-mother proves to be a confederate, not the enemy; Prince Charming in the person of Patrick is accepted, but then discarded, and Rose embarks on her own self-determined odyssey.

In the choice of the name, Rose, for her heroine and her profession of actress, Munro is true as well to feminist folklore. Acting as a means of career and success for women is, in effect, a social reality which has become feminist legend, including many legendary females. In her book *The Female Hero in Folklore and Legend*, Tristram Coffin comments on the history of female as actress since the social rise of the actress Lavinia Fenton as Polly Peachum in John Gay's *The Beggar's Opera* in 1728:

> Bordered by primroses, though it may be, few paths have led young women more directly to reward than the theatre. Whether the aim is "a good marriage," fame or fortune, or simply a place in the sun, for about 300 years acting has been the way. Furthermore, nowhere since the doll house was built has woman attained the old "hunting and gathering parity" more completely than on the boards. There, salaries, publicity, recognition, and success or failure have been, if not "regardless of sex," "regardless of which sex."[16]

Munro's actress Rose also has a suitably mythic name. As Coffin explains in a chapter of her book entitled "Grotesque Roses," Rose is associated with the fairy queen of Celtic legend, with the romantic image of Keats' la belle dame sans merci. An image of the errant seductress of patriarchal design, the Rose figure is still a magical type of some independence. Both of these implied folkloristic identities of Munro's heroine, of actress and Rose are folk-expressive of female ascendancy, and would seem to have been carefully chosen by Munro for their legendary appropriateness.

The Rapunzel story has also intrigued Munro. Susan Brownmiller delineates the importance of hair in the definition of femininity, and that "a woman's act of unpinning and letting down a cascade of long hair is interpreted as a highly erotic gesture, a release of inhibiting restraints"; further, "according to psychologist Bruno Bettleheim, the prince who called to Rapunzel to let down her hair was pleading for rescue from an impotent condition."[17] Certainly, the epitome of femininity is established in the long blonde hair of the fairy princess, and in the fairy princess myth, one of the most powerful symbols of femininity, says Brownmiller, in the Western world.

In unpublished fragments of stories with the titles "Rapunzel" and "Rapunzel, Rapunzel, Let Down Thy Gold Hair" Munro attempts to rework the myth as a critique of the dicta of femininity. Her developing heroine is in revolt against the conventions of romance, of traditional male and female discourse and the symbolic statement of the myth itself. In the following excerpt, there is a perverse denial of the symbol of erotic hair and an equally perverse shift in gender.

> My sister's hair, unbraided, was down on her shoulders, wiry, stiff and yellowy-white, like the whisks of a broom... Her name was Llewelyn... I could remember Aunt Carey saying to me in her mystified, discouraging way, "But that's a boy's name she's calling it, Llewelyn."[18]

Female heroines of popular, modern folk culture are also woven into the consciousness of Munro's central voice; in "Images," for example, the narrator as child fearfully watching the unknown man approach her thinks that she has always known there was a man like this, "So now I saw him and just waited, like a child in an old negative, electrified against the dark noon sky, with blazing hair and burned-out Orphan Annie eyes" (*Dance*, 38). The cartoon strip of Daddy Warbucks and Orphan Annie, identified as "mod marchen" by Tristram Coffin,[19] was a remarkable folk fiction of female indestructability. Annie, along with her faithful dog Sandy and her guardian, Daddy Warbucks, was a crusader against evil, who, Coffin continues, "developed for many Americans the same reality that Tom Sawyer's fence has developed... —a reality which makes her marchenlike adventures part of our legendary past.[20] The characteristic circumstance of Little Orphan Annie and Daddy Warbucks powerfully aligned against the world is present in Munro's "Images" as it is in "Walker Brothers Cowboy" and subtly serves her authorial aims: the expression of childhood enchantment and a developing, independent female mind.

As Alice Munro moves in her art towards the creation of a genuinely female literature, she actively resists the myths and the folk fictions of woman as Adam's rib, the traditional stories of the innocent, slaughtered maiden, the princess confined in the tower or the mound, sleeping beauty, the girl as helper in the hero's flight.[21] As a means of resistance, she selects from the past märchen and myth and, from the present popular figures which begin to suggest otherwise—a solid intrusion in Del Jordan's words of "the legendary into the real world" (178). Thus her protagonists become the mythic controllers of the evil eye, Isis and Cleopatra, Cinderella transformed and la belle dame sans merci, the clever beggar maid, Little Orphan Annie and peripherally even Judy Canova, Barbara Stanwick and Rita Hayworth as Zelda. However insufficient these female images may seem to be, they are at least a first answer to some of Munro's girls and women as they stand in the crumbling doll's house wondering "who do I think I am?"

| | | —

> *It was the long, patient face of the humorist, secretive, ironical.*
> ALICE MUNRO

The reshaping of female identity is central to Munro and it is the threatening void of absent definition which leads her into the realm of irony. The ironic mode has often been discussed as a questioning and relativist one. Wayne C. Booth quotes Kierkegaard's definition of the ironic method as that in which one asks a question, "not in the interest of obtaining an answer, but to suck out the apparent content with a question and leave only an emptiness remaining."[22] As Booth points out, in many modern writers, such as the poetess Sylvia Plath, the ironic vision is a teetering stance between a possibly meaningless universe and a certain meaningless universe—a world, in any event, of cosmic absurdity and black despair.[23]

Munro's irony, in her six works of fiction, does not plunge her into the absurdist's absolute void. B. Pfaus in *Alice Munro* explains that "All of Munro's short stories present the reader with Munro's vision of two worlds which she sees as having an essential and irreconcilable tension between the two sets of values inherent in each world: the chaotic, natural world... and... [the] social garrison of conventionality."[24] Straddling these two worlds, and struggling to compromise them, Munro and her heroines may ultimately find nothing that gives absolute meaning to life in either world, or resolution of situations possible, but in Pfaus' estimation, "the reader can sense Munro's protagonists moving to a more complete and 'whole dense vision of the world.'"[25] Finally, the recurring paradoxical pattern in Munro's stories is "the dramatization of the conjunction of existential desperation and existential possibility within a total vision that is actually much closer to faith than it is to despair."[26]

Faith rather than despair prevails partly because the voyage of the self does not touch on cosmic order or metaphysical concern until Munro's later work. Essentially, the voyage of the self is not that of outward bound man or woman in a universe out of human control, but that of the female psyche confronting herself and society. The teetering stance between order and chaos, convention and nature is largely of a psychological-social character, with the ever-promising possibility of change in the social domain. Also, because the psychological questioning is rooted in gender, in sexuality, in the developing female throughout Munro's six works, its idiom is process. The female body behind the texts offers the possibility of reproduction and completion, rather than nihilism, even in the face of existential *angst*. In her fourth book, for example, Munro's irony approaches a broad existential absurdity. The ironic contrast between Flo in youth and senility is due to the villainy of Time, and the importance of human affairs is ironically reduced to the absurdity of old people as primitive babies. But there is also "faith." The female body behind the Munro text is a naturalistic phenomenon, offering the assurance of cyclic life and regeneration.

The incongruity between discordant realities which is the basis of irony is most often depicted in Munro's fiction, then, as the female conception or expectation of self and sexuality in collision with a male perspective, authority or control—a collision which is threatening and often unsatisfactorily resolved for the woman, but which is never fatal. At points, however, Munro edges close to the ironic void where the self can be lost, in her sketches of the dance of the sexes. When replaying the classical Psyche in search of Eros, her heroines come closest to losing their souls and tumbling into the abyss. Witness Del Jordan with Mr. Chamberlain. Del is Psyche in process, uncertain what to expect of male love, but assuming decadence in this illicit affair, even evil with the greater promise of black romantic beauty. "The layer of reality" which Del gets into (140) is quite the opposite. Mr. Chamberlain's singular, grotesque "Indian" dance is both ugly and prosaic. This ironic situation threatens to injure her sense of self when the postcoital landscape looms large in the absurdist's empty vision.

Helen of "Postcard" is a similar ironic victim of the dance. In her mind, she has lived up to Clare's expectations of her, has been the "good girl," but she has obviously misinterpreted his reality and what she assumed was

his intention to marry her. At the end of the story, she is left in the ironist's questioning vacuum, wondering why.

In Munro's fiction, and these situations, however, irony is ultimately
comic, liberating, and self-affirming for women. Munro extends the folk
tradition of frontier women who objected to their domain as only that
which could be seen from a kitchen window by "using humour to attack the
stereotypes of their ascribed role and status" by, for example, stitching
"onto samplers sardonic reference to their images as may sometimes be
found in museums."[27] The secret, ironic voice of female folk life is intensified, publicized in Munro's fiction. The humor of self-mockery we know as
that of the Negro or Jew in folk America deflecting his enemies through
laughter is played out by the equally oppressed female on Munro's fictional
stage.

Munro assigns to her early female voice and several of her heroines the
humor of ironic self-deprecation, a humor which affirms the self, even as it
seemingly denigrates it. Not an irony of defeat, but one of challenge, protest and self-sustenance. The child in "Boys and Girls" rather sadly learns
that she is "A girl. . . . A joke on me" (*Dance*, 119), but this baptism into
the joke of being female can be constructively used to shore up the female
self. Helen of "Postcard" actually escapes the void, is able to maintain her
self-worth by taking the joke on her, but passing it on to Clare, too, when
she also steps outside the traditional courtship pattern with her ironic chivaree. Del Jordan is rescued from Mr. Chamberlain by absorbing the joke
at her own expense; the gloomy landscape is dispelled when she realizes the
ironic incongruity between her expectation and the mean reality of Mr.
Chamberlain, particularly when he ludicrously gets her to crouch down on
the floor of the car as they re-enter town, yet "He felt enough like himself,
however, to tap me in the crotch with his fist, as if testing a coconut for
soundness" (142). Similarly, the courageous and flashy old maid, Iris,
from "Connection" in *The Moons of Jupiter* is a delight to her female lis-
tener when she takes the joke of being unmarried on herself. Dismissed by
the husband, Richard, as a "pathetic old tart" (17), she contradicts this indictment through ironic recognition of her social status: "I'm with a tour,
dear, did I tell you? Nine old maids and seven widows and three widowers.
Not one married couple. But, as I say, you never know, the trip's not over
yet" (15).

Irony is part of the complex structures of Munro's fiction, worked in different ways to underline the shifting realities of the human and artistic ex-

perience, but it is also communicated as the special medium of women. While men have jealously guarded the comic muse as their own, preferring in Stephen Leacock's words the genteel angel in the kitchen to the disruptive witty woman with the spectacles,[28] Munro indicates that women have managed to avoid self-negation and achieve a measure of self-respect through their largely private humor of ironic detachment. It is an effective alternative to the land of self-pity Roberta feels in "Labor Day Dinner," "rising and sloshing around in her like bitter bile" after her lover comments on her aging body, her flabby arms. Irony, a palliative, begins to surface when she thinks to herself, "She must get away, live alone, wear sleeves" (*Moons*, 137).

In the battle of the sexes, irony and humor is also the medium for the establishment of female equality and for overt protest. The comic catastrophe of "An Ounce of Cure," with its conforming, nonconforming heroine, previews Del Jordan in a similar scenario at the Gay-la Dance Hall finally refusing to accommodate the irony of who she is and what Clive expects her to be, and getting drunk and independent in the process. Her responsibility is to herself in this instance, notably triggered by male humor at passive female expense.

> I laughed hard, unhappily. Responsibility was coming back. That started Bert and Clive telling jokes. Every joke would start off seriously, and would continue so for quite a time, like a reflective or instructive anecdote, so that you had to be always on guard, not to be left stupidly gaping when the time came to laugh. . . . In many of these jokes as in the first one it was necessary for Naomi or me to supply the straight lines, and the way to do this, so as not to feel foolish as I had that time was to answer in a reluctant, exasperated, but still faintly tolerant way, to follow the joke with narrowed eyes and a slight smile as if you knew what was coming. (*Lives*, 158)

A further measure of her equality will be that of ironic exchange, the Pogoesque language she and Jerry Storey play with together.

In the story "Material" from *Something I've Been Meaning To Tell You*, like Del with Jerry, the narrator has been "strong on irony" (26) in dialogue with her first husband, Hugo. They have been equals until he proves himself a successful artist by using female "material" as the subject of his art without conscience or emotional attachment.

When the writer-husband transfers their mutual acquaintance, Dotty, into an artful fiction, the narrator speciously apologizes for her "ironical objections" to the fiction of Dotty. But she is the apologist only after she launches into a sardonically ironic attack against Hugo's own male "artistic" self-legend, his machismo image of himself as lumberjack, beerslinger, telephone lineman, sawmill foreman:

> Look at you, Hugo, your image is not only fake but out-of-date. You should have said you'd meditated for a year in the mountains of Uttar Pradesh; you should have said you'd taught Creative Drama to autistic children; you should have shaved your head, shaved your beard, put on a monk's cowl; you should have shut up, Hugo. (25)

In Munro's later work, as she turns her attention to more complicated narrative structures, she develops complex ironic and feminist patterns that are woven into the fiction, are below the surface, secretive and challenging in the manner of women's folk life and folk art. Irony as extended narrative pattern is brilliantly executed, for example, in such a story as "Mrs. Cross and Mrs. Kidd" from *The Moons of Jupiter*.

In this fiction, feminist irony, melancholy, and complaint about the way things happen to women continue from earlier work. In this most painstakingly patterned story, Munro conveys the awful impotency of the sick and the old, but at the same time she injects a wry feminist design. These two old ladies, who have known one another for three-quarters of a century but who have not been friends, are ironically forced into artificial intimacy in a nursing home. While Mrs. Kidd valiantly struggled against being the conventional, decorative wife, and still resists being "the average, expected old lady" (163), she, like the conventional, maternal and aptly-named "Dolly" Cross, succumbs to the need to nurture, to care *for*; the pathetic human irony is that both old ladies re-experience their children's initial abandonment when their childlike prodigies in the home, Charlotte and Jack, discover one another, leaving the old women to themselves.

In a brilliant final image of Mrs. Kidd propped up against a wall with her legs straight in front of her, Munro visually remarks that the final stage of life for Mrs. Cross and Mrs. Kidd is that of being useless, collapsed and shelved old dolls. With feminist irony and wit, the author leaves us to understand that all women here retain their original, long-standing definitions; they are versions of the dolls their mothers had, "with long, limp bodies and pink-and-white faces and crimped china hair and ladylike smiles" (178).

Similarly, in the story "Eskimo" from *The Progress of Love,* irony is the underlying structural mode. The heroine Mary Jo is involved in a conventional, unconventional sexual relationship with the heart specialist, Dr. Streeter. She is his longtime lover and receptionist and on the surface is contented with a life ordered by his desire. When he sends her off on a vacation alone to Tahiti, as a reward for her devotion in love, the silenced woman, the "bland and unforthcoming" (91) Mary Jo begins to divine, on her plane trip, the underlying realities of her situation. Mary Jo's story is a desperate joke on her, thick with ironic undercurrents.

The tension between the primitive world of nature and chaos, and conventional order is particularly intense in this volume and in this story. Mary Jo assumes her relationship to be civilized, ordered, fair, but when she sees the "primitive" Eskimo girl and her lover on the plane, she knows them as an extension of herself and Dr. Streeter. The male has the absolute authority; he is "the Khan," "the ruler of the tribe" (197), a man of several wives or concubines in the age-old masculine tradition. He controls the "heart." Mary Jo, standing on the edge of the ironic abyss, is in danger of losing her mind, like the Eskimo doll she dreams of whose head comes loose from her body, but she resurfaces to an ironic resolution. The final line of the story, "This is the beginning of her holiday" (207) is equal to the private, ironic messages that folk women sewed into their samplers. The real advantage for women in the sexual game of polygamy is that they ultimately get a rest from the effort of true devotion in love when another woman takes over.

If Munro illustrates that irony comes naturally to thinking women when they are down and out, she also demonstrates the comedy of down and out poorer folk, both men and women, of lesser resources. A significant portion of her humor is attached to the rural folk mind and milieu, to the extremes of an unsubtle and primitive point of view, to exaggeration and the grotesque. A clue to her attitude towards the latter can be seen in a manuscript *Home—October/1973—Notes for a Work* as the authorial persona speculates on a character she calls Irlma, a stepmother she is designing:

She becomes so easily a comic character. I am afraid this is vengeful reporting, in spite of its accuracy. I do not make it clear anywhere that she talks the way she does in the "hot stuff" scene at least partly out of

anxiety, that she always covers up her fright with her voice, with brag-
ging and joking. . . . More kindness is due this character than she is getting. But if I should try to give it, it would not ring true.

And, in a further comment:

> Here is a woman who has seen bad times, work and poverty, many
> deaths, whose recital of the details of death by dropsy and drowning,
> freezing and bloody accidents, is comic and grotesque, but a means of
> protection, not unlike the means I am trying for now.[29]

The comedy of Munro's folk types of limited intellectual and economic
means is that which she delineates above—the grotesque, the primitive,
the bloody. Seemingly exaggerated from a middle-class point of view, it is
the reality of these lives lived on the Flats Road or West Hanratty—outside
of town. The Mother in "Forgiveness in Families" in *Something I've Been
Meaning to Tell You* says her son's life is "so terrible it's funny" (77), and
it is precisely this kind of realization by Munro that contributes to the vein
of primitive comedy in her fiction. The joke which the violent Madeleine
becomes to Del Jordan's mother and father is the natural humor of the Flats
Road given over to the reader. The reality of the lives of these people as
comic grotesquerie—that of the paranoic Joe Phippen or Becky Tyde—is
mainly viewed from superior distance, but not unsympathetically by
Munro. Their preoccupation with the gothic, for example, Uncle Benny
reading his tabloids *(Father Feeds Twin Daughters to Hogs/Woman Gives
Birth to Human Monkey)*, Flo's penchant for stories of severed breasts and
other horrors, is not parody because of Del's and Rose's basic allegiance to
these primitive story-seekers. In fact, during Patrick's visit, when the dis-
comfited superior Rose sees Flo and her family "as the most hackneyed
rural comedy" we believe her to be in well-deserved humiliation for her
pretensions, as the conversation takes its unexpected, hilarious gothic turn:

> She had doubts about what was coming, and rightly so, for then Patrick
> got to hear about a man who cut his own throat, his own throat, from
> ear to ear, a man who shot himself the first time and didn't do enough
> damage, so he loaded up and fired again and managed it, another man
> who hanged himself using a chain, the kind of chain you hook on a trac-
> tor with, so it was a wonder his head was not torn off. *Tore off*, Flo said.
> (*Who*, 89–90)

Who Do You Think You Are? is easily the most comic, in a sustained way, of Munro's fiction to date. In many ways it is a comedy of errors—a farce, lewdly so in the rural realities of Mr. Burns' backside on secret view in the outhouse, in the "performing" of Shortie and Franny McGill; existentially so in the numerous missed or unexpected connections of Rose, perpetually in transit, with the other characters. Patrick, too, is part of the farce, "edgy, jumpy. . . . always under stress—he knocked dishes and cups off tables, spilled drinks and bowls of peanuts, like a comedian" (67), while Hat Nettleton with his bowler hat "for the comic effect" is an extra, a Chaplinesque figure (8).

The real comic core of the novel, though, resides in Flo, a folk character and female clown of extraordinary persuasion. Flo is not comic in a genial sense. She has all the dimensions of West Hanratty. Like the toilet shacks which Rose knows "were supposed to be comical—always were, in country humor—but she saw them instead as scenes of marvellous shame and outrage" (24), Flo is herself part of the outrageous scenery. Rage is her center and Rose often its physical and verbal victim. But as a tartar, lambasting all and sundry, a double-jointed vaudevillian who can lie stiff as a board between two chairs in moments of celebration, a "burlesque" (48) player who gleefully displays Flo's father's stained underwear and, later, as the "comic character" of daunting ludicrousness (191) arriving at Rose's award reception in gaudy costume, she meets with our instincts for farce and our comic approval. If, as she promised herself with the character of Irlma, Munro had meant to convey Flo's comedy as her means of protection, as irony is for the author's more genteel heroines, she succeeds in one of Flo's final scenes. When Rose comes to the Home and brings Flo's old wig to her and together they enact a bizarre comedy of female fashion, Flo becomes for a moment lucidly herself—a survivor—and in that instance part of that larger theatrical company of joking women, including Munro herself, her protagonists and her readers.

In an essay published in 1925 entitled "Women and Fiction," Virginia Woolf considered that,

> It is probable. . . that both in life and in art the values of a woman are not the values of a man. Thus, when a woman comes to write a novel, she will find that she is perpetually wishing to alter the established values. . . . And for that, of course, she will be criticized; for the critic of the opposite sex will be genuinely puzzled and surprised by any attempt to alter the current scale of values, and will see in it not merely a dif-

ference of view, but a view that is weak, or trivial, or sentimental, because it differs from his own.[30]

The current scale of literary values has been substantially and artfully
altered by the fiction of Alice Munro. Her explorations of the "folk" realities of women, their feminine dispositions and their humor, are extraordinary in design, aesthetic effect and simultaneous feminist protest.

| 4 | REGIONALIST

Wawanash County: A Landscape of Mind, A Mythic Place

Nature poetry is seldom just about Nature; it is usually about the poet's attitude towards the external natural universe. That is, landscapes in poems are often interior landscapes; they are maps of a state of mind. . . . The same tendencies can be present in the descriptive passages of novels or stories with natural settings.

MARGARET ATWOOD,
Survival

"Art must be universal," many critics say. It must circumvent such boundaries as sexuality or region and speak to the reader in the exceptional grammar of art, in the language of absolute truths. On the other hand, contemporary writers like Margaret Atwood suggest that there is no truly universal literature, partly because there are no truly universal readers.[1] In the wake of modernism, feminism, and postmodernism, literary theorists and critics, too, are insisting that the so-called "universals" of aesthetic valuing are culturally determined, and dependent on a cultural ideology that is particular to a historical time and place. Linda Hutcheon challenges the concept of universality in art, links it to a patriarchal homogenizing system and concludes, "I no longer read books the way I once did: that eternal Universal truth I was taught to find has turned out to be constructed, not found—and anything but eternal and universal. Truth has been replaced by truths, uncapitalized and in the plural."[2] Arguing as well that Canadian novelists have refigured the *realist regional* into the *postmodern different*, she sees many contemporary regional writers rendering the particular concrete, glorying in "(defining) local ex-centricity" and "translating the existing Canadian emphasis on regionalism in literature . . . into a concern for the different, the local, the particular—in opposition to the uniform, the universal, the centralized."[3]

This is not to say, however, that the best "regional" writers in Canada today whether writing, to use Hutcheon's terminology, realist regional or postmodern different fiction, do not communicate the particular *as* universal or that they and their readers cannot be imaginatively transported into a powerfully engaging and seemingly all encompassing fictive space. The creation of *place*, in fact, is a vehicle for sympathetic bonding between the reader and the writer's fictional world, offering, at the very least, the illusion of shared, hence universal, experience; this is especially true of the fiction of Alice Munro who has a remarkable ability to poeticize a specific place, to sing its praises and hypnotic mysteries, as well as to invoke place as a maternal mythscape. Most importantly, Munro is able to authenticate a fictional female world by expanding her characters' inner lives into place, and by manipulating place as feminist inquiry.

Alice Munro would agree with Eudora Welty, a writer she acknowledges "has been a very big influence"[4] and who stresses the poetic value of the local in fiction:

> It is by the nature of itself that fiction is all bound up in the local. The internal reason for that is surely that *feelings* are bound up in place. The human mind is a mass of associations—associations more poetic even than actual. I say, "The Yorkshire Moors," and you will say, "*Wuthering Heights*" . . . The truth is, fiction depends for its life on place. Location is the crossroads of circumstance, the proving ground of "What happened? Who's here? Who's coming?"—and that is the heart's field.[5]

Munro's "heart's field," southwestern Ontario, around Wingham where she grew up, is mythologized as Huron or Wawanash County and threaded through a great deal of her fiction. For her two major heroines, Del and Rose, and for many of her narrators, as children and adolescents in Ontario, or middle-aged women returning there, the bush landscape and the town hall are the touchstones and genesis of their identities. Their evolution begins in the Orenoch swamp, the Wawanash River, the dusty roads and red brick houses, and Munro and her characters are drawn back, almost compulsively, to review the country of their origins.

In part this is the mystery of place, celebrated, says Eudora Welty, by all the arts: "Where does this mystery lie? Is it in the fact that place has a more lasting identity than we have, and we unswervingly tend to attach ourselves to identity?"[6] We know that for Munro's heroines place *is* very much identity and despite the houses and social conventions which trapped these female characters in the past, they are nostalgic and loyal to their small towns, Jubilee and Hanratty and Dalgleish, because such places are woven into selfness. Theirs is a country of the mind which holds the psyche together in the desperate relativism and unpredictability of modern city life which begins to unfold in Munro's fiction. It is a prevention, so that, as with the narrator of "Tell Me Yes or No," "My life did not altogether fall away in separate pieces, lost" (*Something*, 92). In the canon of her work to date, Munro narrates, with a kind of Whitmanesque over-ego, this psychological truth and the poetry of feeling of her own and her characters' Ontario place.

As a regional writer, Munro moves us through the particulars of locale to inhabit neutral, catholic, and what appears to be androgynous fictional ground. Certainly it is a ground, particularly in her early work, that has been universally lauded for its poetic surface. The depth of feeling in Munro's place, however, belies a mythic reality beyond the surface, one which has gender implications. Psychiatry has argued the importance of the mother as a primary landscape, and the strong possibility that "'the life of the body and the experiences of infancy,... are the reference points of human knowledge and the bedrock of the structures of culture.'"[7] For Munro's heroines in the sexual dance, the struggle to return to place and the poetic evocation of regional ground are highly suggestive of the mythic return to the maternal body, a return which may be for all her readers an archetypal journal, but most importantly, one which is for her female characters the source of female identity.

By her sixth work, *The Progress of Love*, there is even a veiled, partly apprehended understanding of the impulse, as the return becomes more and more difficult to accomplish, as maternal source collapses with the physical aging of the authorial persona and her heroines. Isabel of "White Dump," a partner still in the sexual dance of "most impulsive, ingenious, vigorous couplings" (304), guards her intuition of and longing for mythic maternal source carefully:

Sometimes she thought of her childhood with a longing that seemed almost as perverse, and had to be kept almost as secret. A sagging awning

in front of a corner store might remind her, the smell of heavy dinners
cooking at noon, the litter and bare earth around the roots of a big urban
shade tree. (304)

Nonetheless, the female figure is invested in such an image as "a sagging
awning" and feminine sustenance invoked in "dinners cooking" and the
"bare earth," triggering a longing for the psychic journey back to the place
of one's origin—journeys which are for Munro and her heroines mythic
researches for first felt maternal landscapes and female selfness.

For the female author, as well, who lives the life of the body as the
source and vehicle of reproduction and whose female self is objectified and
splintered by patriarchal fiat, ego is transformational with an ambiguous
sense of boundary, encouraging the investment of self in exterior place.
Landscape and region are easily colored by the psyche. Del Jordan "admits
her shifting sense of self" when she "compares herself to the rigid, pur-
poseful Jerry Storey: 'I whose natural boundaries were so much more ambiguous, who soaked up protective coloration whenever it might be found,
began to see that it might be restful, to be like Jerry'" (Lives, 200). As
Lorna Irvine argues "this sense of ambiguous boundary permeates
Munro's fiction not only because she so often describes women, but also
because she is a woman writer."[8] Self overlaps easily into space and place
for the heroine and her female author; the emotive self can be naturally
projected into place to become interior psychological landscape, to become,
to use the telling, previously quoted phrases of Margaret Atwood and
Eudora Welty, "maps of a state of mind" and the "heart's field."

Beneath the surface, in Munro's fiction, place is a cloaked, subterranean,
mythical and psychological female region. On another level, place is hard
reality, the "proving ground" of dramatic action, of female experience and
feminist event. The critic Bronwen Wallace quotes the following passage
from Munro, "We drove through the country we did not know we loved—
not rolling or flat, but broken, no recognizable rhythm to it; low hills, hol-
lows full of brush, swamp and bush and fields," and excitedly claims, "For
me, the power of Munro's work emerges first from its centre in the flat,
solid, reality of things. Behind everything else she writes, the particular
physical landscape is simply there. It is of course often involved with human emotions... [9] On this plane, Munro "is" and "of" her Ontario region, although always its female author. The "flat, solid reality of things,"
the authenticity of provincial town, country and house, slowly eroding un-

der the weight of modern change, has contributed to what is often called the "documentary realism" of her art. At this level, Munro's fiction is re-markably lifelike—in the "realistic" mode; her point of view is controlled, convincing her reader of being *there* in a palpable and objective, external world.

There is very often introduced, in the traditional way of storytelling, in the early paragraphs of story or chapter. We are placed in the first story of the first volume *Dance* by "Then my father and I walk gradually down a long, shabby sort of street, with Silverwoods Ice Cream signs standing on the sidewalk, outside tiny, lighted stores. This is in Tuppertown, an old town on Lake Huron, an old grain port" (1). In *Lives*, Del's experiences are carefully located on the Flats Road, Jenkin's Bend, Jubilee, the Jericho Valley, and the geography of landscape and the pattern of town are fully detailed; in *Who Do You Think You Are?* Hanratty, Ontario, is the signal of a credible world, beckoning us into it, like the signpost in "Thanks for the Ride": "Mission Creek. Population 1700. Gateway to the Bruce" (*Dance*, 44).

As Munro carefully establishes setting, situates house on precise street corner, unravels the design of town streets, or charts the spatial relationships between hummocks, plains, woods and river in her province, she reconstructs the world through the language of the local and the particular and like a surveyor or map maker lays claim to the perceptible spaces of "real life." Underlining the illusion of such objective register is the recurring image of the map itself and the activity of map making. As her characters move out into new frontiers of provincial towns and cities, they map the territory. Uncle Benny in *Lives*, an explorer in urban Toronto, returns to Jubilee with a map of his journey burnt into his mind; the narrator of "Tell Me Yes Or No" searches out her dead lover's place, declaring, "I have bought a map. I have found your street, the block where your house is" (*Something*, 95).

Felt as an authorial motivation in her work, the aspiration to map making is the reverse side of the coin for the female artist with her chameleon-like permeable boundaries. Mapping the details becomes the female artist's struggle to avoid the obscurity of transformations, to pin down her fiction, and realize the psychological truth of her characters' experiences, so that her art may not slip away becoming so amorphous as to be as "untouchable" as the magic books are to the author-narrator of "Tell Me Yes or No": "They are all flowing together around the [book] store like some varicolored marvelous stream, or wide river, and I can really no more understand what is inside them than I can breathe under water" (*Something*, 97).

As an authorial incentive, the figurative making of map and fording of stream can also be interpreted as part of Munro's regional identity as a writer. Hers is the aspiration of the pioneer cartographer, a sensibility derived from the Upper Canadian pioneer fact of exploration and settlement and the tradition of historical record keeping which, from Susanna Moodie's classic pioneer autobiography to Munro's own father's posthumously published fictionalized accounts of Highland settlements in the Bruce and North Huron counties, *The McGregors*, has been a strong feature of Ontario life. While other first regions of Canada may claim the same, the recording of provincial history is an activity of Munro's region as perceived and extended by her. As she presents small town Ontario beginning to be invaded by tourists and factories, she becomes the natural descendent of Del's Uncle Craig in *Lives*, instructing the reader what came after his recollection and description of the corduroy, and later, gravel roads in Fairmile Township. More than its resident geographer, cartographer and historian, she is, of course, the feminist legend-maker of the dramatic moments in the lives of the locale's inhabitants, placing markers, as it were, "Up the road, not a quarter of a mile" (*Lives*, 25), to memorialize the spot where human drama occurs and which conventional objective, factual and masculine histories, like that of Uncle Craig's, happily destroyed by Del Jordan, ignore.

Moreover, as Munro moves her outward bound female protagonists out of their province and into British Columbia, she remains of Ontario pioneer heart and the author of historical fact. The westward pull of the new frontier has historically seduced many Ontarians, as it did Munro's mother who became a teacher in Alberta before she married, and Munro herself who admits she went West to British Columbia with her first husband for "adventure."[10]

The British Columbia locale explored periodically, particularly in her third and fourth volumes, is a lived one then, but it never achieves in a sustained way the resonance or poetry of her primary landscape of southwestern Ontario town and country. Its reality is a lesser one in Munro's imagination and her uncertainty, her difficulty in grasping it, is reflected in the anxious mental state of Rose in *Who Do You Think You Are?* After she moves back to Ontario from British Columbia, and just as she had spent a lot of time remembering the parts of Ontario when she lived in Capilano Heights, "being faithful, in a way, to that earlier landscape," she tries to remember Vancouver. Rose's subsequent memory seems true, but the details she conjures are less poetry than list (132).

| | | —

In her first volume, *Dance*, as Munro first names her fictional country, she pays the most attention to the provincial scenery outside of kitchen windows and the interiors of houses. Because the authorial sensorium is that of childhood and adolescent discovery, *Dance* is the freshest of Munro's works in uncovering the poetic associations and feelings attached to place. As David Helwig states in his review of *Dance*, "the whole feeling of this part of Ontario is in Miss Munro's book of stories."[11] A felt sense of Ontario in *Dance* depends in part on Munro's amazing ability to capture its surface life, and in her own words, it is texture that she strives for: ". . . I am certainly a regional writer in that whatever I do I seem only able to make things work. . . if I use this. . . this plot of land that is mine. . . . And texture is the thing that I've got to have."[12]

Besides achieving texture, Munro has extraordinary visual control. Several critics have observed that hers is a visually real art, like that of a photographer's or painter's.[13] What she often offers in *Dance*, presented from an objective distance, is a framed landscape or a small townscape, carefully spaced, emotively colored (sometimes by the absence of color), and sensually textured. The felt image of small town Ontario in poetic decay, is caught, for example, in the main street description in "Thanks for the Ride":

It was a town of unpaved, wide, sandy streets and bare yards. Only the hardy things like red and yellow nasturtiums, or a lilac bush with brown curled leaves, grew out of that cracked earth. The houses were set wide apart, with their own pumps and sheds and privies out behind; most of them were built of wood and painted green or grey or yellow. The trees that grew there were big willows or poplars, their fine leaves greyed with the dust. There were no trees along the main street, but spaces of tall grass and dandelions and blowing thistles—open country between the store buildings. The town hall was surprisingly large, with a great bell in a tower, the red brick rather glaring in the midst of the town's walls of faded, pale-painted wood. The sign beside the door said that it was a memorial to the soldiers who had died in the First World War. We had a drink out of the fountain in front. (*Dance*, 46–47)

The art of Munro's description of the plot of land which is hers rests on accurate detailing of native trees, flowers, buildings (details often emotionally charged, like the memorial to the dead soldiers which calls up the Remembrance Day Service and vigil of Ontario town life), but most importantly, on a careful visual composition or patterning, which very often suggests the eye of the painter or the motion of a moving camera. Jubilee in "The Peace of Utrecht," for example, is a series of three images which are validated through the illusion of the upward movements of a roving camera. Jubilee is simply, but unforgettably, "the earth bare around the massive roots of the trees, the drinking fountain surrounded by little puddles of water on the main street, the soft scrawls of blue and red and orange light that said *Billiards* and *Cafe*" (191).

Depth perception, suggesting a retreating camera or a painter's visual magic, is also part of Munro's talent in presenting a place which her reader feels to be real. In "A Trip to the Coast," countryside is viewed to the artist's vanishing point. The eye is led to the retreating pointed trees at the end of the road:

The houses and the store are built of red brick of a faded, gingery colour, with a random decoration of grey or white bricks across the chimneys and around the windows. Behind them the fields are full of milkweed and goldenrod and big purple thistles. People who are passing through, on their way to the Lakes of Muskoka and the northern bush, may notice that around here the bountiful landscape thins and flattens, worn elbows of rock appear in the diminishing fields and the deep, harmonious woodlots of elm and maple give way to a denser, less hospitable scrub-forest of birch and poplar, spruce and pine—where in the heat of the afternoon the pointed trees at the end of the road turn blue, transparent, retreating into the distance like a company of ghosts. (*Dance*, 172)

In "The Time of Death" Munro's final paragraph gives the effect of stepping away from the house, a technique reminiscent of a moving camera fade-out, used not without irony in this tragic story of a poor girl whose hope is to be a movie star:

There was this house, and the other wooden houses that had never been painted, with their steep patched roofs and their narrow, slanting porches, the wood-smoke coming out of their chimneys and dim children's faces pressed against their windows. Behind them there was the strip of earth, plowed in some places, run to grass in others, full of stones, and behind this the pine trees, not very tall. In front were the yards, the dead gardens, the grey highway running out from town. The snow came, falling slowly, evenly, between the highway and the houses and the pine trees, falling in big flakes at first and then in smaller and smaller flakes that did not melt on the hard furrows, the rock of the earth. (*Dance*, 99)

In *Dance* Munro conjures up the details of the Ontario landscape she remembers (from the thirties and forties) and presents them to the eye: the high brick houses with wooden verandahs, the peeling cupola of the town hall, the patches of woodlots still standing, the stubble fields, the trap-lines along the river, the tall, unpainted farm houses. Preserving them in their best design, as a visual artist does, she lures us into believing that her provincial fiction is reality and we are delighted by its integrity.

While the critic may be tempted to describe Munro's control of place as documentary or photographic realism, it does not adequately explain the power and mystery of many of her physical settings, or the overall impression of her locality. A metaphor which illustrates its complexity is Eudora Welty's well-known one of the china nightlight. Often applied to Welty's work, it is equally true of Munro's:

Some of us grew up with the china night-light, the little lamp whose lighting showed its secret and with that spread enchantment. The outside is painted with a scene, which is one thing; then, when the lamp is lighted, through the porcelain sides a new picture comes out through the old, and they are seen as one. A lamp I knew of was a view of London till it was lit; but then it was the Great Fire of London, and you could go beautifully to sleep by it. The lamp alight is the combination of internal and external, glowing at the imagination as one; and so is the good novel.[14]

Like Welty's lamp, Munro's scenery is very often of both internal and external surfaces, and if one looks closely at her "camera" art, it is clear that the "new picture coming through the old" is that of the psychological life of the female protagonist and that the illumination occurs as the landscape animately refracts the character's innermost feelings, mood, or evolving consciousness. In "Thanks for the Ride," the hardy things growing out of the cracked earth as lone survivors is a landscape image of the heroine's gritty will not to be reduced by male use of her. In the three sweeping images of Jubilee in "The Peace of Utrecht," is the faint, felt suggestion of a body being dressed; the act of dressing and undressing is not only the governing event of the story but the ultimate *idée fixe* in the narrator's interior life which places her forever beyond any "ordinary and peaceful reality" (91). Similarly the crazy angles of porches and the falling snow in the final paragraph to "The Time of Death" are landscape extensions of Patricia and Leona Parry's bizarre, obsessive ambition and the falling snowflakes a reflection of innocence turned mean, of the hard, driving fury within the child's mind.

Inner landscape enchantment in a more lyrical form than the naturalistic and grim story of Patricia Parry is also found in *Dance* when the fiction is interpreted directly through the female child's imaginative eye. However mean and imprisoning the external world of skinned foxes, butchered horses and male order is for the girl in "Boys and Girls," the mood is that of a child's amazing discovery of the sensual, natural world about her through her awakened I. Sensitive to the rhythms of seasonal time and filled with a sense of adventure, the child-author interprets the *outside* landscape with the lyric wonder of a female eye. The land is viewed as promising fertility, a maternal promise, in the striking sexual image of childbirth: of opening-out and release: "when spring came. . . . Snow drifts dwindled quickly, revealing the hard grey and brown earth, the familiar rise and fall of the ground, plain and bare after the fantastic landscape of winter. There was a great feeling of opening-out, of release" (120).

"Boys and Girls" pales, however, beside one of the most dramatic and extraordinary combinations of inner and outer surfaces in Munro's fiction, that of "Walker Brothers Cowboy" where the wonderful mental landscape of the child is superimposed, like a transparency, on the literal one. Here is a seemingly naturalistic world—dusty, real, colorless and depressed, but it is simultaneously crayoned in silver and patches of color through the child's imagination. When the epiphany comes in the narrative, the magic of the china light is clicked on in a visionary moment as the woman as child realizes that the territory she has travelled, like her father before her, is as much an enchanted, interior one as it is prosaic country roads—objective and fixed:

> So my father drives and my brother watches the road for rabbits and I feel my father's life flowing back from our car in the last of the afternoon, darkening and turning strange, like a landscape that has an enchantment on it, making it kindly, ordinary and familiar while you are looking at it, but changing it, once your back is turned, into something you will never know, with all kinds of weathers, and distances you cannot imagine. (*Dance*, 18)

In this story, Munro carries the magic spell to a dramatic climax when she gracefully informs her reader in the final paragraph that reality exists at another level beyond physical nature and that landscape is an apt metaphor of the mind's subjective odyssey.

In "Walker Brothers Cowboy," as in other stories in Dance, landscape and psychology are naturally linked for the Munro heroine and for the female artist who knows, like Del Jordan, her "ambiguous natural boundaries." "Walker Brothers Cowboy" is, in effect, a classic expression of the transformational sensibility of the female-as-artist. Lorna Irvine comments on the fluid narrative, on the technique of "memory flowing" in this seminal story, as a narrative structure special to the woman artist.

> The important words here—flowing, darkening, turning strange, enchantment, changing—all suggest secrecy and transformation. In context (similar words appear in almost every story), they reveal with varying emphases certain facts about women's lives: the sense many women have of being suppressed, of living underground; the discrepancy between what one appears to be and what one feels oneself to be; the vagueness experienced by many women about their ego boundaries; the tendency to merge with others.[15]

Many of the techniques Munro uses to achieve "another" interior reality for her female characters are indirect, difficult to penetrate. In an attempt to get at the enigmatic double realities in her art, several critics, including Catherine Sheldrick Ross,[16] have compared her to the magic realist school of painting, to artists like Edward Hopper, Jack Chambers, Alex Colville and Ken Danby. The subjects of magic realist painters are ordinary objects which are painted in a mysterious photographic reality that is described by John Metcalf in his conversation with Alice Munro as "the magic of the ordinary."[17] Geoff Hancock has briefly commented on its literary variety, pointing out that a writer like Robert Kroetsch, sending a group of runaway horses through Woodward's Department store, is actually using a common technique of the painters by juxtaposing real forms in unlikely places (like Arthur Horsfall's giant eggshell floating on Lake Louise). "The combination of the two forms," suggests Hancock, "creates a third meaning, often difficult to explain."[18] In Canadian fiction, he determines, documentary realism is magically reshaping itself as fiction writers instill humour and hyperbole into the landscape.[19]

Munro, while not nearly as extravagant and as bold as Kroetsch (or Jack Hodgins in *The Invention of the World*), is certainly on the skirts of a movement in Canadian literature. Part of the magic of Munro's fictional world depends, too, on the comic thrust of landscape in the literature and art of the new magic realists. The humor Munro instills in place in *Dance* is not hyperbolic or absurdist, however, but of a secretive, ironic, accommodating feminine kind. In essence, by using disarming rather than shocking humor, Munro places faith in Eudora Welty's conviction that "humor, it seems to me, of all forms of fiction, entirely accepts place for what it is."[20] If we readily enter the world of *Dance*, it is partly because we succumb to the good humor as invitation. This is easily demonstrated by the first three stories in *Dance*. The first line of "Walker Brothers Cowboy" is a joking reference to the reality of place itself, and a sly authorial trick: "After supper my father says, 'Want to go down and see if the Lake's still there?'" (1). In the next story, "The Shining Houses," the location of a British Columbian suburb is introduced in full ironic contrast between the raw roads and open ditches of the new subdivision and its pastoral street names— Heather Drive and Garden Place. And in the third story, "Thanks for the Ride," the signpost of Mission Creek (Population 1700. Gateway to the Bruce) which establishes setting, is punctuated with the final comic line, "We love our children" (44).

In these three stories, humor accommodates place, promoting the reader's acceptance of setting but, at the same time, it becomes a magic realist technique. The reader is simultaneously informed that ordinary reality is not to be completely trusted and that the path is open to the interior lives of

Munro's women and the levels of reality (or fiction) she explores through them.

For the author of female psychology, the magic realist approach, with its multiple meanings and levels of reality, serves well the facts of womens' lives, the secrecy and transformation of their behavior and experience. Munro comes closest to magic realist painting in this first volume, and most successfully so, in one of her most visually arresting stories, "Images." In this story, the events are realistic and the landscape is suprareal as a primal extension of the psychology of the female child who is fearful of the death of her mother. The electric source of Munro's china nightlight and the magic realist impression is that of interior space and landscape as psychic agent and receptor.

In "Images" the ordinary circumstance, that of a relative coming to nurse a sick mother, is overlaid with the magic sensibility and vision of the child. From the child's perspective, the landscape outdoors and the interior of the house are bathed in a dazzling world of light and white brilliance. It is a vision flooded with sharp light, suggesting both the technique and deeper meanings in the paintings of Ken Danby and Alex Colville. There is whiteness everywhere and the power of the nursing relative, the totemic female, Mary McQuade, like Garcia Marquez's character Pilar Temera in *One Hundred Years of Solitude* with her trailing smoke, is let loose in the house, tasted even by the child in her food.

Beyond this double vision, there is yet another, a subliminal image under image of a vast expanse of water which conveys a prehistoric sense of flood and the possibility of either genesis or fearful sinking death. This impression comes into focus as the flat fields in the sun turn to water, the sun's rays to lightning; the room is felt to be a vast space of "sweating heat" with the possibility of "magic ice" (31). Mary McQuade is interpreted as an "iceberg"; out beyond the house the child discovers that the "snow is a thin crust like frosted glass" (35); later, the river curves and the narrator loses her sense of direction while the noise it makes seems to come with mysterious, attractive ominousness from down in the middle of it, "some hidden place where the water issued with a roar underground" (37). In "Images" Munro becomes a romancer of the sublime, melting her Wawanash County into the landscape of the unconscious much as Coleridge did when he dreamed of Xanadu in "Kubla Khan." In "Images" landscape imagery is a metaphor for the actual life and death situation the child feels her sick mother to be in, for her own burgeoning, perilous identity as a female child, and, as with Coleridge's pleasure dome, caves of ice and roaring water, a metaphor for artistic inspiration itself. Beyond this, Munro's images expand inexplicably, the mythic level of Jungian mind.

In this sense, "Images" is very close to visual art and to the enigmatic mysteries in works by artists like Alex Colville. The feeling one gets in "Images" is not unlike that of Colville's "Low Tide," where the natural element of water, considered to be the archetypal symbol of the feminine and the unconscious, is the background for a female body. In this painting there is the "feeling that you may be contemplating the Jungian archetype of the Great Mother," suggests Hans Werner. Certainly, Munro's images, here, like Colville's, are not entirely accessible to analysis by language; they "inhabit a silence that must be experienced, and cannot be explained away."[21]

In *Dance of the Happy Shades,* Ontario place is of primary importance in fictions of childhood memory and magic. On one level, Munro's locales are painstakingly realistic, even naturalistic representation, on another, romantic, psychological visions—her art, magically real.

Characteristically, a romantic frame of mind informs Munro's seemingly ordinary realities in much of her early work. Romantic proclivities are apparent in her faith in interpreting the world through the poetic eye of childhood, her reflective stance substantiated philosophically when she quotes Wordsworth's dictum, "Poetry is emotion recollected in tranquility" in an interview with Allan Twigg,[22] her melancholy over the passage of time, her regionalist attitude that the artist derives her inspiration from an intimate and continuous association with the place of her birth, and most importantly, her attraction to primitivism and the unconscious.

Contributing to the romance of the unconscious in her work is the black romantic angle of vision—the gothic—which, introduced in *Dance,* will also contribute to Del Jordan's view of her world in *Lives,* and which has feminist implications. In "The Peace of Utrecht," for example, townscape has the same dark "attractive ominousness" of the mysterious, supernatural landscape poems of Coleridge and Keats—poems which pulled their readers out of sensible reality into threatening, desolate "gothic" interior worlds. In Munro's townscape, we can see as well the standard split in the romantic literary imagination between the good magic of the picturesque and the black magic of the gothic. The primitively seasonal rhythm of life in Jubilee is reassuring to the returned narrator, but the brick house is also the place which imprisoned her legendary "Gothic Mother," and the decaying streets of the town are at once a picturesque and a dreamlike world of gloomy houses and psychic foreboding:

> I drove up the main street . . . and turned into the quiet, decaying streets where old maids live, and have birdbaths and blue delphiniums in their gardens. The big brick houses that I knew, with their wood verandahs and gaping, dark-screened windows seemed to me plausible but unreal. (*Dance*, 196)

Behind Munro's romanticism, her landscapes of gothic mind, is also the literary tradition of the gothic novel begun by such eighteenth-century British writers as Ann Radcliffe and Monk Lewis. The original gothic mode of fiction with its primary emotions of fear and terror, its crude villains pursuing palpitating heroines, was primarily a sexual fantasy fiction which tellingly projected the repressed feeling of a society which placed woman on a pedestal, denied her sexuality and romantically idealized her as morally superior to and more sensitive than the male. As the heroine of gothic fiction escaped the imprisonment of her tower, she was often placed in threatening landscapes of roaring cataracts and majestic mountains. Unconsciously projected into the heroine's dangerous situations were the primitive passions the eighteenth century denied her. Obviously, the gothic heroine is not in her eighteenth-century dress in Munro's fiction but she and her fiction of psychological projection are very much alive in the supra-real story of seemingly ordinary life, "Sunday Afternoon," from *Dance*.

While superficially a critique of middle-class provincial society conveyed through the person of the summer maid Alva, the story becomes one of mindscape when Alva, as captive occupant of the carefully ordered stucco house, like the imprisoned gothic heroine in her tower, begins to feel herself in an unreal world of sun and water as those "long, curtained and carpeted rooms, with their cool colours seemed floating in an underwater light" (163). As Alva walks down the long corridor wondering in a dreamlike way if she is there or not, she becomes the literary descendant of the gothic heroine, her fear muted and implicit, not theatrically tortured as in the gothic tales of old, but she is as much in the trapped, feminine quandary as the heroines of Radcliffe and Lewis who took symbolic mental flight through subterranean caves and castle labyrinths. Alva's potential seducer is a male guest at a party, and by the end of the narrative the island of Georgian Bay, the summer place Alva hoped would offer some release, is subtly underscored as a mythic fearful place of further humiliation for the girl when the guest, a modern villain, slyly promises that he will see her there.

Feminist critics have established that gothic fiction written by women in the last two centuries, both at a popular and literary level, is a genre apart as Female Gothic and as such, is primarily concerned with definitions of female sexuality and the role of the female in patriarchal culture. Partly a subversive fiction, it nonetheless apes the values and images of male culture. Juliann E. Fleenor explains, "Female Gothicists had adopted the anti-rationalistic Gothic both to reproduce and yet challenge the patriarchal world in which they lived. . . . [23] Fleenor points out that it is in the Gothic novel that female writers could first accuse the "real world" of falsehood and deep disorder. It is in the spirit of this tradition that Munro creates a subliminal gothic mindscape in "Sunday Afternoon." Although the fiction reproduces the status of women in patriarchal culture, it is meant as feminist accusation.

Gothic mindscape is not to be overlooked in *Dance* and poses an intriguing question about the region Munro writes from. The mythology of small town Ontario as gothic is persistent and to some degree is its own mystery, although partly explainable through the social reality Munro herself depicts of a long-standing, genteel, and repressed Protestant class and the crumbling architecture of gothic churches and romantic Victorian culture they inhabit. While the Victorian sensibility may be passing, the absolute moral code and civilizing manners of the Fathers of Confederation and their wives are well rooted in Ontario ground, with vestiges of their attitudes filtering through Munro's heroines, including a Calvinist apprehension about the primitive and barbaric potential of man and, more importantly, woman.

This gothic terror of the primitive is not new to Canadian literature, nor is Northrop Frye's now well-worn argument that Canadian poetry began with a response to the land as vast wilderness: that the deep terror in confronting the frontier and a northern land was felt as "the riddle of the unconscious in nature" producing a "garrison mentality,"[24] and a literature where civilized small towns provided social and psychological refuge from the primitiveness of an awesome landscape. Frye's contention, while now almost a cliché of literary criticism, is well worth mentioning here because it is validated to some degree in the landscape of gothic mind which creeps into *Lives of Girls and Women.*

In *Lives* the tension between country and town, the Flats Road and Jubilee, is that of the primitive versus the civilized; and as Jubilee becomes a shelter to Del Jordan and her mother, it is not far removed from Susanna Moodie's "one woman garrison" in the Peterborough bush.[25] Neither is this acute struggle between nature and culture unnaturally felt by Del and her mother and Mrs. Moodie. It is a natural psychological extension of the maternal principle and the mother as first felt landscape. As Julia Kristeva explains, "the maternal body is the place of a splitting, which, even though hypostatized by Christianity, nonetheless remains a constant factor of social reality. Through a body, destined to insure reproduction of the species, the woman-subject, although under the sway of the paternal function. . . is more of a *filter* than anyone else—a thoroughfare, a threshold where "nature" confronts "culture.""[26]

Female Gothicists are most aware of the maternal body. In fact, the conflict with the all-powerful Mother is at the heart of their fiction. Consequently, the relationship between mother and daughter is a key one, as it is in *Lives,* with the mother often acting as the psychological double for the questing heroine,

> For the mother represents what the woman will become if she heeds her sexual self, if she heeds the self who seeks the power that comes with acting as the mother, and if she becomes pregnant. The ambivalences surrounding the conflict with this awesome figure are in part shaped by the twofold knowledge that to become the mother is to become the passive and perhaps unwilling victim of one's own body.[27]

For Del Jordan—and her mother—and the ghost of Susanna Moodie—fear of sexuality and the female body is projected onto the natural world. The Flats Road outside of town where Del first lives is introduced as seemingly neutral, but it is potentially a savage place. True to Munro's romantic realist style, though, the setting is socially real gothic: la belle dame sans merci is the prosaic down and out child beater, Madeleine; the gothic reality of the place is literally accredited through the newspaper headlines of Uncle Benny's tabloids. If this is the way it *really* is outside of town, at the same time the Flats Road landscape incorporates an underlying, treacherous, unconscious power. The fear of the black well of the unconscious (the fearful imagery of wells and deep holes recurs in *Lives*) is read into the bush by Del, just as Uncle Benny's primitive lifestyle symbolizes for her the swallowing of daylight order: "The deep, deep, layered clutter and dirt of the place swallowed light" (3). Such danger is apparent in our immediate introduction to the Grenoch Swamp, with its treacherous quicksilver holes and the vast, unfathomable frontier universe of space which was "black, hot, thick with thorny bushes, and dense with insects whirling in galaxies" (2). In *Lives* the layers of the mind are suggestively superimposed on objective reality. The Flats Road, and bush beyond, are symbols of primal energy and sexuality, its chaos and danger. The town, in its intricate design, is representative of order, reason and control.

This is Del's foremost interpretation of the environment, one which is inherited from her mother whose sexual puritanism, reason and genteel town aspirations place them both *at the end* (6) of the Flats Road. Because the Flats Road is known to her as the projection of her mother's puritan, Anglo-Saxon mind, Del's point of reference and safety is the Christian pastoral image of Sandy Stephenson's donkey which stands "like the illustration to a Bible story, pasturing in the stony corner of a field" (5). The gothicity of the Flats Road is heightened by the good/evil dichotomy of ideal Protestant vision—a dichotomy which is a characteristic of the Female Gothic genre[28]—generating in full steam the sublime terror of Del who, after reading Uncle Benny's tabloids, will reel "out into the sun, onto the path that led to our place, across the fields... bloated and giddy with revelations of evil, of its versatility and grand invention and horrific playfulness" (4).

While Del Jordan, unlike her mother, will come to suspect the town itself as being as gothic as the Flats Road, later, seeing through her mother's eyes, she will rather predictably revive Mrs. Moodie's state of mind as she interprets Jubilee as a fort in the wilderness:

> My mother would never let this sighting [The Town] go by without saying something. "There's Jubilee," she might say simply, or, "Well, yonder lies the metropolis," or she might even quote fuzzily, a poem about going in the same door she went out. And by these words, whether weary, ironic, or truly grateful, Jubilee seemed to me to take its being. As if without her connivance, her acceptance, these streetlights and sidewalks, the fort in the wilderness, the open and secret pattern of the town—a shelter and a mystery—would not be there. (*Lives*, 58)

Although Del meets with some equanimity the primitive folk reality and sexuality her mother will not have, in her initial fearful willingness to interpret the bush as gothic she is her mother's and Mrs. Moodie's natural daughter. And while the "garrisoned mentality" of Mrs. Moodie, her decorum and her suppressed sexuality, may seem terribly regressive to the modern reader, it is well to remember that within the confines of her domestic role, Mrs. Moodie was an adventuress. After all, she did come to Canada and confront the wilderness. A living heroine of gothic fiction, she retreats into civilized order but at the same time travels out beyond its limits.

Similarly, Del's mother is a traveller of "bright ruthless forces" which pushes her out into the wilderness beyond the town, into the country "with no recognizable rhythm to it" (57). Although she drives in "grand terror" all the time "as if she would not be surprised to see the ground crack open ten feet in front of her wheels" (55), she still drives, preferring to sell encyclopedias on the Jericho Road to keeping house. In effect, she is a participant in what Ellen Moers has called the *travelling* heroism of the Female Gothic, a mode which from Ann Radcliffe on she determines has been primarily a female adventure fantasy. Her claim is that Radcliffe used the Gothic novel "to send maidens on distant and exciting journeys without offending the proprieties. In the power of villains, her heroines are forced to do what they could never do alone, whatever their ambitions... spy out exotic vistas, penetrate bandit infested forests" (the Gothic novel becoming a feminine substitute for the picaresque);[29] following suit, Alice Munro uses a muted gothic form and sensibility to explore Del Jordan's potential as a modern, adventurous reflection of her mother, making Ontario gothic clearly a landscape of feminist mind in *Lives* and Alice Munro, as author, a writer firmly rooted in this mental soil.[30]

Unlike her mother who is a daytime voyager with her sexual urges firmly garrisoned, Del will go on to willingly experience sexual passion— but Munro has her do so in accordance with a genteel Upper Canadian, puritan psychology. Del will be seduced by titillating gothic fantasies of sexual evil, and in the very tradition of gothic fantasy, via versions of the gothic villain. Through Uncle Benny, who is described in gothic fashion as a man with "heavy black moustache, fierce eyes, a delicate predatory face" (2), she is introduced to the mythic, puritan-inspired world of gothic horror, its erotic possibility and male-directed evil. Reading his tabloids, she discovers *Virgin Raped on Cross by Crazed Monks;* via the seedy Mr.

Chamberlain she actually enters this landscape of perverse and forbidden sexuality (out in the bush), an encounter which is overlaid in true Ango-Saxon gothic tradition with fantasies of Mediterranean and Southern European licentiousness.

The spirit of Ann Radcliffe's *The Mysteries of Udolpho* and *The Italian* steals into Del's adventure when Mr. Chamberlain as conventional villain reveals that he has been in Italy during the war and knows its decadence. Both Del and her mother imaginatively travel this country through this information and Mr. Chamberlain's exotic experience further excites Del to the possibility of erotic adventure with him as she rubs her "hipbones through the cool rayon" considering, "If I had been born in Italy my flesh would already be used, bruised and knowing" (128). Del's gothic bubble begins to deflate when Mr. Chamberlain's sexuality proves to be both prosaic and self-indulgent, but Munro has her ride out the black romantic state of mind in her relationship with Garnet French, reaching a milestone in her development towards independence when she transfers the romantic egoism of gothic villainy to herself. In "Baptism" she remains excited by the romantic opera *Carmen* but not by the fantasy of voluptuous surrender to a man:

> *Et laisser moi passer!* I hissed it between my teeth; I was shaken, imagining the other surrender, more tempting, more gorgeous even than the surrender to sex—the hero's, the patriot's, Carmen's surrender to the final importance of gesture, image, self-created self. (*Lives*, 153)

In the end, however, Del's voyage out cannot be accomplished by the dark sublime; whether a woman defines herself as active romantic subject wailing for her demon lover or passive object of a mysteriously violent, attractive, evil male (Del's view of Garnet), the romantic state of mind is too closely tied to sexual contest of patriarchal imagination and the pyrrhic victory of one ego over another, as Del discovers with Garnet. While there is no hint of solution given to Del's future sexual relations, in the final chapter, "Epilogue: The Photographer," Munro clearly tells us that she has been in the process of surrendering the gothic mode, of liberating her heroine from adventure as virginal gothic fantasy, making possible adventure as self-created sexually-liberated fact. In contrast to Miss Farris and Marion Sherriff who as real people are still doomed, gothic maidens drowning themselves in the Wawanash River (due to male misuse), Del Jordan survives her baptism by water, fighting underwater as though through a dream, to emerge into a daylight landscape stripped of romantic color: "As I walked on into Jubilee I repossessed the world. Trees, houses, fences, streets came back to me, in their own sober and familiar shapes" (199).

The exorcism of the gothic is also symbolically expressed through Del's final fantasy, the fictional novel she carries in her head of the aspirant travelling gothic heroine Caroline, who, like Radcliffe's heroines moving from setting to setting in magic transport like fairy tale creatures, slips "along the streets of Jubilee as if she was trying to get through a crack in an invisible wall, sideways" (204). In Del's story, Caroline's antagonist and fateful seducer is the gothic villain full blown, a photographer in black who captures the terrifying illusion of people as they will be in time, not as they are. Symbol, in part, of the collective gothic imagination of small town Ontario, part of the other dreamlike, psychological Jubilee "lying close behind the one" (206) Del walks through every day, he is also this place's outdated, romantic paternal fantasy of the way to adventure. Both he and the victimized Caroline must be gotten rid of so that Del Jordan will be free to continue to take up her own modern picaresque by taking the next bus out of town. At the conclusion of the novel, Jubilee seems well named as Del's gothic novel recedes in the natural light of Bobby Sherriff's house. Having "lost faith in it" (208)—her own gothic fiction, Del is now open to self-directed possibilities.

As a footnote of gothic villainy, the photographer in "The Epilogue" is one of Munro's more complex symbols. On one level, he is surely the face and function of the artist herself: his ugly, futuristic picture-making an expression of Munro's own artistic fear. Munro knows that her gothic Ontario place is the wellspring of her creative imagination and its inner magic. To leave regional space behind and to transport her heroines into the new wilderness, the metropolis, as Del and Munro's fiction seem to be heading, presents not only a feminist frontier, but an aesthetic one. The question which Munro asks herself is whether she the artist, will, like Del, in moving out of the Jericho bush, leave behind instinct and unconscious inspiration, a world for Del, "not far from what I thought animals must see, the world without names" (184) to gain in the town and city, merely one of inconsequential surfaces, of "callous importance" and "sober shapes" (199). Will she as future "unromantic" artist only capture, like the photographer, cheap and flat images of dulled and stupid faces, pregnant brides and adenoidal children?

Although Munro's fear of sordid art does not materialize, this prognostication is important because in *Something I've Been Meaning to Tell You,* as she moves her characters out of Ontario and into cities of the sixties, she largely abandons romantic picturesque setting and the gothic mysteries of town and bush in favor of a greater psychological and social realism. This transition is reported by the middle-aged narrator, Dorothy, in "Marrakesh," as she accepts with interest the process of modernization:

> Dorothy herself as a young girl—. . . . How she hated change, then, and clung to old things, old mossy rotten *picturesque things.* Now she had changed, herself. She saw what beauty was, all right; she acknowledged the dappling shadows on the grass, the gray sidewalk, but she saw that it was, in a way, something to get round. It did not matter greatly to her. . . . this town had been Town to her when she was a child. . . But if those houses were all pulled down, their hedges and vines and vegetable plots. . . obliterated and a shopping centre put up in their place, she would not turn her back. . . because there was in everything something to be discovered. (*Something,* 131)

Although Munro does not totally discard an earlier Ontario life—seven of the thirteen stories are set in Ontario—its magic landscape does begin to melt away and, like the mother in "The Ottawa Valley" whom the narrator sees "turning strange, indifferent, darkening" (195), characters, not landscape, take on their own interior realities. In a story like the lead one, the house is "pulled down" and old Et's decayed psyche exposed, fulfilling the author's promise of greater realism at the end of *Lives.* In the very first story we discover what Et herself does: that what showed in her sister's photograph was equal to her real face, that the "qualities of legend were real" (5).

There is still a sense of earlier Ontario life in this story and others like "The Found Boat," "Executioners," "Winter Wind" and "The Ottawa Valley," but those earlier expanded landscapes have shrunk, and are losing force. While an impression of springtime Ontario countryside is recaptured in "The Found Boat," as two girls help a gang of boys rebuild a boat on the Wawanash River, it loses its authority to a dour Calvinist mentality projected through biblical metaphor and allusion to Eden passing (the girl is named Eva), the Flood and the underlying idea of Original Sin. The passage from childhood to adolescence here is a painful Calvinist image and a repetition of Munro's steady, melancholy complaint about the denial of adventures to females in this kind of society. In "Winter Wind," too, there is little interior landscape magic; rather, it seems purposely nullified as wilderness is turned to tame bush by the matter-of-fact narrator:

> From my grandmother's bedroom window you could look across the CPR tracks to a wide stretch of the Wawanash River, meandering in reeds. All frozen now, all ice and untracked snow. Even on stormy days the clouds might break before supper time, and then there was a fierce red sunset. Like Siberia, my grandmother said, offended, you would think we were living on the edge of the wilderness. It was all farms, of course, and tame bush, no wilderness at all, but winter buried the fence posts. (*Something*, 154)

Similarly, the gothic setting of Ontario town and bush is demythologized in the two black tales of Ontario, the lead one and "The Executioners." In the first, the gothic town has become a commercial commodity for tourists and Munro moves from previous ironic invitation to place to outright parody of place when she names the town Mock Hill. In the second, the gothic wilderness mythology has become an obvious frontier fiction, an unbelievable place where, according to the mocking Robina, wolves in the winter have been known to eat babies. Like Margaret Atwood in *Lady Oracle*, Munro plays here in these two pseudogothic tales with the comic/Gothic,[31] a subgenre of Female Gothic, where terror and angst are modified by humor.

Munro does not completely succeed, however, in ridding herself of the conventions and sensibility of Female Gothic in these stories of an earlier time and place. The gothic character of the imprisoned and repressed heroine is clearly retained and at first glance, would seem to be an anachronism in a volume which projects a sixties urban obsession with psychoanalysis, as the author probes the primal depths of her characters' psyches by moving them out of the bush and into the actual and figurative houses they inhabit. Exploring their psychological architecture, Munro, a modern, urban literary architect, uses interior space, and images of doors and windows, not landscape, as reflections of her subjects' interior lives.

This technique, the imagization of interior space, is nonetheless a contemporary mindscape of Female Gothic, a modernized expression of female repression in male dominated culture. As Fleenor expresses it, "The writer's feelings are frequently illustrated by the image of enclosed space, an image which conveys repression and frustration. . . . Spatial imagery, images of enclosed rooms or houses, suggests either the repressive society in which the heroine lives or the heroine herself, and sometimes, confusingly both" (12). Further, Claire Kahane points out that at the centre of Female Gothic lies the ambivalence about the all powerful, all embracing mother and that "the heroine's exploration of her entrapment in a Gothic house. . . can be read as an exploration of her relation to the maternal body which she, too, shares, to the femaleness of experience, with all its connotations of power over and vulnerability to, forces within and without."[32] In the lead story, the childish old Et has not assumed maternity; she closes the front curtains of her sewing establishment tight, pinning the crack so that men cannot see in, secreting herself and her private passions. In "Executioners," the murder of Stump and Howard Troy is psychologically housed in the narrator's mind, the burning house itself a metaphor of her own deep and vengeful passion:

> I was the one who had first seen the fire from my upstairs window, seen something beautiful, a flush in the corner of the night landscape, separate from the glow of the town lights, a warm spreading pool. That was the house giving off such light, through its cracks and windows. (*Something,* 121)

In these two stories, internal space or the maternal house is strongly represented by images of windows and doors, connoting both female vulnerability and the power of suppressed rage and identity. By the end of "Executioners" the black magic of an earlier time and place seems almost an illusion to the mature narrator who ironically persists in being safely housed, occupying in isolation the seventeenth floor of a high rise apartment building. Despite such a contemporary entrapment in "Executioners," Munro insists in both these stories that the gothic house is crumbling, with female passion rightly and powerfully, leaking through.

As Marilyn Julian observes, "fascinating are the windows in these stories. Characters peer out of them or stare into them. . . . Romance. Ideals, Disillusionment. Attempted Escape. Reality. . . . Always there is the figurative shattering of window glass. . . ."[33] The nerves of the characters pulled taut—captured by the recurrent threat of shattering glass in this collection—are not only symptoms of feminine struggle, but of the urban dislocation and alienation of both sexes. The six stories set in British Columbia are intense, desperate, psychological dramas, their middle-aged narrators trying to come to grips with an uprooted lifestyle and the new religions of modern urban life: materialism, sexual liberation, and strange cults. Madness is a constant threat. In transit or temporary residence, divorced and unsettled, the city dwellers find little truth or beauty in the places they are presently in. Characters like the narrator of "Tell Me Yes or No" and Mr. Lougheed in "Walking on Water" look backwards to the past for a steadier foothold. For the old man, his real life is the dream of his rural childhood, and for both, the city is bizarre and artificial, a Hollywood set, a circus. Country, too, is beginning to be this. As seen by Mr. Lougheed,

> The weight of life, the importance of it, had some way disappeared. Events took place now in a diminished landscape, and were of equal, or no, importance. Mr. Lougheed riding on a bus through the city streets or even through the countryside would not have been much amazed to see anything you could name—a mosque, for instance, or a white bear. Whatever it looked to be, it would turn out to be something else. Girls at the supermarket wore grass skirts to sell pineapples and he had seen a gas station attendant, wiping windshields, wearing on his head a fool's hat with bells. Less and less was surprising. (*Something*, 67)

The feminist adventure in the city is still in this volume weighted in favor of men, but in modern, urban technological society, dispossession cuts across sex in the masquerade of the city. The female character of "Tell Me Yes or No," in a new city [Victoria] is equally as shocked and disoriented as Mr. Lougheed:

> And the shops so strange to anyone from an industrial/ university town, someone used, in spite of shopping-centre dress-ups, to some commercial modesty and functionalism. Turn-of-the-century ice-cream parlors. WILD WEST SPORTING GOODS. HAWAIIAN CASUALS, with palms in tubs. Tudor teashops with flimsy gables... Candy stores with false fronts like miniature castles. These masquerades are too various, too tiring. (*Something*, 93)

In *Something I've Been Meaning to Tell You*, there is no magical or mysterious cityscape equal to the Ontario landscape of mind of her first two volumes. There is only the city as preposterous setting and the private, imprisoning psychological houses of individuals. There are brief mappings of streets and descriptions of facades of buildings on this new urban and provincial frontier, but no consistent mythology of place. Munro's new urbanites are in their own mental cages but they are also very much like those people imagined by the youthful narrator travelling outside of "The Ottawa Valley"—"Outside of my own town—this far outside of it... seeming to be floating around free" (183).

In *Who Do You Think You Are?*, the city and modernity are as intrusive as in *Something I've Been Meaning to Tell You*. The reader's first introduction to the *idea* of city is the childhood rhyme excitedly chanted by the young Rose as she grows up in Munro's Wawanash County in the small town of Hanratty: "Two Vancouvers fried in snot/Two pickled arseholes tied in a knot!" (12). Bizarre, comic, deliciously obscene, the city is a Gordian carnival knot to be untangled. And Rose is admirably suited for the part, as she blossoms into an independent, modern professional actress who spends her gypsy life moving in and out of towns, cities and country places. Unlike the middle-aged narrators of the last volume who are voyeurs out of control as they travel out of old, familiar country spaces into modern ones, Rose learns to take charge, becoming in the process a contemporary, urban heroine, an active participant in the modern circus, to whom all life, whether in country or city place, is legitimate theater. With Rose, outside moves in—and place, as townscape and landscape, becomes little more than backdrop for house, apartment, train, hospital, library, legion, nursing home, which, appropriate to the heroine's calling, become theatrical sets to the scenes of modern manners played out within them.

In recognition of *Dance*, Beth Harvor has said that "Using Virginia Woolf's guidelines from *A Room of One's Own*, that she [Munro] belongs to the Jane Austen rather than to the Charlotte Brontë tradition."[34] This is truer of the fourth book than the first as Munro and her heroine investigate the various strata of society, observing with realism and irony, class deportment and styles of living.

Rose is herself a cool, economic heroine constantly balancing the virtues of richness versus poverty, considering what to buy and what to pay. Hers is the material mindedness of the poor country mouse come city mouse, and an accurate representation on Munro's part of an urban, technological

social phenomenon. A fiction based on sociological truth, this novel is not
without Munro's characteristic magic as the enchantment of the earlier dis-
coveries of country and town is transferred to the new material of modern
drawing room interiors—to exotic foods and clothing and interior designs.
Detailed landscape portraits are no more; in their place are extravagant surfaces of taste (the acquiring of taste is a theme of the novel) and color which
express, with a kind of Keatsian glamor, Rose's sugar plum vision as she
experiences the extravagances of aspirant and actual middle-class life. Gor-
geously imaged and reflected in Rose's little girl's story of the fairy prin-
cesses is Rose's own romance with such goods as imported black cherries,
Camembert cheese and sheets covered with stylish garlands of blue and yellow flowers.

> There was a white princess who dressed all in bride clothes and wore
> pearls. Swans and lambs and polar bears were her pets, and she had lil-
> lies and narcissus in her garden. She ate mashed potatoes, vanilla ice
> cream, shredded coconut and meringue off the top of pies. A pink prin-
> cess grew roses, and ate strawberries, kept flamingoes... on a leash.
> The blue princess subsisted on grapes and ink. The brown princess
> though drably dressed feasted better than anybody; she had roast beef
> and gravy and chocolate cake with chocolate icing, also chocolate ice
> cream with chocolate fudge sauce. (*Who*, 147)

Like the initial obscenity of the childhood rhyme, however, there are
also "rude things" in this garden of delights; an excess of taste and digestion, the modern place is market, carnival surfeit and an obscene joke. In
Who Do You Think You Are? the invitation to a contemporary circus is extended, accepted and played out with some pleasure by Rose; but after the
final act, when the tent comes down, there is only empty space and the return trip back—home to Wawanash County. The value of home has altered, however, from *Dance* and *Lives* and even those Ontario stories in
Something I've Been Meaning to Tell You. The circus has come to the
country too in the form of factories and crazy religious cults discovered by
Rose in her country retreat in "Simon's Luck." For the theatrical Rose, in
fact, it has always been there in the comic and grotesque players of the
horsewhippers, the freakish Becky Tyde, and the parade-walking Milton
Homer.

In the end, as for most of Munro's characters, it is Wawanash County which offers Rose her psychological stability, but not through its outward features and external reality. From the beginning, the physical surface of Hanratty has had little meaning for Rose; a character who sees the world in social terms, her Hanratty is one of social structure:

> They lived in a poor part of town. There was Hanratty and West Hanratty, with the river flowing between them. This was West Hanratty. In Hanratty the social structure ran from doctors and dentists and lawyers down to foundry workers and factory workers and draymen; in West Hanratty it ran from factory workers and foundry workers down to large improvident families of casual bootleggers and prostitutes and unsuccesful thieves. (*Who*, 4)

By the conclusion of the novel, Hanratty, like the country place Rose flees to in her interlude with Simon, has lost its original shape, has become corroded by technological change. The Hanratty Rose discovers when she comes to put Flo away in the Home is an unrecognizable one of highway bypasses, new aluminum and mercury vapor street lights. What Rose is made to see, then, is the evanescence of physical "properties" and the changeling, flirtatious face of material reality. The ultimate truth for her is Munro's characteristic psychological one that place is the source of identity—but here, not as physical setting. Instead, as I have pointed out in Chapter Two, place becomes the memory of those people whom Rose comes to understand constitute her Self; however treacherous and tasteless their disguises may have been, it is only they, as she knew them, who define her humanity and ultimately sustain her person as she moves into the future.

In *The Moons of Jupiter* place has a new expansiveness. Several of the stories, "Connection," "The Turkey Season," Accident," "Labor Day Dinner," "Visitors," "Hard-Luck Stories" include obvious, local, familiar Ontario settings but "Dulse" is located in New Brunswick, and "Bardon Bus" partly in Australia; the overall impression of the volume is that of an author and her characters moving out and beyond old borders and boundaries, beyond province, nation, and as the title of the volume suggests, the world itself.

For Urjo Kareda, "The most beautiful stories here are those that return us to the idiosyncratic world of Munro's previous stories—rural Western Ontario and the town she usually calls Dalgleish."[35] As in her earlier fictions, familiar landscape provides background identity and psychological roots for contemporary women in social and sexual transition. The narrator-wife in "Connection," a typical Munro heroine in conflict with her husband, resists his amputation of her past.

> Background was Richard's word. Your background. A drop in his voice, a warning. . . . When he said Dalgleish, even when he wordlessly handed me a letter from home, I felt ashamed, as if there were something growing over me. . . . He wanted me amputated from the past which seemed to him such shabby baggage. . . . (*Moons*, 12–13)

There is a spare pastoral poetry, too in the stories of Ontario place, in the "flat, solid reality of things" that mentioned at the beginning of this chapter, so pleased the sensibility of Bronwen Wallace in Munro's earlier work. Beyond the Maitland River and its cedar banks in "The Stone in the Field" are,

> pasture hills covered with purple-flowering milkweed, wild pea blossom, black-eyed Susans. Hardly any trees here, but lots of elderberry bushes, blooming all along the road. They looked as if they were sprinkled with snow. One bald hill reached up higher than any of the others. (*Moons*, 24)

With the exception of "Bardon Bus," however, in this volume as in her last two, the emotional lives of the heroines rarely invade or merge with particular landscape descriptions. In "Bardon Bus" the extravagance of Australian vegetation is a reflector of the heroine's passionate, perhaps final, sexual fling, the gully "like an oval bowl, ringed with small houses and filled with jacaranda, poinciana, frangipani, cypress and palm trees. Leaves like fans, whips, feathers, plates; every bright, light, dark, dusty, glossy shade of green," (119); discoverable here is the luxurious sensuality of a woman's climacteric passion.

More common than full interior landscapes in *The Moons of Jupiter* is the authorial technique of drawing an object out of location, out of the "heart's field," and investing it with the full power of a literary figure, not as a symbol, but as an indirect emblem of the central female voice. Emblems, tokens, antiques, artifacts, and relics are embedded in the narratives as predictors of the characters' emotions, just as these words themselves specify the central female dilemma of the volume, of moving through menopause into old age. "I think maybe we're destroyed already," Ruth says dreamily. "I think maybe we're anachronisms. No, that's not what I mean. I mean relics. In some way we are already. Relics" (157). In "Dulse," then, the New Brunswick landscape is given over to "long, dark, ragged leaves of dulse, oily—looking wet even when dry" (58), a mermaid gift of new experience and future possibility for the melancholy Lydia, a kind of emblematic possible antidote even to the physical, sexual drying up that awaits her.

The stone in the heart's field is also a central figure, as Mount Hebron cut down for gravel, as the boulder rolled away in "The Stone in the Field," and as absent rubble in "Visitors." When the aging Wilfred and Alfred return nostalgically to the site of their family home, they find nothing: "Conservation people. They don't leave one stone of the foundation, or the cellar hole, or one brick or beam. They dig it all out and fill it all in and haul it all away" (212). In a larger sense, the foundation stone is the familiar, cultural and regional background of Alice Munro's well established Protestant and Anglo-Canadian world, a world that begins to break down here for some of her more adventurous and urbane heroines in a discomfiting but not entirely unwelcome way. Frances of "Accident" and Roberta of "Labor Day Dinner" travel beyond Mount Hebron through their lovers. Under a picture of Jesus walking by the Sea of Galilee, Frances discovers something of the Finnish community and its family life through her lover Ted from northwestern Ontario, and Roberta from "Labor Day Dinner" wonders at her lover George from Timmins, the son of a Hungarian shoemaker, discussing the history of architecture and denouncing the pointed arch as a Christian marvel.

In *The Moons of Jupiter*, Munro's heroines continue to be transforming in every sense: physically, emotionally and socially; moreover, they are strongly defined as travelling heroines in constant physical motion both in fact and in memory. Even Mrs. Kidd, confined to a home for the aged, conceives of herself as a traveller within its walls: "She prayed no nosy person would come along until she could recover her strength and get started on the trip back" (180). Because of this, place in *The Moons of Jupiter* becomes, very much, in Eudora Welty's words, "the crossroads of circumstance." Characters cross paths in casual relationships in stories such as "Dulse" and "Hard-Luck Stories." As Munro's women move through places, fate and circumstance acquire a new unpredictability. Fear of natural disasters is an underlying anxiety in the volume and accident itself is highlighted in "Accident" and "Labor Day Dinner." The sensibility of *The Moons of Jupiter* is, of course, an aging one, one that acutely understands the inevitability of natural disaster for everyone, and the cosmic possibility of another space beyond the physical.

Munro's women are fearful, but at the same time they are interested in, intrigued even, by natural process. Theirs is that essentially female interest in physical metamorphosis, and as Lorna Irvine comments of Munro's previous women, that "peculiarly female concern with bodily boundaries."[36] Ultimately in *The Moons of Jupiter*, place is a pastiche of shifting grounds—of changing physical boundaries—and, as such, is emblematic of the psychological and physiological gates which several of Munro's heroines are passing through in this work. In *The Moons of Jupiter*, as with all of Munro's fiction to date, setting can be seen as an extension or projection of a female point of view.

In the collected short stories *The Progress of Love*, place has a stronger presence than in *The Moons of Jupiter*, is close to *Dance of the Happy Shades* in the feeling attached to locale, but here setting is not presented primarily as pictorial art as it was in the first volume, that is, as single textured photographs of townscape and landscape. Munro and her heroines are in the winter of their lives, and as they progress physically, edging closer to the end of reproductive sexuality, their author underwrites the text as the female body more than ever before. Place and the body are hardly separable, linked, in fact, through a pastoral mythic context of a northern garden. As Annette Kolodny has argued in *The Lay of the Land*, the pastoral myth is an informing metaphor of feminine design in American life and letters. The most cherished fantasy for America, since its inception, has been: "a daily reality of harmony between man and nature based on an experience of the land as essentially feminine—that is, not simply the land as mother, but the land as woman, the total female principle of gratification—enclosing the individual in an environment of receptivity, repose, and painless and integral satisfaction."[37]

Although Munro's Canadian landscapes are not always specifically or explicitly gendered female, their mythopoesis is primitively seasonal, and the rhythms of the lives of her rural and small town Canadian characters tied to the female principle of Mother Earth and her reproductive powers. The motif of seasonal change is strong in *The Progress of Love*, with springtime and summer garden backdrops receding as winter visions predominate. There is a new impression, that of northerness in this volume. Northerness is a feature of life in the skating party in "The Moon in the Orange Street Skating Rink," in the Eskimo couple in "Eskimo," in the Icelandic poetry of "White Dump," and most dramatically, in the winter landscape of "Fits" and the symbolic extension of snow-bound worlds in the white dump of candy of "White Dump." The Canadian garden is primarily one of rock and infertile frozen space and in this capacity, is a telling extension of the condition of female aging that occupies Munro.

In "White Dump" the Canadian landscape is analogous to the Old Norse, Sophie, to a white dump of "silica quarry," "snowfield," "white marble" (*Progress*, 306)—to bedrock candy—that is difficult to penetrate. In this story, the character Sophie, a female goddess and fertility figure in the mythic substructure of the fiction, shrivels symbolically with the vast Precambrian landscape she inhabits:

> They hovered in the air, a thousand feet or so off the ground. Below were juniper bushes spread like pincushions in the fields, cedars charmingly displayed like toy Christmas trees. There were glittering veins of ripples on the dark water. That toylike, perfect tininess of everything had a peculiar and distressing effect on Sophie. She felt as if it was she, not the things on earth, that had shrunk, was still shrinking—or that they were all shrinking together. This feeling was so strong it caused a tingle in her now tiny, crablike hands and feet—a tingle of exquisite smallness, an awareness of exquisite smallness. Her stomach shrivelled up: her lungs were as much use as empty seed sacs; her heart was the heart of an insect. (*Progress*, 296)

Mother Earth, the maternal principle, and the life of the body are in deadening repose and icy stasis, a condition mimicked even in the situations of male characters. In "Monsieur les Deux Chapeaux," Colin, after realizing he has not killed his brother, is revived into life through a psychological thawing: "Colin felt dizzy with the force of things coming back to life, the chaos and emotion. It was as painful as fiery blood pushing into frozen parts of your body" (83).

Retrospective journeys back to "Wawanash County," to maternal source, to female identity are as evident here as in *Dance* and other volumes but they have now also become largely deadening returns, a predication of female endings rather than beginnings. The return to the country past, to Ramsay on the Ottawa River, unearths the image of the hung grandmother for the narrator of "The Progress of Love." The narrator of "Miles City, Montana" reviews the drowning death of a child, Steve Gauley, who is conspicuously without a mother in a childhood pastoral past of southern Ontario, who may even have died because of the maternal void. The narrator herself is nostalgic for home, for Ontario, as she is reminded of it by a Washington landscape, but her wish for the days when she was little is also a death journey to the remembered turkey farm where "the turkeys are on a straight path to becoming frozen carcasses and table meat" (93). Childhood here, in "Miles City Montana" even in the present, is a dead deer, a lady deer—dead female meat.

In "A Queer Streak," female beginnings are also a dead end; the early drama of Violet's life in South Sherbrooke Township is introduced through "a lack of motherly feelings" on the part of Violet's mother, Aunt Ivie, who has "lost" three baby boys (208). Lost childhood, with its landscape as female is treacherous, affording no maternal protection or inspirational model of femaleness for the authorial sensorium. Violet's wading into water is a symbolic desolate excursion for her, as well, into the life of the female body, into symbolic maternity, a potential death trap where she will become the "waste ground."

> "Lost" meant that somebody died. "She lost them" meant they died. Violet knew that. Nevertheless she imagined. Aunt Ivie—her mother— wandering into a swampy field, which was the waste ground on the far side of the barn, a twilight place full of coarse grass and alder bushes. There Aunt Ivie, in the mournful light, mislaid her baby children. Violet would slip down the edge of the barnyard to the waste ground, then cautiously enter it. She would stand hidden by the red-stemmed alder and nameless thornbushes (it always seemed to be some damp, desolate time of year when she did this—late fall or early spring), and she would let the cold water cover the toes of her rubber boots. She would contemplate getting lost. Lost babies. The water welled up through the tough grass. Farther in, there were ponds and sinkholes. She had been warned. She shuffled on, watching the water creep up on her boots. She never told them. They never knew where she went. Lost. (208–9)

The pastoral dream is recounted with some springtime possibility in "Jesse and Meribeth "through Jessie's happy playfulness on the Maitland River and excursions with Mary Beth: "We filled our hands with the silk from burst milkweed pods, the softest-feeling thing there is on earth, then let it all loose to hang on other dry weeds like bits of snow or flowers" (163). But even here the pastoral world is inflected with "snow" and there is certainly no maternal protection from the snake in the garden, from Mr. Cryderman, the contemptuous, threatening seducer of Jessie in the summer-house, "a shady and neglected," "wonderfully secret" womblike pastoral retreat (182). Mary Beth's mother is dead, and the waifish Jessie's is unknown in the fiction.

In *The Progress of Love* the maternal body physically, psychologically, and mythically is dying, in ruins, a wreck. Mythically, the wrecked landscape is also that of Mother Earth defaced and overcome by modernity and the machinery of men. The stone in the field of *The Moons of Jupiter* has been replaced by the recurring landscape reality and mindscape of the machine in the garden in these stories, signifying the death of the power of female fertility and underscoring the powerlessness of Munro's heroines at the hands of men, in the game of love.

Cars litter these stories and country landscapes as symbols of masculine control and authority. David's visit to Stella's aged father in "Lichen" revolves around conversations about cars. Still learning "to be a man" (53) for the older man, David asserts himself with an updated masculinity as a driver of a foreign Japanese car, and is acknowledged by the patriarch who knows of and values this progress, even in the dying garden world on the clay bluffs overlooking Lake Huron: "Small cars were not a sign of any of the things they used to be a sign of. Even here on the bluffs above Lake Huron at the very end of life, certain shifts had registered, certain shifts had been understood..." (52).

Men are assertive drivers of both cars and women. The mother in Callie's legendary bloody childbirth in "The Moon in the Orange Street Skating Rink" has both husband and driver at her death. Violet in "A Queer Streak" is "rescued," quixotically shoved out of her possibly tragic life without a man by an anonymous male driver, by Wyck, when she runs her car off the road. She is ensnared symbolically in the maternal garden, and into the traditional female experience of a male-centered domestic life:

She walked around and looked at where her wheels were, then stood by the car waiting for somebody to come along and give her a shove.

But when she did hear a car coming, she knew she didn't want to be found. She couldn't bear to be. She ran from the road into the woods, into the brush, and she was caught. She was caught then by berry bushes, little hawthornes. Held fast. (234)

Dan, a gigolo, is especially good at repairing motors in "Circle of Prayer," but not interested in having and holding fast. His association with cars and machinery is an extension of masculine sexual control, of the sex act itself, as Trudy feels the impact of heavy trucks passing their house at night: "Trudy got so used to the noise and constant vibration she said she could feel herself jiggling all night, even when everything was quiet. . . . They woke up at the bottom of a river of noise. . . . There was the smell of diesel fuel in the air" (266). As Trudy and Dan say their last goodbyes, their sexual relations eclipsed forever, the machine in the garden is rendered harmless—an aimless object in the garden landscape: "She felt serene. She felt as if they were an old couple, moving in harmony, in wordless love, past injury, past forgiving. It was between four-thirty and five o'clock; the sky was beginning to brighten and the birds to wake, everything was drenched in dew. There stood the big, harmless machinery, stranded in the ruts of the road" (267).

Wrecked vehicles, in particular the wrecked car, is also a metaphor of the ruined female body, discarded by men with their preference for new models. As soon as the snow has gone, Ross in "Monsieur les Deux Chapeux" invests the landscape with car parts as he wrecks and reassembles bodies in much the same fashion as male lovers in others of these fictions discard and revisit women. "Ross had two cars to wreck and one to build" (63). Even in his craziness, Ross is a driver of women, a persecutor of Wilma Barry who dropped out of school and married at seventeen because "Ross was too much for her" (62). Car parts and female body parts are one and the same in the minds of men. Callie's vagina, penetrated by Edgar and Sam in "The Moon in the Orange Street Skating Rink" is imagized through the point of view of a man driving a car: "Cold and sticky where Edgar had wet her, dry otherwise, with unexpected bumps and flaps and blind alleys—a leathery feel to her" (146).

In "Fits" the wrecked car merges with the landscape, a frozen wilderness of Canadian garden where "winter comes down hard on the country, settles down just the way the two-mile ice did thousands of years ago" (110). Here, as in the mythopoeic "Images" from Dance, landscape has a magical psychic life and seems almost a protagonist in its own right. Robert has married Peg, and by so doing, has put a lid on his passions. When his next door neighbor murders his wife and kills himself, Robert feels the cracks in his and Peg's orderly existence, the emotional dangers beneath the frozen crust of a controlled daily life.

Typically, the landscape becomes Munro's and Robert's testing ground of his fear of the unconscious and the irrational:

> He walked here and there, testing. The crust took his weight without a whisper or a crack. It was the same everywhere. You could walk over the snowy fields as if you were walking on cement. (This morning, looking at the snow, hadn't he thought of marble?) But this paving was not flat. It rose and dipped in a way that had not much to do with the contours of the ground underneath. The snow created its own landscape, which was sweeping, in a grand and arbitrary style. (127)

While cars had threatened Robert's composure, "nosing along the street, turning at the end, nosing their way back again" to view the house of murder, "making some new kind of monster that came poking around in a brutally, curious way" (126), he is momentarily restored while "walking on this magic surface" (130).

His terror resurfaces with the intrusion once again of machinery in a frozen landscape space: a "congestion of shapes with black holes in them." As he traverses a "long slanting shelf of snow" (130), these shapes come into view:

> He was so close he could almost have touched one of these monstrosities before he saw that they were just old cars. Old cars and trucks and even a school bus that had been pushed in under the trees and left. Some were completely overturned, and some were tipped over one another at odd angles. They were partly filled, partly covered, with snow. The black holes were their gutted insides. Twisted bits of chrome, fragments of head-lights, were glittering. (131)

When Robert dismisses with relief the mysterious cars as "nothing but old wrecks" (131), he exorcises the enigma of the retired Weebles' passionate tragedy, superficially dispenses with them as gutted out, worn down old characters, and removes himself from the passion of their exit and their gruesome physical destruction. His is, however, something of a masculine illusion. Robert has accepted the maternal principle, or the male version of it, the comforting mother receptacle of Peg and the landscape of soothing, blanketing snow—the still center that receives him and that Munro explains men expect of women.[38] He is nonetheless apprehensive because he senses that Peg has deceived him. The female as author insists that the snow is littered with physical wreckage, that the landscape of mythic maternal source is a ruined body predictive of everyone's final condition, of the physical carnage of the Weebles' remains. This bloody and somewhat indecent knowledge is secreted by Peg; she does not tell Robert of having seen Mr. Weebles' shot-off head; she continues to project the maternal ideal, the smooth, undifferentiating blankness, what Plato called the *chora*—the mother receptacle of all things; it is, after all, what Robert expects, although he is uneasily *taken in.*

The landscape and the human body are inextricably fused in *The Progress of Love.* The skin of the earth is equal to the skin of women, and as a springtime, pastoral promise, sadly dead-ended for some of Munro's heroines. In "Eskimo," Mary Jo, trapped within the womblike machine, the airplane, and within her relationship as a pseudowife-mother with the suggestively named Dr. Streeter, struggles for voice, to determine to say what she wants. On this trip towards independence, she is "wearing new clothes from the skin out" (192), but the best she can finally muster for herself is the dream of the maternal garden with blue flowers, "like snowdrops" (207), only partly understood: "'in the garden' means something else, too, which Mary Jo will have to concentrate hard on to figure out" (207).

Beneath the skins of these fictions and read into the pastoral landscape are metaphors of the female body as rusted out, stripped down, worn vehicles and receptacles. In "Monsieur les Deux Chapeaux," the smell of spring in the air and the clouds of pollen create the backdrop for the rusted body of Ross's car; the dream of the garden is complicated in "Eskimo" by a first visionary entry into a badly maintained ladies room, with "an irregular, surprising patch of rust where the enamel has worn away at the bottom of the sink" (206). Although images suggestive of worn out bodies, patchy skin and rusted genitals communicate melancholia as a dominant mood of this volume, in the last story "White Dump," Munro expresses the magic that she believes comes at the end of reproductive life.[39] There is something of a surprising reversal in this final winter vision. Magically and mythically, the landscape of snow melts into that of a dump of candy, the view from the air of the Ontario landscape into that of a child's Christmas, the professor Sophie into that of Venus and the Fairy Queen. As the end story, finalized by Icelandic inscription: "It is too late to talk of this now: it has been decided" (309), "White Dump" also makes a claim on the innocence of new beginnings.

| | | —

For the devotee of the documentary who applauds regional fiction as the mirror representation of place, Munro's Ontario settings are a high artistic achievement. However, the power and importance of Munro's place, as is true of place generally in fiction, cannot entirely be its literal transcription of reality; rather the power of place resides in the art of its reconstruction and the uses the writer puts it to. As Eudora Welty once noted, the very term "regional" is a careless term, as well as a condescending one, because what it does is fail to differentiate between the localized raw material of life and its outcome as art. "Regional" is an outsider's term;[40] the insider, the artist, knows herself only to be writing about life, with region as the starting point of her human and aesthetic understanding. In this case, the artist's private place, Alice Munro's Ontario, is the source of her vision and the poetics of her prose; it is also an expression of her first truth that place is the psyche's fortress. A subjective landscape, a region, and often metaphor, of female mind and body, Wawanash County, and its sister places, unfold, like Faulkner's country of the American south, accruing their own mythic realities. The country of childhood landscape enchantment in *Dance*, adolescent gothic romance in *Lives* and tragicomic theater in *Who Do You Think You Are?* becomes one of shifting middle-aged boundaries in *The Moons of Jupiter* and of dying fertility in *The Progress of Love*. In the final analysis, the fictional world that Munro creates is an expanding, visionary location but at the same time always recognizably hers. It would seem that Munro knows very well the secret of many great writers before her: that the permanence of art is insured as it passes into legend, and that the magic source of legend itself is place.

THE SHORT STORY WRITER
AS FEMALE
Forms and Techniques

The short story is her house.
BETH HARVOR

One critical question which has kept resurfacing when the forms
of Munro's fiction have been under discussion is the following: can Munro
legitimately be called a novelist or is she "just" a short story writer? Even
in recent criticism that recognizes the postmodern tendency to usurp traditional genre boundaries, the question continues to be rearticulated. Linda
Hutcheon comments, "perhaps 'postmodern' is the best way to describe the
genre paradoxes in the work of Michael Ondaatje (are they biography? fiction? poetry?) or Alice Munro (are they short-story collections? novels?)"[1]
What constitutes a novel, of course, has become increasingly open to debate. There is a world of difference, for example, between the Victorian
novels of Charles Dickens, with their easily discernible traditional elements
of plot, characterization, chronological event and recognizable setting, and
those of Alain Robbe-Grillet in which the annihilation of these conventions
is the raison d'être, or the enormously complex intertextual fictions of
Robert Kroetsch where borders and boundaries, both as fictional subject
and form, are continuously addressed, parodied and reinvented. Nonetheless, in the past there have been certain reasonable expectations of the

novel, one of the most obvious being that of narrative order. The expectation of the novel has been that it must cohere structurally, even if it has been designed to offer the illusion of chaos.

Adopting this traditional standard, Canadian critics, in the past, have speculated on whether Munro's longer narratives, *Lives* and *Who Do You Think You Are?* meet this requirement. There would seem to have been some differences of opinion. *Lives*, for example, is described by one reviewer as "episodic, repetitive... a scrapbook of anecdotes" and, finally, as a collection of "highly enjoyable autobiographical sketches."[2] On the other hand, Rae Macdonald discovers a controlled structure in the narrative which

> is constructed from chapter to chapter around a series of parallel crises. . . . As the chapters go on and Del grows up, a sense of tension grows; each crisis seems more serious, less easily resolved. . . . The reader finally perceives that the repeated crises have been partial illusions masking a creeping decay and that day-to-day life is a greater illusion, "deep caves paved with kitchen linoleum." As with Uncle Benny, it is Munro's triumph to "make us see."[3]

While, for Macdonald, Munro's *vision* is finally what integrates the novel, for John Moss, "consummate use of point of view" is largely responsible for the novel's cohesive resonance and "sustaining hold" on the reader:

> The Del who remembers and relates is not the same person at a different point in time, but another person who includes the known and unknown complexities of the younger Del within her, and whose unconsciousness and inner life have continuity that is impossible for her ongoing conscious self. Munro does not simply tell a story from a particular perspective in time but includes the experience of the intervening years implicitly in the tones and attitudes of the narrating voice; and sometimes briefly intrudes as if from another reality, creating dimensional resonance like the echoes of memory within the reader's mind.[4]

These three observations are in their own way equally perceptive. Nor are they as different as they might first seem. A major assumption of all three readers is that *relativity* is the cornerstone of Munro's artistic method. Just as a good scrapbook is unified through the relative arrangement of pictures and mementoes, the structure of *Lives,* as Macdonald and Moss respectively claim, is defined by its *parallel* crises and *parallel* points of view. *Relativity* is a central aesthetic concept for Munro. Hers is a variegated art like the squares the mother crochets in all shades of purple in "Images." In relation to one another, they become an afghan and a visual whole. In *Lives* Munro chooses to juxtapose seemingly disconnected episodes, and places her fiction in a modern novelistic tradition. James Carscallen rightly connects *Lives* as a novel of seeing, in "which a girl is slowly learning what she must see to be a writer," to the tradition of the *Bildungsroman* [the novel of education], and matches it with Joyce's *A Portrait of the Artist As a Young Man:* "in it... there are great gaps in time between the chapters, and each of these chapters contains a variety of experiences that come together when the hero, or the reader, sees a meaning in them. This is the kind of story and the kind of book Munro tends to write..."[5] Some narrative order is also apparent in the novel-like *Who Do You Think You Are?,* though its structure would seem to be serendipitous, as Munro recollects the publication of the manuscript. In an interview with Carole Gerson, she explains that she originally submitted a text with two main characters, "six Rose stories and five Janet stories" but feeling these stories needed to be "linked" about one character, she halted publication until she was able to deliver a complete series of stories about Rose. From Munro's point of view, *Lives* is an "episodic novel," *Who Do You Think You Are?* "linked stories."[6] Although Munro exhibits some concern about ordering fiction in a traditional way, she develops narrative strategies in these "novels" that depend on *vision* and *correspondence* rather than explicitly linked chapters.

Both works approach, at least in a minimal way, the modern disruptive method of Joyce whose fictional form has been identified by French feminist critics as *l'écriture féminine,* in which the traditions of Western narrative are undermined. For Julia Kristeva, finding in psychoanalysis the concept of *jouissance*—the sexual pleasure that is associated with early experience of the maternal body—writers like Joyce and Mallarme re-experience playful maternal *jouissances* by constructing texts against the rules and regulations of conventional patriarchal writing. When attributed to women, *jouissance* is considered to be of a different order from the pleasure of men; women's *jouissance* carries with it the notion of fluidity and diffusion. For Kristeva's sister critics, Luce Irigaray and Hélène Cixous, the female libido is cosmic, her sexuality is autoerotic, the "geography of her pleasure" much more diversified than that of the male. Irigaray further comments on women's problematic relationship to (masculine) logic and language: "'She' is infinitely other in herself. That is undoubtedly the reason she is often called temperamental, incomprehensible, perturbed, capricious. . . . In her statements—at least when she dares to speak out—woman retouches herself constantly."[7] If sexuality is for the female contiguous and relative, then for Alice Munro as a female author writing the body, fictional "novelistic" structures built on correspondences and juxtapositions without ends and closure are much more natural texts than the traditional narratives of linear logic extended into climax.

Critics who concern themselves with *l'écriture féminine*, such as Cixous, have also stressed that the motives behind feminine literary texts have risen from libidinal rather than sociocultural forces,[8] and that the typical feminine gesture is to produce in order to bring about life and pleasure. Fractured texts of surrealist and avante-garde writing with puns, typographic breaks and coded allusion heighten *jouissance*.[9] Munro's fiction is not, as a canon, of the radical, structurally subversive avante-garde, but her fiction is rich with coded allusions, the names of her characters being the most obvious source of secret meaning.[10] By her sixth work, *The Progress of Love*, she is also moving in a more radical direction and demonstrating that her libidinal energy does not direct her to a garden of pleasurable maternal play. In this collection, the forms of her fictions break down from her earlier work in the fractured forms of discourse embedded in the texts. Songs and rhymes are playful, ironical, critical interjections and allusions as they always have been, but here there are now, more obvious, sudden passages of displaced interior thought, dialogue and self-talk. In "Circle of Prayer," this passage follows the objective description of Trudy throwing a jug at her daughter.

> You threw a jug at me that time. You could have killed me.
>> Not at you. I didn't throw it at you.
>> You could have killed me. (*Progress*, 255)

In "A Queer Streak," Violet has words settle on her, "like cool, cool cloths, binding her."

> It was not your purpose to marry him.
> It was not the purpose of your life

Not to marry Trevor. Not the purpose of your life. . . .
A golden opportunity.
What for?
You know what for. To give in. To give up. Care for them. Live for
others. (*Progress*, 232)

Conventional social structures and language bind Violet, just as conventional language and narrative structure are binding Munro. Nor is the
fractured form of discourse meant in play. In *The Progress of Love*, the maternal body is dying, the female libido struggling to bring about life and
pleasure, and insertions of this kind suggest a deadening, disintegrative,
schizophrenic state where language and reality split, and the ego shifts into
a self-enclosed space, without function in the external world.

As Violet's discourse demonstrates, libidinal force is not Munro's only
energy; her motivation is also sociocultural. The narrative "disordering" of
her fiction is indicative of writing the body, but her invention of Violet's
self-talk is also a rational, critical comment on the impact of the concept of
the maternal body on society, of the social dictum that women should live
for others: "You know what for. To give in. To give up. Care for them.
Live for others." Although Munro's sociocultural perspicacity may be lib-
idinally-inspired, on one level her diction displays feminist directed socially
real comment. Critical comments on sociosexual attitudes throughout all of
her work pinpoint Munro's fiction—on one level—as being the province of
the sociocultural observer and critic, and move her fiction in the direction
of social realism. Furthermore, her concern with the actual, with ordinary
women in childhood, adolescence, love, marriage, parenthood and infidel-
ity have long been the traditional subject matter of the realist writer.

Yet, as many critics have suggested, to label the form and genre of
Munro's fiction as realistic is highly misleading. "Actual" and "ordinary"
are dangerous descriptors of Munro's art. Her approximations of "real
life," her painstaking attention to the ordinary details of her physical environment, to every "layer of speech and thought, stroke of light on bark or
walls, every smell, pothole, pain, crack, delusion" (*Lives*, 210) is nothing
short of miraculous. As Catherine Sheldrick Ross observes,

[Munro] wants to present ordinary experience with such intensity that it
stands revealed as something extraordinary. This is why the stories are
always pushing toward that moment when "these things open; frag-

ments, moments, suggestions, open, full of power." When "these things open," the reader catches a glimpse of other levels of experience—powerful legendary shapes that lie behind the ordinary life...[11]

Ross's and Munro's language is revealing. The artist is giving birth, her fictions as I have previously discussed, opening, often in the mode of the romantic writer, into mythic subtexts which are filtered through her central voice of the physically and socially metamorphosing woman.

Clearly, the form of Munro's art is equal to onion-skinned layers of multiple meanings and levels of reality. Clearly, too, to interpret her art as simple extensions of reality or mirror reproductions of life-as-it-is-lived, to argue, with a Victorian sensibility, for a singular mimetic relationship between art and life, is highly suspect, particularly in the new age of postmodern writing and thinking. Recent critics have, in fact, veered off in another direction, emphasizing the nature of Munro's art at a more esoteric level of art *as art*. Louis MacKendrick prefaces *Probable Fictions: Alice Munro's Narrative Acts* with the following:

> The literary dimensions of her fictions, not their approximations of life-as-it-is, are the collective focus of this collection. Munro's stories retain probability and authenticity, while they also delight the attentive reader with their fictionality; their realities are constructs of rare skill and masterful invention, a facsimile at best. However "real" or "true to life" the residual impression of her writing remains, Munro's probable fictions firmly show that Art is necessarily grafted on from some other reality.[12]

The emphasis on fictive reality as "narrative acts" of another world, another dimension, has been the preoccupation of the postmodern "novelist" whose "novel" has become metafiction and who, as he writes about writing, sometimes believes that fictive language itself, metalanguage, has its own reality. Munro's work begins to be seen in this light by Tim Struthers when he stresses the reader's awareness of the "fictiveness of the fictions themselves" in *Something I've Been Meaning to Tell You*, concluding, "We recognize that we are reading not just complex psychological fiction but fiction that investigates itself, self-referring fiction, stories about storytelling-metafiction."[13] Similarly, Gerald Noonan in "The Structure of Style in Alice Munro's Fiction," sees considerations on art debated in the content and structure of Munro's fiction, including a challenging of art's ability to present real life, a challenge that is embedded primarily in structure.[14]

The recurring presence of the narrator-as-artist and Munro's self referring narrative acts predict yet another dimension of her art, one which broadens in the complexities of her later work, and invites further critical study. At the same time, Munro's fictions are not totally self-enclosed worlds entirely divorced from life-as-it-is-lived; thus they cannot be defined exclusively as the metafictions of the postmodern writer, particularly if postmodern is given to mean, as it does for many critics, beginning at a stage beyond realism. To insist Munro's fiction do is to encourage the possibility of ignoring the full female, feminine and feminist implications of her art. Her art is very much grafted on from the female experience and its social, psychological and physical realities. It is even arguable that the new literary directions of many writers towards probable, uncertain fictions, of stories within stories and subtexts underlying texts, of self-reflexive artistic fictional acts may be accredited to or influenced by the female imagination, born of the uneasy socially marginalized condition of being a woman, and the libidinal *jouissance* of women as defined by the French critics, that of diffusive sexuality which fictively retouches the self. The Canadian author and critic, Robert Kroetsch, affirms this influence when he answers the question on how feminism, which he sees as one of the genuine ideologies of the moment, has influenced contemporary male writers such as himself:

I think it goes back to a kind of unease that we can see almost as a subtext behind the ways we have of picturing the world or telling a story, even writing a poem; those ways were based on male supremacy, on premises that the male experience was somehow superior to the female experience. Upsetting that has made an unease in male writers which is very useful, a very good thing.[15]

| | | —

The short story is itself an interesting choice of form on Munro's part, and if there has been some doubt about how to assess and "name" Munro's longer prose works, there never has been any doubt about her talent with the short story: she has given the genre a new status. An earlier critic, Kildare Dobbs, claimed in a review of her third book,

"Alice Munro has it in her to become one of the best storytellers now writing"[16] and by 1983, Judith Miller prefaces *The Art of Alice Munro* with the following, "Alice Munro, with the 'recklessness' which Yeats tells us the creative writer must have, has shown us again and again the possibilities of the short story as literary genre."[17] Partly because of the precise lucidity of her style, Munro's natural narrative gift is the short story form. As a work in miniature, the short story, like a needlepoint square, demands flawless execution. While we can overlook artistic bumps and flaws in the novel because the whole may be greater than its individual parts, this is not true of the short story. In Munro's own storytelling language, it asks for "well-proportioned magic" and "no possibility anywhere of mistake" (*Dance*, 29).

Yet Munro, fashioning her novels by juxtaposing interludes, arranging them like the mother in "Walker Brothers Cowboy" who makes new clothes by cleverly cutting and matching pieces of old, climaxing each with an *epiphany*, a moment of *vision*, uses in her early work the same thread and stitching for both genres. Martin Knelman's observation that *Lives of Girls and Women* is constructed entirely out of "tiny moments of recognition and illumination"[18] is also true of Munro's early collections of short stories. In her later work, particularly *The Moons of Jupiter* and *The Progress of Love*, the fine craftsmanship remains but with Munro showing us even greater possibilities of the short story as a literary genre. Finely woven complex thematic patterns, encoded symbols, language and allusions compete with visionary moments and expand within the boundaries of the short story form. And here, too, there are gender implications. The Canadian author and critic David Helwig intuits this early on in Munro's career when he speculates about *Dance*: "Her art consists of an expansion inward, rather than outward, the discrimination of tone and language that makes a small event within a provincial society an important human matter. It is perhaps an essentially feminine art...[19] Expanding inwards, pushing the boundaries of the short story form to its limits, layering multiple meanings and experience within the form is very likely a "feminine art." The occupation of interior spaces is a physical reality for women and well understood as a favorite fictional stratagem for female authors. As Beth Harvor has claimed, the short story is Alice Munro's house.

If the short story form is a female choice of fictional house, what then of its architectural design and the materials Munro chooses to build with? Are these, too, sexual choices—and further, do they belong to a tradition of female authoring? A key question in feminist criticism today, one which touches Munro, is that of a female aesthetic. Does women's writing have its own unique character—is there a female or feminist mode of writing that consistently demonstrates psychological, textual and technical differences? The reclamation and study by feminist scholars of literary texts written by women suggests proof positive, the full scale studies of the genre of the Female Gothic being a case in point. Neither is the question itself a revolutionary new insight. As Elaine Showalter has pointed out, female aestheticism became a dominant intellectual issue for authors and critics during and after the suffrage campaigns and the First World War. Showalter also suggests the enormous difficulty of relating gender to fictional technique: "It is another thing altogether to talk about female style when you mean female content. And it is the hardest of all to prove that there are inherent sexual qualities to prose apart from its content. . ."[20]

The complete separation of style and content in Munro's art is ultimately not possible, nor perhaps even desirable given the gestalt of the artist's creative process. Neither is it possible here to answer the question of Munro's relationship to a contemporary female aesthetic in a full-scale way. The following analyses are meant only as opening observations on the gender related artistic concerns and techniques in Munro's literature, often advanced through female custom, situation and female physicality, and a possible source for comparative feminist studies. Other studies would seem to be well under way. Barbara Godard, for example, has made several points in "'Heirs of the Living Body': Alice Munro and the Question of a Female Aesthetic," including making the connection between patchwork quilting, the key image in many women's texts, and the intertextuality of narrative techniques in contemporary writing by women.[21]

There is necessarily some overlap from other chapters here. My central argument throughout has been that Munro's art is informed by being female. Her folk art and her irony are natural expressions of her gender, her use of landscape and place are bound up with the female psyche, and fictional form and content develop in a variety of ways from writing the body. Munro's "style" and "techniques," touched on in other chapters, are ostensibly the subject here, and can best be "got at" in a Munro-like manner through description and exploration of a list, a record if you will, of Munro's recurring aesthetic interests and those of her artist-protagonists. These include *pattern, time, light, image, symbol* and *language*.

| | | PATTERN

> *We leave my mother sewing under the dining-room light, making clothes for me against the opening of school. She has ripped up for this purpose an old suit and an old plaid wool dress of hers, and she has to cut and match very carefully...*
>
> ALICE MUNRO,
> "WALKER BROTHERS COWBOY"

Munro's affinity for the short story is natural because of her female "status" and was undoubtedly conditioned by her years of writing apprenticeship daily interrupted by the care of her children. The short story is, in fact, the most rewarding accessible fictional medium in a quick-paced modern world, particularly for both busy housewife-writer and reader. As a superior art in Munro's hands, it is also carefully *designed* and *tailored* in continuum with the ancient, domestic female arts and crafts tradition of the rural life, and Munro's own country background. Behind her art is the heritage of the "country producers" Mary R. Beard defines in *On Understanding Women*. Traditionally, rural women have known themselves as

country producers, all working... at the home, garnering harvests, cooking meals, minding offspring, caring for the sick beside their own hearths and answering calls from afar,... carding, dyeing, shaping clothes, blankets, rugs, transforming flax and wool into sheets, towels, garments, household decorations and comforts, spinning as they guard the flocks by day, knitting as they lead them to shelter by night, conceiving designs for textile ornamentation, embroidering, comparing work with neighbours, judging art, training maidens in domestic crafts... endlessly washing ... mending, combining and recombining old clothes into new with fancy stitching.[22]

We know that Munro is both crafty and economical with her fictional material, reusing *relatives*, the likes of the spinster aunts who themselves are imaged reworking old clothes in "The Peace of Utrecht." The designs of her stories are also carefully embroidered, often as an intricate pattern of visual connections. One of the most explicit and simpler examples of this is the short story "Red Dress—1946," which is *patterned* by the juxtaposition of primary colors, red and blue. As the narrative develops and the tension in the elementary psyche of the young heroine quickens, colors accrue a symbolic value. Red is the symbol of the girl's passion, of her mental uncertainty about her female maturation and of her sturdy, active physical good health, while blue is the symbol of fineness and delicacy, of female passivity, of childbirth and the conventional role of women.

The weaving of these colors through the story is so fine that the craft is largely unnoticed by the reader. Initiating an impression of *pattern* in process both psychologically and aesthetically, Munro quietly begins with descriptions of cut-up red velvet pattern pieces and a repetitive use of the word "pattern" itself. The mother, anxious for her daughter's social success at her first dance, is then described fitting her daughter's dress, colored blue, in her fitting position, as if in childbirth: "her legs were marked with lumps of blue-green veins. I thought her squatting position shameless, even obscene" (148). Lonnie, the narrator's less anxious and more conforming friend, is aligned with the mother; she is "light-boned, pale and thin; she had been a Blue Baby." Later, the mother will remember fondly her own dress "with royal blue piping down the front" (148). While Lonnie gets icy hands before an exam and will wear a pale blue crepe dress to the dance, the narrator herself in a ritual of preparation attempts to escape the forthcoming dance by symbolically and ironically, trying to catch a cold, to turn herself blue, "I pictured my chest and throat turning blue, the cold, greyed blue of veins under the skin" (151).

Stuffed finally into her own red velvet dress, she becomes an outrageous captive and unconventional golliwog doll, but we fear the dye is cast anyhow in favor of a stereotypic female role for her when Munro, at the conclusion of the story, has her offer the boy who rescues her and walks her home, half a Kleenex—which "probably has ink on it" (159).

Trailing color through the narrative is a technique for ordering and visualizing theme in "Red Dress—1946." It is, however, one of Munro's more elementary efforts. The novel *Who Do You Think You Are?* is of much more complex design, its structure conceived almost as a dressmaker's art. It is as if a dressmaker's tissue paper *pattern*, a transparency of connecting lines and images, rests on top of the narrative material. Certainly beneath it the reader apprehends the outlines of the corporeal, physical human shape, which, as a subliminal and almost surreal impression, is itself defined by the pattern of juxtaposed images of human anatomy and *relative* anatomically-shaped objects which provide the texture for the fictional cloth.

Blood is itself a thick and constant image, visualized first by Rose as a royal beating: "Someone knelt, and the blood came leaping out like banners" (1). A circulatory pattern persists through Rose's mother's description of her own impending death in the following clotting image: "I have a feeling that's so hard to describe. It's like a boiled egg in my chest with the shell left on" (1). Munro then subtly picks up this thread of biological, imagistic connections in the description of the mother's few possessions left to Rose—egg cups which carry veinlike designs: "She had nothing to go on but some egg cups her mother had bought, with a pattern of vines and birds on them, delicately drawn as with red ink; the pattern was beginning to wear away" (2). The pattern of egg shape and lung is further expanded by recurring references to such objects as scalded strawberries, the vegetable eggplant, and by a culminating description of the foundry disease which infects the coughing workmen on benches outside of Flo's store, as well as Rose's father: "When he realized they were out, there would be a quick bit of cover-up coughing, a swallowing. . ." (3). In "Royal Beatings" features of the human body emerge; in this first chapter, the lung and neck begin to surface, as do the body systems of circulation, respiration and digestion, the latter through the author's detailing of bathroom noises and preferred foods.

As the chapters develop, the anatomical *pattern* of a dressmaker's art persists. Hands appear in the hand of the father in "Royal Beatings" and in Flo's memory the hands, only, of the woman who fed her chocolate cake and may have had second sight; and in "Wild Swans" the groping, disembodied hand of the man on the train is a dramatic image. The head emerges, rotten, in the portrait of the old woman in "The Home," whose hat has melted into her hair; the breasts in the television production of *The Trojan Women*; Rose's navel is even lovingly addressed in love-making by the "Mad Satyr," Simon. Drops of blood congeal, too, in color pattern. Nancy and Rose sell their blood together. Patrick's birthmark is like a red tear.

Most importantly, the underlying human form is given substance by rhetorical and imagistic references to the somewhat shocking vision of beaten or mutilated meat, established early in the fiction in the beatings of Rose, Becky Tyde and her butcher father: "So they began to beat him and kept beating him until he fell. They yelled at him, *Butcher's meat!* and continued beating him while his nightgown and the snow he was lying in turned red" (8). Women in particular are tenderized and sliced by the butcher's hand. "Hold out your hand," the father says. The biological pattern blackens, turns ominous and gothic as Franny's face is smashed, Ruby Carruthers ages into mutilation and death with one breast gone, and by "Spelling," "every magazine rack in every town was serving up slices and cutlets of bare flesh" (185). This is a pattern of feminist protest at being the one without power, of feeling as Rose does, "ashamed of, burdened by, the whole physical fact of herself, the whole outspread naked digesting putrefying fact" that could make her "flesh... seem disastrous; thick and porous, grey and spotty" (173). Yes. Beyond this, however, is the overwhelming theme of woman's and man's mortality, and that acute universal apprehension about "how death would slice the day" (54).

A pattern of human physicality is also a peripheral design of *The Progress of Love,* advancing steadily from other volumes as one of feminist protest and despair. The fine, white skin of women, seen by Susan Brownmiller as one of the ideal attributes of femininity[23] surfaces as a topic and pattern in the lead story. Marietta is emotionally affected by the domestic German woman making strudel and connects this domestic art, uncomfortably, with skin: "The dough for the strudel hung down over the edge of the table like a fine cloth. It sometimes looked to Marietta like skin" (9). Phemie is similarly fascinated by her Aunt Beryl's futile attempts to recover skin and face, "patting the cream on her face with puffs of cotton wool, patting away until there was nothing to be seen on the surface" (17). The face of woman as feminine artifice is attacked by Munro who suggests the tyranny of its convention and reflects on the consequences of it being stripped away. The skin of the strudel, a "fine cloth" hangs perilously and is juxtaposed with the image of Marietta's mother, powerless in marriage, hanging herself. There is danger, too, when Beryl scrubs her face clean, revealing its reality: "... there was such a change that I almost expected to see makeup lying in strips in the washbowl, like the old wallpaper we had soaked and peeled. Beryl's skin was pale now, covered with fine cracks, rather like the shiny mud at the bottom of puddles drying up in early summer" (17). The pattern of stripped skin is extended beyond the body through the imagery of peeling wallpaper Phemie discovers in revisiting the family home. In her anger at not getting beyond the contemporary layer with its pattern of a life-sized naked couple when she attempts to peel it, she expresses Munro's protest against the sexual dynamics of femininity and culture that penalize the aging woman. "Why is it?" says a frustrated Phemie to her current middle-aged lover, "Just tell me, why is it that no man can mention a place like this without getting around to the subject of sex in about two seconds flat?" (27). At the same time, Munro is as frustrated as Phemie at not being able to see the underlying patterns of previous wallpapers, about not getting to the heart, fictively, of what women really are, as well as at having the layers of wallpaper adhere to one another the way that three generations of women have suffered the code of femininity.

In *The Progress of Love* there is also artistic anxiety about patterning itself, about taking control of the creative process. Physical body parts are strewn on the skins of these fictions, even as the skin of women is a constant motif. In "Lichen," female genitals and pubic hair are severed in a photographic image and defined as a kind of external fungus. In "Fits" a decapitated male head closes the story, the Weebles's bodies having been exploded as a surface mystery. In the tradition of female authors as studied by Susan Gubar,[24] Munro projects her female physical self as text, with skin, metaphorically the blank page. In "Lichen," the death of the reproductive life is equal to the severed genitals which are forced onto the page with anxious despair. In "Fits" Munro explodes bloodily onto the page, recreating the tyranny of the male master who, as Mr. Weebles, controls women—and the female artist's creativity—and takes her fictive revenge against him. As Gubar explains, for many twentieth century female authors, writing feels "as if the ink was pouring onto the page like blood";[25] the artistic process feels like helpless subjugation, like a woman's helplessness with a man; artistic creation feels like a violation, "a belated reaction to male penetration rather than a possessing and controlling."[26] Consequently, the female author often presents herself as a wounded victim. Like Charlotte Brontë who suffers from a "secret, inward wound" at the moment she feels "Ambition,"[27] Stella (and Munro) in "Lichen" "felt the old cavity opening up in her" (55). In "Miles City, Montana" Munro uses the image of the wounded deer, as Emily Dickinson did in several of her poems, to express artistic creation as violation. The pattern of peeled, wounded and pierced skin is a complex one in this collection; as exterior surface, skin is both the artist's parchment, written into the text as uneasy script, and the face of woman in society. Paradoxically and ingeniously, by using skin as the material of her pattern, Munro creates the illusion of easy artistry, of an undifferentiated smooth surface, with no obvious evidence of pattern at all.

Women sewing, crocheting, quilting, wallpapering, performing to pattern, themselves *patterning*, is a subtle feature of Munro's fiction. A domestic sensibility, designing by pattern informs the intricate, complex connection of colors, images, object correspondences and rhetorical references which hold her fictional material together.

| | | TIME

> *Memory is important in Alice Munro's writing, since she is obsessed by time.*
> **KILDARE DOBBS**

Underlying Munro's volumes is the romantic's sensibility to the passage of time. An elegiac apprehension, it contributes to the impression of poetry in her prose. Often she is quite explicit about time's authority, as in the lead story "Walker Brothers Cowboy" of her first volume. Here is the child's father describing geological time:

> Then came the ice, creeping down from the north, pushing deep into low places. Like *that*—and he shows me his hand with his spread fingers pressing the rock-hard ground where we are sitting. His fingers make hardly any impression at all and he says, "Well, the old ice cap had a lot more power behind it than this hand has.". . . The tiny share of time we have appals me, though my father seems to regard it with tranquillity. (*Dance*, 3)

The hand of time, its squeezing grip on individual life, is an obvious preoccupation. One could even argue that death is Munro's greatest protagonist. Lurking behind every page is accidental and untimely death or death by murder. Death is explicitly and repeatedly brought forward as fictional event. In such pseudo-ghost stories as "A Trip to the Coast" and "Something I've Been Meaning to Tell You" it is clearly the dominating force.

Technically, Munro best handles this emotional sensitivity to the evanescence of human time through point of view and imagery. The present of her narratives, given to the reader through the Proustian convention of "remembrances of times past," allows the lyric immediacy of the moment to be felt and importantly known because it is simultaneously apprehended as already lost. Her point of view engenders romantic art—as does her control of single or accumulated images. The scissors of the travelling scissorsman, Old Brandon, in "The Time of Death" is an effective, emotive image of time's cruel cut. The surplus of images of physical body parts in *Who Do You Think You Are?* conveys a similar impression. A good example of the way Munro is able to brilliantly invent a *vision* of human mortality can be seen in the following still-life portrait from "A Trip to the Coast." Beautifully arranged, with a slightly comic-macabre touch (the grandmother's teeth), its message concealed by the semblance of ordinary, daily life, its mood that of dry apprehension, it is a deathwatch passage which is vintage Munro:

> The kitchen was empty; the clock ticked watchfully on the shelf above the sink. One of the taps dripped all the time and the dishcloth was folded into a little pad and placed underneath it. The face of the clock was almost hidden by a yellow tomato, ripening, and a can of powder that grandmother used on her false teeth. Twenty to six. She moved towards the screen doors; as she passed the breadbox one hand reached in of its own accord and came out with a couple of cinnamon buns which she began to eat without looking at them; they were a little dry. (*Dance,* 174)

The cool, calculated style here is fine reminder that Munro, while melancholy about life's passage, is no maudlin sentimentalist.

Moreover, time, an emotional consideration, is also a complex intellectual and aesthetic one. One question she poses as the artist-narrator is that of the "pure" reality of the past when it is recorded through anecdote, history, myth and legend. Mary in "The Shining Houses" understands the "remembered episodes" of grandmothers, aunts and Mrs. Fullerton to be of a "pure reality that usually attaches to things which are at least part legend" (*Dance,* 19). In part, this is a Keatsian aesthetic affair. Like the figures on Keats' grecian urn, frozen in static beauty, Munro's fictional episodes are caught, aesthetically arranged life, "safely preserved in anecdote, in a kind of mental cellophane" (*Dance,* 193). While for Munro as artist, the present-in-past narrative can become pure and immortal art (beauty is truth, truth, beauty), the legendary past can also intrude in uncomfortable and objectionable ways into what seems the greater reality of the moment for Munro's heroines.

In *Lives*, the parable of the wise virgins from the Bible, the historical record of Christian beginnings and its collective memory is read to Del by Naomi's father and interpreted subjectively by each of them. Naomi's father reads the Bible by "fixing his pale eyes on your forehead as if he expected to find the rest of his thought written out there" (129), and Del rejects his interpretation of sexual caution because it contradicts her determination for sexual adventure in the present.

For Del in this situation, and for Alice Munro as female artist, the collective historical and mythological past as represented by the Bible is problematic because of its masculine bias. What is more reliable is individual female memory which is entirely subjective and changeling, but which, for Alice Munro, remains in each singular expression a kind of pure and unblemished Keatsian moment out of time. Although this search for reality through private memory is the fictional métier of modern psychological writers of both sexes, it is particularly attractive to the female author who necessarily gravitates to the highly subjective narrative forms which Alice Munro uses—autobiography, personal reminiscence and the diary-like letter.

It is also important to understand that the mythos of time itself expressed through narrative is perilous for the female writer. In *Time and the Novel*, Patricia Tobin explains that the old-fashioned novel was structured according to chronology—to time as progressive event. She further points out that its source is the history of man as genealogical time: "The identity and legitimacy of the individual" is guaranteed "through the tracing of his lineage back to the founding father, the family's origin and first cause. . . . He extends the paternal promise of purpose throughout his progeny, bestowing upon them a legacy that contains within this structural unity a whole history of meaning." Predictably, claims Tobin, this "same lineal decorum pervades the structure of realistic narrative."[28] Although Munro has a historical impulse and often structures her fiction continuously through events, she is uneasy with the masculine concept of linear time. Her longer narratives are episodic but each episode is its own separate illumination. Privately, she expresses anxiety about working with the novel form because, as she puts it, "I can't work in continuity because I don't actually feel it in life. I feel funny jumps."[29] Munro even intuitively attacks the masculine concept of time within her fiction. In *Lives*, at least, the historian Uncle Craig seems the archetypal Calvinist father described by Patricia Tobin as "keeping records of the past in linear shape, in precise chronological sequence of annals and history,"[30] and when his historical annals of Wawanash County are water-soiled, Del Jordan does not try to save them. Instead, she symbolically discards them with a "brutal, unblemished satisfaction" (*Lives*, 53).

Similarly, in the short story "The Office," Munro moves her narrative forward through the continuous events of realistic fiction, but by the conclusion of the story, its structure seems almost an ironic innuendo when the author acknowledges that it is the overbearing Mr. Malley who most naturally can "build up" the legends of his life (71) in a straightforward way, and that she, as female author, is not entirely comfortable with her act of fictional arrangement:

> I have not yet found another office. I think that I will try again some day, but not yet. I have to wait at least until that picture fades that I see so clearly in my mind, though I never saw it in reality—Mr. Malley with his rags and brushes... breathing sorrowfully, arranging in his mind the bizarre but somehow never quite satisfactory narrative of yet another betrayal of trust. While I arrange words, and think it is my right to be rid of him. (*Dance*, 73–74)

As with chronology, Munro cannot entirely dismiss genealogical time and its measure of family line, but she does substitute matriarchal female relationships for orderly, patriarchal descent. This is strongly presented in the lead story "The Progress of Love" in her sixth work. There is an amazing structural complexity in this story, as Munro, in a comparative study of three generations of mothers and daughters, juxtaposes time periods, disrupts—ironically—the linear, temporal notion of progress and establishes an emotional continuum between women. These time shifts, sometimes presented as vignettes within the last daughter's, Phemie's, "present" experience, also bring into relief and texturize the individual, emotional, sexual landscape of each woman as she exists within her own time-frame.

Here Munro is uncomfortable with traditional historical causality, with simple linear cause and effect, what Jane Gallop would characterize as "phallocentric economy."[31] Rather, the connections between female generations seem very often to be slippery collisions of affect. Female sexuality which "is of the register of touching, nearness, presence, immediacy, contact"[32] underlies Munro's historical approach.

Sometimes, through matriarchal relationship, the flux of nonlinear time is even expressly felt in Munro's writing. Witness May in "A Trip to the Coast" who, seeing her grandmother coming around the corner, feels a "queer, let-down feeling that seemed to spread thinly from the present moment into all areas of her life, past and future. It seems to her that any place she went her grandmother would be there beforehand: anything she found out her grandmother would know already" (Dance, 175). The concept of time at play here is both feminist and beyond feminism. Scientific and modern, it echoes Newtonian physics and the theory of relativity, and the premises that only relative motion can be detected or even defined, that time and space have no absolute significance. They depend on the motion of the observer. Here they depend on the grandmother who will die, not on the stilled May. In flight from temporality and death, Munro's instinct is to reserve motion, suspend action, place her characters even outside of gravity. Thus we have Flo as a still life and a space woman in Who Do You Think You Are? suspended in gravitational defiance between two chairs "like an airship, an elongated transparent bubble, with its string of diamond lights, floating in the miraculous American sky" (21).

The earthly world outside of scientific abstraction is, however, the greater reality in Munro's work as she acknowledges, by human necessity and romantic inclination, the continuity of life through organic time, which, cyclical and evolutionary, is also the biological imperative of the female body. The periodicity of "funny jumps" is what move the female animal through her creative cycle and Nature's time. Consequently, the "flow" of life, of living organic substances and metamorphic nature is felt through Munro's fictional structures. It is experienced in the canon of her fiction to date in the stages of the growth of the authorial persona from childhood on. It is experienced in the double, even triple, vision of the several Del Jordans projected in point of view and discribed by John Moss in the passage quoted at the beginning of this chapter. The circular pattern of Del's memory, like ripples after a stone is thrown into water, is also the shape of time in Who Do You Think You Are? In this fiction, there is the careful meeting of an updated present (which is already past) and the "immediate" past at the "end" of each chapter but one, the dreamlike "Wild Swans." The continuous, organic, circular view is also expressed in such temporal signposts in her fiction as seasonal change ("the rhythm of life in

Jubilee is primitively seasonal " (*Dance*, 194))), in the biological processes of animal and human life embedded in her fiction, and in the repetitive return of her heroines to their first places.

It is most noteworthy in her strong fictional attachment to autobiography and its posture of first person narration, a narrative formula, which, according to J. Hillis Miller, acutely reflects a circular concept of time. This is the way Miller describes the autobiographical process:

> The protagonists live their lives in ignorance of the future. The narrator speaks from the perspective of the end. The reader enjoys both these points of view at once. He experiences the novel as the reaching out of the protagonist's point of view towards the narrator's point of view, as if at some vanishing point they might coincide.
>
> This reaching out towards completeness, in which the circle of time will be closed, is the essence of human temporality. . . . [33]

For the female writer, historical and genealogical time may hold little truth. What is most real to her may be what Barbara Godard identifies as "'crone-ology', youth and age contained within a cyclical whole."[34] What then will the female writer like Alice Munro do to provide *order* in her fiction and the lives of her female protagonists? She may acquiesce to the tradition of chronological time in conventional, realistic narrative, as Alice Munro does in an early piece like "An Ounce of Cure" yet all the while speculating on and defensively measuring her fiction as she imposes fictional order on absurd life:

> What was it that brought me back into the world again? It was the terrible and fascinating reality of my disaster; it was *the way things happened*. . . . But the development of events on that Saturday night—that fascinated me; I felt that I had had a glimpse of the shameless, marvelous, shattering absurdity with which the plots of life, though not of fiction, are improvised. (*Dance*, 87–88)

She may, like Munro, listen to the rhythms of her own body, and measure life through fiction in organic stages. Even though she may be unable to shatter or rearrange time in fiction in completely radical or unorthodox ways, as some contemporary male writers are doing, she may not need to. Time as flux, with amorphous boundaries, may satisfy her. And if she is the genuine artist that Alice Munro is, she may even in her novels about women prove herself a visual genius by creating an impression of the time-lapse camera capturing the growth of an artistic persona and a variety of female characters, not always in full, fleshed out succession, but from a variety of imaginative and distinctive angles.

| | | LIGHT AND IMAGERY

> *I loved light. . . . When I saw the car lights sweep my ceiling I got up to look down on them through the slats of my blind. I don't know what I thought I was going to see.*
> ALICE MUNRO,
> "HOW I MET MY HUSBAND"

> *Among branches*
> *a bird lands fluttering*
> *a soft gray glove*
> *with a heart.*
> ROO BORSON

The play and pattern of light and dark, of shadow and shade, is one of Munro's more significant visionary techniques. Even in a prosaic story like "An Ounce of Cure" she manages a moment of poetry when the narrator puts out the lights and puts on the record player—"The curtains were only partly drawn. A street light shone obliquely on the windowpane, making a rectangle of thin dusty gold, in which the shadows of bare branches moved, caught in the huge sweet winds of spring. It was a mild black night when the last snow was melting" (*Dance*, 79). Like an expert photographer, Munro very often arranges black and white contrast (such is our visual-emotional impression of Et and Char in "Something I've Been Meaning to Tell You"), or subtly withholds or floods her subjects with light. In her earlier work, as above, the result can be merely a charming or picturesque still, or an illuminated, mysterious three-dimensional image of magic realist proportion as with "Images."

This interest and obsession with light also has feminist implications. Many of Munro's earlier heroines live behind windows boarded up, or with curtains drawn, windows with blinds which obscure or fracture light. In this posture they are both the watchful passive female artist outside the active reality of life and the entrapped, repressed isolated Victorian heroine who inhabits a shady, limbolike interior world. As fractured psyches living in the half-light, they—Miss Marsalles, old Et, Dorothy, Alva, even the Spanish lady ("I ask for a gin and tonic. The glass catches the sunlight, reflecting a circle of light on the white mat. This makes the drink seem pure and restorative to me, like mountain water") (*Something*, 146) are glassed in genteel characters, outside the clear daylight of self-directed masculine adventure and expression. Some of Munro's farm women obviously do better than her more Victorian heroines. Rural heroines like Nora Cronin and Mary McQuade are painted turning their faces to the sun with a measure of brilliant light and "manly" independence. Del Jordan, of course, in the conclusion of her novel, attempts to walk out of the "leafy shade" (200) and the gothic box into "real" life and "radiant" light (210). Rose, it would seem, has succeeded in having done so, although as a television personality, she still remains a character within the box and behind the glass.

Although the girl-woman standing at the window or peeping Alice in Wonderland-like through the keyhole is a conventional Victorian image of woman, it is a historical posture which contributes to, perhaps even commands, Munro's visual talents and her imagistic imagination. She is not primarily a symbolic writer until her later work, and would have difficulty in being conventionally so if she is to remain faithful to her female reality, since a great many poetic symbols and symbolic patterns are emotively charged with masculine values. On the other hand, Munro's images are neither dead nor disaffecting. If they are symbolic at all, they may seem to Munro to be private, found, contextual symbols, yet some may even be particularly compelling because they also stand as metaphors for a collective female imagination or experience. At the very least, there are certain recurring images in Munro's art which feminist critics have discovered in other female writers.

One of these is glass itself. Grace Stewart explains:

The female artist has an affinity for images of imprisoning glass—the bell jar, the bottle, the glass vase, or the spun glass illusion. Since women traditionally depend on others for support and long for approval of sexual identity, the image they project to society is of paramount importance. They live in glass houses. The artists who break out crash against the pane or cut themselves on the glass, destroying their artistic dexterity. Those who don't escape suffocate under the bell jar.[35]

Some epiphanic and dramatic climaxes of distraught women in Munro's fiction depend on such glassy images. The pink glass bowl shatters in "The Peace of Utrecht" with Maddy unable to claim her life. Dorothy's disturbed vision of the new woman and the new morality in "Marrakesh" is of silent, locked-in figures in a lighted glassed-in porch. Beyond these specific images of glass, Munro's major impulse as a writer is to struggle in an investigative, feminist way with the *face of things* and what lies beyond their ordinary, superficial realities.

Bird imagery is also peculiar to women writers and to Munro. Ellen Moers confides that of "all the creatures—the flowers, the insects, the cats—that women writers use to stand in, metaphorically, for their own sex," it is their birds who have made the greatest impression on her. She further speculates that women may be particularly fond of birds because "they are a species of the littleness metaphor by which women define themselves" or "because they are tortured as little girls are tortured" or because they are "beautiful and exotic creatures" and "universal emblems of love."[36] Munro does use birds as some of her most compelling images. There are at least two in *Lives*. One is that of Pork Child's peacocks who preview Del's own springtime initiation into sex; with a dollop of female irony and aggression, Munro shows Del's contradictory emotions towards masculine sexuality and its grandeur:

> The hens were easily forgotten, the sullen colors of their yard. But the males were never disappointing. Their astonishing, essential color, blue of breasts and throats and necks, darker feathers showing there like ink blots, or soft vegetation under tropical water. One had his tail spread, to show the blind eyes, painted satin. The little, kingly, idiotic heads. Glory in the cold spring, a wonder of Jubilee. (*Lives*, 132)

Through the bird metaphor, Del delivers a slap towards the male of the species—who is beautiful, but also blind and idiotic. Later, in the loss of her virginity she herself becomes the bird through an image which startles her female reader into wariness. After viewing in the morning light the place of her affair where the peonies have been broken and her blood has dried on the ground, she creates a fiction for her mother about the blood, explaining, "I saw a cat there tearing a bird apart. It was a big striped tom, I don't know where it came from" (189).

In *Who Do You Think You Are?* Rose, too, thinks and experiences in terms of birds. The plastic swan napkin-holder on Flo's kitchen table which disturbs her is the cheap domestic, lower-class equivalent of the Grand Duck middle-class lifestyle that Jocelyn, Rose's friend, experienced as a child. By the time she was thirteen, the author explains, with tongue-in-cheek irony, "Jocelyn had probably the largest collection in the world of rubber ducks, ceramic ducks, wooden ducks, pictures of ducks, embroidered ducks" (103). The duck collection is obviously symbolic of female role, of a predictable, cute dream for a cute daughter by a middle-class mother who had these "rotten coy little names for all the parts of your body" (105). Female is further associated with bird when later, Rose, divorced and with a a a lover, exercises a concubine's imagination when she envisions herself in her Emperor's nightingale outfit, a "caftan-nightgown sort of robe with a pattern of birds on it, in jewel colours" (146); still later, she will move from feeling as "light and welcome as a humming bird" (158) to dreaming of a Victorian birdcage, an image which is painfully evocative to female authors and their readers. Stimulated by the tour of the Home, in which she will put Flo, Rose dreams,

> Someone was taking her through a large building where there were people in cages. Everything was dim and cobwebby at first, and Rose was protesting that this seemed a poor arrangement. But as she went on the cages got larger and more elaborate, they were like enormous wicker birdcages, Victorian birdcages, fancifully shaped and decorated. (*Who*, 188)

Ellen Moers perfectly expresses the female significance and authority of Munro's use of the caged bird image when she points out, "From Mary Wollstonecraft's *Maria*—to Brontë's *Jane Eyre*—to Ann Frank's *Diary of a Young Girl*—I find that the caged bird makes a metaphor that truly deserves the adjective female. And I am not at all surprised by George Eliot's and Virginia Woolf's delight in Mrs. Browning's version of the caged bird metaphor in *Aurora Leigh*.[37]

In female writers, the bird metaphor as symbolic of "free flying" also serves to underline aspirations to female independence; and this is used with remarkable skill by Munro for Rose in the dreamlike sequence "Wild Swans." As she often does, Munro introduces us to the thematic idea of the episode in the first line of "Wild Swans" when she has Flo issue a warning about being trapped into sexual bondage: "Flo said to watch out for White Slavers" (56). As a prelude to the sexual encounter of the young Rose with the minister on the train, Munro then includes a minuscule version of the same tale in the black romantic story of the trapping undertaker of the small town who purportedly lures young women into his hearse and who in mild weather signals his intention to capture fair, swanlike maidens with the imagistic refrain: "Her brow is like the snowdrift/Her throat is like the swan" (58).

Building on the legendary fairy-tale character of the gothic undertaker and his virgin swans, Munro goes on to explore the implications of modern sexual life for women in her bird imagery when Rose's orgasmic climactic moment with the minister is conveyed through the liberating image of wild swans:

> The gates and towers of the Exhibition Grounds came to view, the painted domes and pillars floated marvelously against her eyelids' rosy sky. Then flew apart in celebration. You could have had such a flock of birds, wild swans, even, wakened under one big dome together, exploding from it, taking to the sky. (*Who,* 64)

What Rose is experiencing is sex without love, and the fantastic freedom in its pleasure for the new woman. The old entrapped swan housed in the romantic, womb-tomb metaphor of old, the undertaker's hearse "'Some women are taken in,'" she [Flo] said. . . . She liked to speculate on what the hearse was like inside. Plush. Plush on the walls and the roof and the floor. Soft purple, the color of the curtains, the color of dark lilacs" (58) is replaced by the image of Rose as the wild swan in miraculous, adventurous, graceful free flight.

There are many images which are more natural to women than to men, including those which evolve as extensions of her female anatomy and childbearing function. They include the bell, the egg, the shell or, as with the description of the undertaker's hearse, womblike interiors. Others identified by Ellen Moers are the precious box—the jewel case, and the small or exquisite object such as the jewel, the pebble, the coin, got at in a Freudian way very often through the image of the deep sea diver. In Munro's work, these prove to be some of her best, most breath-taking images.

In "A Trip to the Coast" (a story filled with birds), "the sky was pale, cool, smoothly ribbed with light and flushed at the edges, like the inside of a shell" (*Dance*, 174). In the same story Hazel, bound for a life of sleazy spinsterhood, is visualized in a sad, lyrical moment: "Her bleached head disappeared into the skirt of her dress with a lonesome giggle like the sound of a bell rung once by accident, then caught" (180), and the young girl May feels the sudden new, unexplored power of her own female hostility which she means "to hold for a while and turn it like a gold coin in her hand" (185). In "The Found Boat" the child Eva, riding the Flood, momentarily counters a masculine Calvinist imagination by supposing, in a visionary way, to be "riding in a Viking boat—Viking boats on the Atlantic were more frail and narrow than this log on the Flood—and they had miles of clear sea beneath them, then a spired city, intact as a jewel irretrievable on the ocean floor" (*Something*, 103); and in *Who Do You Think You Are?* Rose's misgivings about marrying the conservative, but rich, Patrick are expressed in her image of his love like an egg, not of a creative, fruitful kind, but of a heavy, masculine and wealthy variety: "It was as if he had come up to her in a crowd carrying a large, simple, dazzling object—a huge egg, maybe, of solid silver, something of doubtful use and punishing weight—and was offering it to her, in fact, thrusting it at her, begging her to take some of the weight of it off him" (79). Similarly in "Labor Day Dinner" in *The Moons of Jupiter* the young girl Angela has a creation vision of her father scooping out sand and her mother rolling into the hole: "When it is finished her mother rolls over, giggling, and fits her stomach into it. In her stomach is Eva, and the hollow is like a spoon for an egg" (148).

The recognition of female/feminine imagery brings us to a larger and crucial question about gender metaphor and the art of Alice Munro—a question which is already under careful study by other feminist critics; that is, if certain images and imagistic patterns are most natural to the female author as extensions of female anatomy, what of the world at large as depicted by her? In particular, does the topography of her landscapes suggest her own physicality? This is particularly relevant to Munro as a "regional" writer. For Ellen Moers "the female landscape knows no nationality or century"; it is very often sexually suggestive, even by the names imposed on it. She mentions George Eliot's and George Sands's inventions, the Black Valley, the Divide, the Red Deeps.[38] I would not argue that all of Munro's landscapes need to be seen primarily from this perspective, but some very definitely convey sexual content. The creation history expressed by the father in "Walker Brothers Cowboy" to the female child, for example, in the imagery of hand and ice cap gouging deep places (*Dance,* 3) is suggestive of sexual encounter. Similarly, the child exploring the Wawanash River in "Images" interprets the waterscape as the thrusting of an arrow into slippery banks:

> Then we went along the river, the Wawanash River, which was high, running full, silver in the middle where the sun hit it and where it arrowed in to its swiftest motion. That is the current, I thought, and I pictured the current as something separate from the water, just as the wind was separate from the air and had its own invading shape. The banks were steep and slippery and lined with willow bushes, still bare and bent over and looking weak as grass. (*Dance,* 36–37)

Perhaps more singularly female features of Munro's landscapes are those images reminiscent of female anatomy, of attractive, dark, impenetrable bushy areas. The landscape is "black, hot, thick with thorny bushes, and dense with insects whirling in galaxies" for Del Jordan (2) in *Lives.* The earth-mother Stella's domain in "Lichen" includes "a jungle of wild blackberry bushes," (*Progress,* 32), a bushy area she steps out of wearing nothing underneath her clothes. For Mary, Mrs. Fullerton's chaos in "The Shining Houses," is an "uncut forest and a jungle of wild blackberry and salmonberry bushes" (*Dance,* 24). Certainly in this last story, the geometric designs of streets and boxy houses is seen as male order; female reality is "dark, enclosed, expressing something like savagery in... disorder" (24). In any case, Munro seems very much aware that the external world can be interpreted through one's subjective state and physical condition. Rose's interpretation of townscape at a moment of sexual climax in "Wild Swans" is just such a classic occasion.

> She could not believe this. Victim and accomplice she was borne past Glassco's Jams and Marmalades, past the big pulsating pipes of oil refineries. They glided into suburbs where bedsheets, and towels used to wipe up intimate stains flapped leeringly on the clotheslines, where even the children seemed to be frolicking lewdly in the schoolyards, and the very truckdrivers stopped at the railway crossings must be thrusting their thumbs gleefully into curled hands. (*Who,* 64)

Light and image are not necessarily sexually connotative words, sexually determined ideas or even ideals. As Del Jordan discovers in *Lives*, the meaning of the biblical parable of the wise virgins who carried lamps without oil and missed their chance, simply meant prudence to her, not sex as it did to Naomi's father. On the other hand, the mythological image of the lady with the lamp is a long-standing one attributed to women, whether as well-oiled virgin in the Bible or as such a real, active modern nursing heroine as Florence Nightingale. Similarly, the woman in the looking glass has become a literary sexual stereotype, at least in the Victorian imagination. In the Tennysonian heroine, the Lady of Shalott, and in Lewis Carrol's Alice, we discover the Victorian female attempting to escape her social place and face through the glass. These images of women demonstrate the connections often made between *light* and *its reflection* and the state of being female—connections Munro herself, however unconsciously, also makes in her fiction. Such a fascination contributes to her extraordinary skill as a *visual* artist.

| | | SYMBOL

> *You mean why has he got two hats on? I don't know. I honestly don't know. Maybe he forgot.*
>
> ALICE MUNRO,
> "MONSIEUR LES DEUX CHAPEAUX"

In the course of Munro's art, visionary techniques, such as the use of imagery, have become progressively more complex as visualized objects have become coded, often allusively, with multiple meanings. The critic W.R. Martin senses this development occuring in *The Moons of Jupiter* where he sees some of the new force and resonance of these stories coming from a "fuller command of allegory and symbol."[39] For Martin, poetic symbols now have a new importance, indicated, for example, in story titles, and coinciding with a detached omniscient point of view.

> Whereas before the titles tended to announce themes, such as "Mischief" and "Providence," or point to central incidents such as "Royal Beatings" and "Spelling," now one finds titles like "The Stone in the Field," "Dulse," and "The Moons of Jupiter" which contain meanings that defy complete definition: they name objects that are symbols. Alice

Munro probably aspired to symbolism from the beginning. She has said: "Things are symbolic but... their symbolism is infinitely complex and never completely discovered." When we come to stories such as "Prue," "Labor Day Dinner" and "Mrs. Cross and Mrs. Kidd," we shall see that Alice Munro evolves a mode that dispenses altogether with a reflector such as Del or Rose, and uses detached omniscience in the narration. It therefore relies almost wholly on the value of image, symbol and dramatic incident.[40]

A peculiar feminist feature of Munro as a symbolic writer is her profound attachment to objects and the wonder and the pleasure with which she presents them. Hélène Cixous, as one of several feminist critics, has considered this empathetic attentiveness to objects a demonstration of idliberated female discourse in contemporary female authors. Cixous celebrates, for example, the Brazilian writer Clarice Lispector "for an extraordinary female attentiveness to objects, the ability to perceive and represent them in a nurturing rather than dominating way."[41] It is true that one cannot read any short story by Alice Munro without being moved by the poetry of the objects of her prose. Like the girl children in "Day of the Butterfly" discovering the exquisite pleasure of the jewelled tin butterfly in the Cracker Jack box, the Munro-reader is captivated by the poetic image-object in story after story. Munro's allusive attachment of meaning to objects, too, is of the playful, secretive avant-garde sensibility assigned by French critics to *l'écriture féminine*.

In her last two collections of stories, Munro is more seriously the symbolic or emblematic writer. Emblem would seem to be a much more appropriate term because Munro's objects are often richly feminine in source—poetically *decorative* in the fashion of girls and women—even as they are imbued with symbolic meaning which is often of a feminist nature. "The Moon" in "The Moon in the Orange Street Skating Rink," for example, is an unforgettable light *fixture*, a found, poetic domestic emblem of what women are and what the senior Edgar will become for his wife Callie, a fixture or doll at her affectionate disposal. As Edgar is connected with the moon, he is connected with the doll, imagized in the dough dolls manipulated by a woman on television (*Progress*, 159). The doll itself is an image and symbol of female and femininity; it is the decorative object that women are required to be and an extension of mothering. Tracing the image of the doll in the work of Margaret Atwood, Sylvia Plath and Katherine

Mansfield, Susan Gubar concludes that "the heroines of women's fictions have played with dolls to define themselves."[42] As Callie, in old age, continues to play with Edgar as she did when they first met, she takes control and fulfills the prophecy of her power in sexual relationships when she got on the train, a young girl in boy's clothes, to become an adventurer with Sam and Edgar: "At that moment, he [Sam] saw power—Callie's power, when she would not be left behind—generously distributed to all of them" (*Progress*, 157). There is an ironical feminist social reversal in Callie's power when Edgar becomes, after his stroke, the "polished ornament" (158), the old doll, dressed and undressed by his wife. Still, from a feminist point of view, Callie continues to enact the maternal ritual; her life is static: she is in "a sorry female state" (160). In this fiction of complicated intersecting and coded symbols which is characteristic of Munro's later work, there are obviously no pat resolutions, no easy conclusions to sexual and human affairs.

The moon in the Orange Street skating rink, like many of Munro's emblems, also, finally, has a range of meanings. It is not only a fixture, it is an illumination on moments of what seem to be pure happiness in life, a light on life's most memorable, rationally unfathomable, events: "The moment of happiness he [Sam] shared with them remained in his mind, but he never knew what to make of it. Do such moments really mean, as they seem to, that we have a life of happiness with which we only occasionally, knowingly intersect? Do they shed such light before and after that all that has happened to us in our lives—or that we've made happen—can be dismissed?" (160). Edgar himself, as fixture and as doll becomes an emblem of this very thing when Callie concludes the narrative with "He's happy" (161).

As Munro's work matures, images and objects become symbols laden with meaning which interconnect allusively and add even greater depth to her stories.

| | | LANGUAGE

> *What an examination of the texture of her [Munro's] prose*
> *reveals, in particular, is the centrality of paradox and the ironic*
> *juxtaposition of apparently incompatible terms or judgements:*
> *"ironic and serious at the same time," "mottoes of godliness*
> *and honor and flaming bigotry," "special, useless knowledge,"*

"tones of shrill and happy outrage," "the bad taste, the heartlessness, the joy of it." This stylistic characteristic is closely related to the juxtaposition, in the action, of the fantastic and the ordinary, her use of each to undercut the other.

HELEN HOY

Munro's use of language can be seen to be operating on at least two, although not always separate, basic levels. First there is the language of her folk or ordinary characters and, second, there is the contextual language of the artist-persona. Popular idiom and dialectal phrases, particularly Canadian Irishisms, provide realistic texture to her dialogue. At the same time, the language of the artist, as Helen Hoy points out, is characterized by paradox and ironic juxtaposition,[43] and serves to underline the tension between the fantastic and the ordinary, or romance and realism, in Munro's fiction. It insists, too, on the concept of the *relativity* of human experience. This handling of language as contradiction and paradox is also read by feminist critics in textual analysis as part of the struggle of female authors to invent a female language and aesthetic. Rachel Blau Duplessis succinctly generalizes: "the 'female aesthetic' will produce artworks that incorporate contradiction and nonlinear movement into the heart of the text."[44] In Munro's art, language is certainly a philosophical and aesthetic problem which is special to the artist as female—a problem which is most acutely felt by the heroine Del Jordan in *Lives*.

One of the oldest themes in the novel and an obvious aesthetic and philosophic canon of the fictionalizer is that language is the creator of reality. Del's natural impulse is that of the artist: to penetrate the true design of things, to create order out of chaos, to shape the world through the artistic medium of language. Del not only reads everything that she can get her hands on, she listens carefully to all that is said in an effort to make connections between the spoken word and its ultimate reality. She begins, as all thoughtful children do, by exploring the mysterious possibilities of these connections. "Heart *attack*" she wonders, about the cause of Uncle Craig's death: "It sounded like an explosion, like fireworks going off, shooting sticks of light in all directions, shooting a little ball of light—that was Uncle Craig's heart, or his soul" (*Lives*, 39).

As she develops as a female, she recognizes that the social environment is an untrustworthy disseminator of values and that its supposed objective truths do not interpret her reality. She relies instead on her own subjectivity, depending on literature and language to help her create some order. Finally, what she comes to realize is that language itself in its subjectivity and limitedness is perilous. The language of the Bible is interpreted differently, weighted by various ministers; and in her physical relationship with Garnet French, she understands that words will destroy their communication—they are the enemy.

Nor can the conjunction of language and woman and artist be overlooked in this fiction, for when Del destroys in fear the article in the newspaper which claims, negatively, "For a woman, everything is personal; no idea is of any interest to her by itself, but must be translated into her own experience; in works of art she always sees her own life, or her daydreams" (150), she is experiencing a distrust of language because of its biased interpretation of her as a woman, and repelling a statement which unfairly denies her credibility as a female artist because she may be inclined to interpret reality subjectively. Indeed, as a woman, as the *Other*, her own subjective states are all that she has to rely on.

"Fiction," says Barbara Godard, "is the exploration of the linguistic body traversed by the solid body of the writer in an effort to free woman's body from the male fantasies which have dispossessed her." For Godard, "Munro is in quest of a body experienced by women as subject of their desires not as object of men's desire and of the words and literary forms appropriate to this body."[45] Joseph Gold, too, discovers a feminist consciousness in Munro's fiction struggling to find a language to express itself, including the use of the double entendre as a means of both satire and female expression. In the seduction of Rose on the train in *Who Do You Think You Are?* "Rose's orgasm blows up Ontario. The very language of this episode, its clearly coded disguise, is itself a satiric commentary on the requirement of genteel expression."[46]

Obviously, Munro, or any author who is deliberately evoking the female imagination, has the problem of a culturally shaped, a male shaped, linguistic body as a mode of communication. Clearly, too, Munro's language is often ironically coded with a layer of meaning meant primarily as female expression. In "Bardon Bus" from *The Moons of Jupiter*, clues to the quest itself for appropriate language are tucked into the narrative. The anthropologist lover of the narrator investigates language groups and brings them home to the woman—"word derivations; connections he found" (113). The narrator herself is operating by a code, calling her lover X—"The letter

X seems to me expansive and secretive. And using just the letter, not need-
ing a name, is in line with a system I often employ these days" (112). X is
coded with several connotations, all of which define the narrator's conception of self and attitude towards the man. The mark X represents the signa-
ture of an illiterate person (read woman has no language of her own); X is
the symbol of a kiss (read physical love); X is the symbol of an unknown
number (read the inaccessibility of the man); X is the symbol of Christ or
Christian (read the connection between the narrator's concept of love and
its Christian connection, introduced early in the hymn—"He's the Lily of
the Valley/The Bright and Morning Star./He's the Fairest of Ten Thou-
sand to My Soul" (111). Finally, X means to delete, to cancel—to obliter-
ate. All of Him and his language and his love are wiped out by the narrator
and by Munro in a single coded stroke. Earlier in her fiction Munro implied
that the comprehension that language cannot be absolutely relied on may
be the special knowledge of the female artist; certainly, it is the final, positive step in Del's maturation both as a human being and a writer. Her last
significant experience is when Bobby Sherriff, the man who has been in the
mental asylum, asks her in for tea, and in his moment of parting, wishes
her luck. And then "he did the only special thing he ever did for me... he
rose on his toes like a dancer, like a plump ballerina. This action, accompa-
nied by his delicate smile... seemed also to have a concise meaning, a stylized meaning—to be a letter, or a whole word, in an alphabet I did not
know" (211). The special message Del divines from Bobby is that in the
dance of the sexes, language is a private and mysterious matter which invites, compels the best translation possible by the female artist who, above
all, is acutely aware of the vagaries and perilousness of *the word*. By "Bardon Bus," however, the investigation has become much more fulsome.
Munro continues to do what Barbara Godard anticipates of Del Jordan,
"Her work will be in alphabets and fictions as well as in matter. She will
work hard to explore the possibilities for language to relate to reality. To do
so she will dissect and demystify, rewrite tradition to include women's lives
while sounding out the limits of language. A, alphabet, origin. Origin in
language... "[47] The origin of women in language.

| | | —

Clearly, contemporary feminism has altered the modes of perceiving of
writing women and their readers. If, in the past, women have been fictively

defined in terms of male experience and discourse as the fixed and objectified other, in the present, armed with this knowledge, women are struggling to be reinstated within the text as autonomous subject. Writing the
female body as subject and technique, writing the linguistic body as gender
coded wordplay, the female author desires, and dares to desire, to be self-
made as woman and as artist. Certainly Alice Munro is of this order. In her
fiction, woman's acculturated distance from her own sexuality and the un-
dervaluing of the feminine role she has been asked to play are both well
understood, and in an attempt at revisioning and redressing the female self
in fiction, Munro authors such aesthetic interests as pattern, time, light,
imagery and symbol with female, feminine and feminist valuing.

Furthermore, by juxtaposing relative visions of diverse female characters
and *relations*, by expanding the parameters of the short story genre in the
likes of the lead fiction in *The Progress of Love* to include intersecting female generations: grandmother, mother, daughter, Munro has begun to
develop the somewhat *novel* perception of not only female self as history,
but also the self *within* a diffuse, sexual historiography of touching and re-
touching female. As France Théoret explains, many women who are writing now are concerned with form and they "want to place themselves right
from the start, outside the unary definition of the subject." The body of
Munro's work as "novel"-in-progress, her mixed media of often interre-
lated, multilayered, autobiographical "short stories" of female life illustrate, as well, Théoret's conclusion that "this women's writing has not
found a name for a multiple form of writing which splinters the concept of
literary genre."[48]

Beyond the female self, there is, of course, the male body of physicality,
language, and patriarchal place and space which women and the female artist are struggling with, and often against. This is the dance of the sexes, a
central metaphor in the art of Alice Munro. Although Alice Munro protests
mightily that women are disadvantaged, wronged, and "setup" (*Progress*,
31) in the traditional positioning of male-lead and female-led dance, she offers no pat answers about the steps to be taken. Instead, she continues to
wonder, in her characteristic way, at the amazing paradoxes of the dance itself, its incredible fictions, its future possibilities. The knowledge that the
reader finally gleans from the fiction of Alice Munro is that in art, as in
life, the dance of the sexes is a changeling, complicated and above all, a per-
versely inviting affair.

| | | NOTES

INTRODUCTION

1 An interview with Alice Munro, February 15, 1981.
2 Simone de Beauvoir, *The Second Sex*, trans. H.M. Parshley (New York: Alfred A. Knopf, 1968), p. 70. All further references in the text are to this edition.
3 Alice Munro, *Something I've Been Meaning to Tell You* (Toronto: The New American Library of Canada, Ltd., 1975), p. 36. All further references in the text are to this edition.
4 Munro, *Lives of Girls and Women* (Toronto: The New American Library of Canada Ltd., 1974), p. 146. All further references in the text are to this edition.
5 Psychoanalysis has stressed in the past the inherent differences between man and woman due to sexual physiology and function. The sex act for man is outgoing and consequently, all male activity has about it this quality of external performance. Women are acted upon in the sex act and after giving birth to children, breastfeed; therefore, woman is naturally passive and nurturing. See *Modern Woman: The Lost Sex*, eds. Ferdinand Lundberg and Marynia F. Farnham (New York and London: Harper Brothers, 1947), pp. 170–71.
6 Elaine Showalter, "The Feminist Critical Revolution," *The New Feminist Criticism*, ed. Elaine Showalter (New York: Pantheon Books, 1985), p. 9.
7 Showalter, "The Feminist Critical Revolution," p. 9.

8 Showalter, *A Literature of Their Own: British Women Novelists from Bronte to Lessing* (Princeton: Princeton University Press, 1977), p. 13.

9 The Female Gothic is an ambivalent mode, very much rooted in patriarchal paradigms. Juliann E. Fleenor explains "The Gothic is a form created by dichotomies and the subsequent tensions caused by the dialectic between the patriarchal society, the woman's role, and the contradictions and limitations inherent in both." See *The Female Gothic*, ed. Juliann E. Fleenor (Montreal-London: Eden Press, 1983), p. 16. Alice Munro also explained in interview that in the beginning of her writing career, she carried with her for some period of time, a powerful, archetypal novel she wanted to write. In her own words, in this novel, the romantic girl has gotten engaged to a worthy, ordinary, young man, thinking that she will be absorbed into real life this way. But another character, "Moral Authority Preacher" is determined the marriage will not take place because he senses the evil, the power of the girl. He is, of course, madly in love with the girl but doesn't recognize it. She is in the same position. She puts a curse on him—it works—he is doomed to death, whereupon she understands that in order to repeal the curse she must take it on herself. And she dies. He then does a kind of "Heathcliff thing"—lives out a life of lonely usefulness, but dies, as Heathcliff does, wedded to her.

  The good-evil girl of this gothic fiction is a characteristic of Female Gothic, the "ambivalence towards the female (good and evil)" having been internalized. "The ambivalence toward the female self leads to feelings of self-disgust and self-fear rather than fear and disgust of something outside her." See Fleenor, *The Female Gothic*, p. 12. The heroine is, of course, in her split personality, a reflection of patriarchal values, here in Munro's latent fiction, personalized as Moral Authority Preacher.

10 Munro, *Dance of the Happy Shades* (McGraw-Hill Ryerson Ltd., 1968), p. 76. All further references in the text are to this edition.

11 Annette Kolodny, "Dancing Through the Minefield," *The New Feminist Criticism*, (New York: Pantheon Books, 1985), p. 161.

12 Linda Hutcheon, *The Canadian Postmodern: A Study of Contemporary English-Canadian Fiction* (Toronto: Oxford University Press, 1988), p. 12.

13 Susan Brownmiller, *Femininity* (New York: Fawcett Columbine, 1984), p. 14.

14 Brownmiller, *Femininity*, p. 215.

15 Susan Gubar, "'The Blank Page' and the Issues of Female Creativity," *The New Feminist Criticism*, ed. Elaine Showalter (New York: Pantheon Books, 1985), p. 296.

16 Maggie Humm, "Feminist Literary Criticism in America and England," *Women's Writing*, ed. Moira Monteith (Great Britain: Harvester Press, 1986), p. 105.

17 Hutcheon, *The Canadian Postmodern*, p. 6.

18 Showalter, *A Literature of Their Own*, p. 9.

19 Adele Wiseman, Chinada: Memoirs of the Gang of Seven (Dunvegan, Ont.: Quadrant Editions, 1982), p. 114.

CHAPTER ONE

1 For an analysis of this early work, see Robert Thacker, "'Clear Jelly': Alice Munro's Narrative Dialectics," in *Probable Fictions: Alice Munro's Narrative Acts*, ed. Louis K. MacKendrick (Toronto: ECW Press, 1983), p. 37.
2 See Virginia Woolf: *Women and Writing*, ed. Michele Barrett (New York: Harcourt Brace Jovanovich, 1980), p. 17.
3 Elaine Showalter, "Killing the Angel in the House: The Autonomy of Women Writers," *The Antioch Review* 32, no. 3, (June 1973), p. 341.
4 Showalter, letter to Joyce Johnson, McGraw-Hill Book Company, New York, 8 February 1973, Correspondence Series, *The Alice Munro Papers: First Accession*, (Calgary: University of Calgary Press, 1986), p. 15.
5 Brownmiller, *Femininity*, p. 115. See also Mary Field Belenky, Blythe McVicker Clinchy, Nancy Rule Goldberger, Jill Mattuck Tarule. *Women's Ways of Knowing, The Development of Self, Voice and Mind* (New York: Basic Books, Inc., 1986).
6 Brownmiller, *Femininity*, p. 119.
7 "The Yellow Afternoon" is an unfinished piece written in the summer of 1951 and housed in the Alice Munro papers, University of Calgary Special Collections. See Uncollected Short Story Series, *The Alice Munro Papers: First Accession* (Calgary: University of Calgary Press, 1986), p. 168.

CHAPTER TWO

1 *Something I've Been Meaning to Tell You*, p. 22.
2 Arthur Miller, *Psychology and Arthur Miller*, interviewer Richard I. Evans, (New York: E.P. Dutton, 1969), p. 56.
3 Brownmiller, *Femininity*, p. 224.
4 Munro, *The Progress of Love* (Toronto: McClelland and Stewart, 1986), p. 16. All further references in this text are to this edition.
5 Lorna Irvine, "Women's Desire/Women's Power: *The Moons of Jupiter*," in Lorna Irvine, *Sub/Version* (Downsview, Ontario: ECW Press, 1986), p. 93.
6 Brownmiller, *Femininity*, p. 24.
7 An interview with Alice Munro, 15 February 1981.
8 See John Metcalf, "A Conversation with Alice Munro," *Journal of Canadian Fiction*, 1, no. 4 (Fall 1972), p. 58.
9 Hallvard Dahlie, "The Fiction of Alice Munro," *Ploughshares* 4, no. 3 (Summer 1978), p. 57.
10 Barbara Frum, "Great Dames," *Maclean's* (April 1973), p. 38.
11 An interview with Alice Munro, 15 February 1981.
12 Munro, "The Peace of Utrecht," *Dance of the Happy Shades*, p. 204.
13 An interview with Alice Munro, 15 February 1981.
14 John Moss, *Sex and Violence in the Canadian Novel: The Ancestral Present* (Toronto: McClelland and Stewart, 1977), p. 60.

15 See J.R. Struthers, "Reality and Ordering: The Growth of a Young Artist in Lives of Girls and Women," *Essays on Canadian Writing*, no. 3 (Fall 1975), pp. 33–46; W.R. Martin, "Alice Munro and James Joyce," *Journal of Canadian Fiction* (1979), pp. 120–26.

16 Brownmiller, *Femininity*, p. 215.

17 Munro, *Who Do You Think You Are?* (Scarborough: Signet, 1978), p. 13. All further references in the text are to this edition.

18 Robert Kroetsch, "Prologue," *Mosaic*, xiv/2 (Spring 1981), p. vii.

19 Urjo Kareda, "Double Vision," review of *The Moons of Jupiter*, *Saturday Night* (November 1982), p. 63.

20 Munro, *The Moons of Jupiter* (Toronto: Macmillan of Canada, 1982), p. 7. All further references in the text are to this edition.

21 Bronwen Wallace, "Women's Lives: Alice Munro," in *The Human Elements: Critical Essays*, ed. David Helwig (Ottawa: Oberon Press, 1978), p. 56.

22 Irvine, "Changing is the Word I Want," in *Probable Fictions: Alice Munro's Narrative Acts*, ed. Louis K. MacKendrick (Downsview, Ontario: ECW Press, 1983), p. 99–111.

23 Kareda, "Double Vision," p. 63.

24 W.R. Martin, *Alice Munro—Paradox and Parallel* (Edmonton: University of Alberta Press, 1987), p. 186.

25 Ann Barr Snitow, "The Front Line: Notes on Sex in Novels by Women," in *Women, Sex and Sexuality*, eds. Catherine R. Stimpson and Ethel Spector Person (Chicago: University of Chicago Press, 1980), p. 161.

26 Snitow argues that women write about sex differently than do men. There is still a common male insistence that "sex is an animal function, a distinct drive, an organ with a private life" resulting in a limited view of the sexual experience in male authors. Females and female authors, on the other hand, are particularly dependent on male protection and affection and diffuse "the sexual moment into all aspects of social experience." See Snitow, "The Front Line," p. 162.

27 Munro, *The Progress of Love* (Toronto: McClelland and Stewart, 1986), p. 11.

28 Phyllis Chesler, *Women and Madness* (New York: Avon Books, 1972), p. 17.

29 See Showalter, *The Female Malady: Women, Madness and English Culture, 1830–1980* (New York: Penguin, 1985), p. 4.

30 Sandra M. Gilbert and Susan Gubar, *The Madwoman in the Attic: The Woman Writer and the Nineteenth-Century Literary Imagination* (New Haven, Conn: Yale University Press, 1979), cited in Showalter, *The Female Malady*, p. 4.

31 Gilbert and Gubar in Showalter, p. 4.

32 Showalter, *The Female Malady*, p. 238.

33 Snitow, "The Front Line: Notes on Sex in Novels by Women," in *Women, Sex and Sexuality*, eds. Catherine R. Stimpson and Ethel Spector Person (Chicago: University of Chicago Press, 1980), p. 162.

34 Snitow, "The Front Line," p. 170.

35 Snitow, "The Front Line," p. 174.

CHAPTER THREE

1 Leslie Fiedler, *Cross the Border—Close the Gap* (New York: Stein and Day, 1971), p. 65.

2 Alice Munro, *The Newcomers Script*, television series. *The Alice Munro Papers: First Accession*, (Calgary: University of Calgary Press, 1986), p. 184.

3 Claire R. Farrar, "Images and Genres," *Women and Folklore* (Austin: University of Texas Press, 1975), p. x. All further references in the text are to this edition.

4 Ellen Moers, *Literary Women* (London: The Women's Press, 1963), p. 67. All further references in the text are to this edition.

5 E.D. Blodgett, "Prisms and Arcs: Structures in Hebert and Munro," in *Figures in a Ground*, eds. Diane Bessai and David Jackel (Saskatoon: Western Producer, 1978), p. 111.

6 Moers points out that the subject of birth was first brought to literature by some male novelists, Zola and Tolstoy (who made it gruesome), but women writers didn't begin to write about birth until the twentieth century. Pearl Buck and Sigrid Unset were pioneers of the subject. See Moers, *Literary Women*, p. 92.

7 See Donald H. Akenson, "Ontario: Whatever Happened to the Irish?" *Canadian Papers in Rural History: Volume III* (Gananoque, Ontario: Langdale Press, 1982), pp. 204–56.

8 An interview with Alice Munro, 15 February 1981.

9 See Ian Pringle and Enoch Padolsky, "The Irish Heritage of the English in the Ottawa Valley," *English Studies in Canada* VII, no. 3 (Fall 1981), p. 347.

10 Alan Dundes explains the new directions in folklore scholarship. Dundes claims the family as the smallest folk group, points out that folk groups may be religious, occupational, or ethnic groups and that the "folk" can no longer be considered synonymous with the rural or lower class. Illiteracy is no longer a criterion for the classification of "folk" and mass culture is as much folk as insulated country worlds traditionally interpreted as such. See Alan Dundes, *Interpreting Folklore* (Bloomington: Indiana University Press, 1980), p. 17.

11 Dundes, *Interpreting Folklore*, p. 47.

12 Catherine Sheldrick Ross, "'At Least Part Legend': The Fiction of Alice Munro," in *Probable Fictions: Alice Munro's Narrative Acts*, ed. Louis K. MacKendrick (Downsview, Ontario: ECW Press, 1983), p. 114.

13 Dundes, *Interpreting Folklore*, p. 93.

14 E.A. Budge in Dundes, *Interpreting Folklore*, p. 109.

15 See Stith Thompson, *The Folktale* (New York: Holt, Rinehart and Winston, 1946), p. 485. The clever peasant girl is folk tale motif (#875)—a riddle solver brought before the king.

16 Tristram Coffin, *The Female Hero in Folklore and Legend* (New York: The Seabury Press, 1975), p. 158.

17 Brownmiller, *Femininity*, p. 61.

18 Munro, "Rapunzel, Rapunzel, Let Down Thy Gold Hair" Uncollected Short Stories Series, *The Alice Munro Papers: First Accession* (Calgary: University of Calgary Press, 1986), p. 161.

19 Coffin, *The Female Hero*, p. 149.

20 Coffin, *The Female Hero*, p. 152.

21 See Thompson, "Index of Motifs," pp. 481–500.

22 Wayne C. Booth, *A Rhetoric of Irony* (Chicago: University of Chicago Press, 1974), p. 252.

23 Booth, *A Rhetoric of Irony*, p. 253.

24 B. Pfaus, *Alice Munro* (Ottawa: The Golden Dog Press, 1984), p. 7.

25 Pfaus quotes Munro as delineating the writing process as "a straining of something immense and varied, a whole dense vision of the world, into whatever confines the writer has learned to make for it," p. 7.

26 Pfaus, *Alice Munro*, p. 11.

27 Farrar, "Images and Genres," p. xiii.

28 Stephen Leacock, "The Woman Question," *Essays and Literary Studies* (London: John Lane, 1917), p. 115.

29 Munro, "Home, October, 1973. Notes for a Work," Uncollected Short Stories Series, *The Alice Munro Papers: First Accession* (Calgary: University of Calgary Press), p. 151.

30 Virginia Woolf, *Collected Essays*, vol. II (London: The Hogarth Press, 1966), p. 146.

CHAPTER FOUR

1 Hutcheon, *The Canadian Postmodern*, p. xi.

2 Hutcheon, *The Canadian Postmodern*, pp. viii–ix.

3 Hutcheon, *The Canadian Postmodern*, p. 19.

4 Metcalf, "A Conversation with Alice Munro," p. 57.

5 Eudora Welty, "Place in Fiction," *The Eye of the Story* (New York: Random House, 1977), p. 118. All further references in the text are to this edition.

6 Welty, "Place in Fiction," p. 119.

7 Joel Kovel in Annette Kolodny, *The Lay of the Land: Metaphor as Experience and History in American Life and Letters* (Chapel Hill: The University of North Carolina Press, 1975), p. 5.

8 Irvine, "Changing Is the Word I Want," p. 101.

9 Wallace, "Women's Lives: Alice Munro," p. 54.

10 An interview with Alice Munro, 15 February 1981.

11 David Helwig, "Dance of the Happy Shades," *Queen's Quarterly* 77 (Spring 1970), p. 128.

12 Metcalf, "A Conversation with Alice Munro," p. 56.

13 One of the most important articles to this effect is J.R. (Tim) Struthers, "Alice Munro and the American South," in *The Canadian Novel Here and Now*, ed. John Moss (Toronto: N.C. Press, 1978).

14 Welty, "Place in Fiction," pp. 119–20.

15 Irvine, "Changing Is the Word I Want," p. 106.

16 See Ross, "'At Least Part Legend,'" p. 112.

17 Metcalf, "A Conversation with Alice Munro," p. 58.
18 Geoff Hancock, "Magic Realism, or, the Future of Fiction," *Canadian Fiction Magazine* 24/25 (Spring/Summer 1977), p. 4.
19 Hancock, "Magic Realism," p. 6.
20 Welty, "Place in Fiction," p. 126.
21 Hans Werner, "Nothing Phoney," *Canadian Art* 4, no. 3 (Fall 1987), p. 76.
22 Alan Twigg, *For Openers: Conversation With 24 Canadian Writers* (Madeira Park, B.C.: Harbour Publishing, 1981), p. 19.
23 Juliann E. Fleenor, ed. *The Female Gothic* (Montreal: Eden Press, 1983), p. 13.
24 Northrop Frye, "Conclusion," ed. Carl Klinck, *Literary History of Canada* (Toronto: University of Toronto Press, 1965; rpt. 1967), p. 830. All further references in the text are to this edition.
25 Frye, "Conclusion," p. 839.
26 Julia E. Kristeva, *Desire in Language* (New York: Columbia University Press, 1980), p. 238.
27 Fleenor, *The Female Gothic*, p. 16.
28 Fleenor discusses this dichotomy briefly and the "notably Protestant origins" of the Female Gothic, p. 10.
29 Moers, *Literary Women*, p. 126.
30 The gothic elements in Munro's "female" art are also discussed by Barbara Godard, "'Heirs of the Living Body: Alice Munro and the Question of a Female Aesthetic" in *The Art of Alice Munro: Saying the Unsayable*, ed. Judith Miller (Waterloo, Ontario: University of Waterloo Press, 1984), pp. 43–71.
31 See Sybill Korff Vincent, "The Mirror and the Cameo: Margaret Atwood's Comic/Gothic Novel, *Lady Oracle*" in Fleenor, *The Female Gothic*.
32 Claire Kahane in Fleenor, Introduction, *The Female Gothic*, p. 23.
33 Marilyn Julian, "Something I've Been Meaning to Tell You," *Tamarack Review* 63 (October 1974), pp. 82–83.
34 Beth Harvor, "The Special World of the W.W's: Through Female Reality with Alice, Jennifer, Edna, Nadine, Doris and All Those Other Girls," *Saturday Night* (August 1969), p. 33.
35 Kareda, "Double Vision," *Saturday Night* (November 1982), p. 63.
36 Irvine," Changing Is the Word I Want," p. 104.
37 Kolodny, *The Lay of Land*, p. 4.
38 Alice Munro, See Chapter One of this text, *Alice: The Woman behind the Art*.
39 Alice Munro, See Chapter One of this text, *Alice: The Woman behind the Art*.
40 Welty, "Place in Fiction," p. 132.

CHAPTER FIVE

1 Hutcheon, *The Canadian Postmodern*, p. 5.
2 Marigold Johnson, "Mud and Blood," *The New Statesman* (26 October 1973), p. 619.
3 Rae McCarthy Macdonald, "Structure and Detail in Lives of Girls and Women,"

Studies in Canadan Literature 3 (Summer 1978), p. 210.

4 John Moss, "Alice in the Looking Glass, Munro's *Lives of Girls and Women*," *Sex and Violence in the Canadian Novel: The Ancestral Present* (Toronto: McClelland and Stewart, 1977), p. 56.

5 James Carscallen, "Alice Munro," in *Profiles in Canadian Literature* 2, ed. Jeffrey M. Heath (Toronto and Charlottetown: Dundurn, 1980), p. 74.

6 Carole Gerson, "Who Do You Think You Are? A Review/Interview with Alice Munro," *Room of One's Own* 4, no. 4 (Winter 1979), pp. 2–3.

7 Luce Irigaray in Ann Rosalind Jones, "Writing the Body: Toward an Understanding of L'Écriture féminine," *The New Feminist Criticism*, ed. Elaine Showalter (New York: Pantheon Books, 1985), p. 364.

8 Jones, "Writing the Body: Toward an Understanding of L'Écriture féminine," p. 365.

9 Showalter, Introduction, *The New Feminist Criticism*, p. 9.

10 W.R. Martin has referred to the alluding nature of the names of Munro's characters. See W.R. Martin, *Alice Munro: Paradox and Parallel*, p. 190.

11 Ross, "At Least Part Legend," p. 112–13.

12 Louis MacKendrick, *Probable Fictions: Alice Munro's Narrative Acts* (Downsview, Ontario: ECW Press, 1983), pp. 1–2.

13 Tim Struthers, "Alice Munro's Fictive Imagination," *The Art of Alice Munro: Saying the Unsayable*, ed. Judith Miller (Waterloo, Ontario: University of Waterloo Press, 1984), p. 103.

14 Gerald Noonan, "The Structure of Style in Alice Munro's Fiction," *Probable Fictions*, pp. 163–180.

15 Robert Kroetsch, *Labyrinths of Voice: Conversations with Robert Kroetsch*, interviewers Shirley Neuman/Robert Wilson (Edmonton: NeWest Press, 1982), p. 34.

16 Kildare Dobbs, "New Directions for Alice Munro," *Saturday Night* (July 1974), p. 28.

17 Judith Miller, *The Art of Alice Munro: Saying the Unsayable*, Introduction, p. iii.

18 Martin Knelman, "The Past, the Present and Alice Munro," *Saturday Night* (November 1979), p. 16.

19 Helwig, "Dance of the Happy Shades," *Queen's Quarterly* 77 (Spring 1970), p. 128.

20 Showalter, *A Literature of Their Own*, p. 258.

21 Barbara Godard, "'Heirs of the Living Body,'" p. 52.

22 Mary R. Beard, *On Understanding Women* (London: Longmans, Green and Co., 1931), p. 10.

23 Brownmiller, *Femininity*, p. 53.

24 Susan Gubar, "The Blank Page," p. 303.

25 Gubar, "The Blank Page," p. 303.

26 Gubar, "The Blank Page," p. 302.

27 Gubar, "The Blank Page," p. 303.

28 Patricia Tobin, *Time and the Novel* (Princeton: Princeton University Press, 1978), p. 9.

29 An interview with Alice Munro, June 1982.

30 Tobin, *Time and the Novel*, p. 7.

31 Jane Gallop cited in Lorna Irvine, "Women's Desire/Women's Power: *The Moons of Jupiter*" in Irvine, ed. *Sub/Version* (Downsview, Ontario: ECW Press, 1986), p. 94.

32 Gallop in Irvine, "Women's Desire/Women's Power," p. 94.

33 J. Hillis Miller cited in Patricia Tobin, *Time and the Novel*, p. 23.

34 Godard, "'Heirs of the Living Body,'" p. 46.

35 Grace Stewart, *A New Mythos—The Novel of the Artist as Heroine* (Montreal: Eden Press, 1979), p. 176.

36 Moers, *Literary Women*, p. 245.

37 Moers, *Literary Women*, p. 251.

38 Moers, *Literary Women*, p. 255.

39 Martin, *Alice Munro: Paradox and Parallel*, p. 131.

40 Martin, *Paradox and Parallel*, p. 131.

41 Hélène Cixous cited in Ann Rosalind Jones, "Writing the Body: Toward an Understanding of L'Écriture féminine," *The New Feminist Criticism*, p. 365.

42 Gubar, "The Blank Page," p. 303.

43 Helen Hoy, "'Dull, Simple, Amazing and Unfathomable': Paradox and Double Vision in Alice Munro's Fiction," *Studies in Canadian Literature* 5 (Spring 1980), p. 100.

44 Rachel Blau Duplessis, "For the Etruscans," *The New Feminist Criticism* (New York: Pantheon Books, 1985), p. 278.

45 Godard, "'Heirs of the Living Body,'" p. 43.

46 Joseph Gold, "Our Feeling Exactly: the Writing of Alice Munro," *The Art of Alice Munro: Saying the Unsayable*, ed. Judith Miller (Waterloo, Ontario: University of Waterloo Press, 1984), p. 8.

47 Godard, "'Heirs of the Living Body,'" p. 71.

48 France Théoret, "Writing in the Feminine: Voicing Consensus, Practising Difference," *A Mazing Space*, eds. Shirley Neuman and Smaro Kamboureli (Edmonton: Longspoon and NeWest Press, 1986), p. 363.

| | | BIBLIOGRAPHY

UNCOLLECTED WORKS OF ALICE MUNRO

During the course of her writing career, Alice Munro has written several short stories which have been published but which, at the time of this publication, do not appear in her major collections. Students might be encouraged to consider those that are easily available, from a feminist point of view. Uncollected stories in order of writing include:

"The Dimensions of a Shadow," *Folio* 4, no. 2 (April 1950): 2–8.

"Story for Sunday," *Folio* 5, no. 1 (December 1950): 4–8.

"The Widower," *Folio* 5, no. 2 (April 1951): 7–11.

"A Basket of Strawberries," *Mayfair* (November 1943): 32–33, 78–80.

"The Idyllic Summer," *The Canadian Forum* 34 (September 1955): 131–33.

"The Edge of Town," *Queen's Quarterly* 62, no. 3 (Autumn 1955): 368–80.

"How Could I Do That?" *Chatelaine* (March 1956): 16–17, 65–70.

"The Dangerous One," *Chatelaine* (July 1957) 48, 50–51.

"Home," *New Canadian Stories* 74, eds. David Helwig and Joan Harcourt. [Ottawa] Oberon Press, 1974: 133–53.

"Characters," *Ploughshares* 4, no. 3 (1978): 72–82.

"Wood," *The New Yorker* (24 November 1980): 49–54.

"The Ferguson Girls Must Never Marry," *Grand Street* 1, no. 3 (Spring 1982): 27–64.
"Oh, What Avails," *The New Yorker* (16 November 1987): 42–52.
"Meneseteung," *The New Yorker* (11 January 1988): 28–38.
"Five Points," *The New Yorker* (14 March 1988): 34–43.
"Oranges and Apples," *The New Yorker* (24 October 1988): 36–48.
"Hold Me Fast, Don't Let Me Pass," *The Atlantic* (December 1988): 58–66
"Differently," *The New Yorker* (2 January 1989): 23–36.
"Goodness and Mercy," *The New Yorker* (20 March 1989): 38–48.

SELECTED BIBLIOGRAPHY

Akenson, Donald. "Ontario: Whatever Happened to the Irish?" *Canadian Papers in Rural History: Volume III* (1982): 204–56.
Allentuck, Marcia. "Resolution and Independence in the Work of Alice Munro." *World Literature Written in English* 16 (November 1977): 340–43.
Bailey, Nancy. "The Masculine Image in Lives of Girls and Women." *Canadian Literature*, no. 80 (Spring 1979): 113–20.
Barrett, Michele, ed. *Virginia Woolf: Women and Writing*. New York: Harcourt Brace Jovanovich, 1980.
Beard, Mary. *On Understanding Women*. London: Longmans, Green and Co., 1931.
Beauvoir, Simone de. *The Second Sex*. H.M. Parshley, trans. New York: Alfred A. Knopf, 1968.
Belenky, Mary Field and Blythe McVicker Clinchy and Nancy Rule Goldberger and Jill Mattuck Tarule. *Women's Ways of Knowing: The Development of Self, Voice and Mind*. New York: Basic Books Inc., 1986.
Blodgett, E.D. "Prisms and Arcs: Structure in Hebert and Munro." *Figures in a Ground*. Diane Bessai and David Jackel, eds., pp. 91–121, 333–34. Saskatoon: Western Producer, 1978.
Booth, Wayne C. *A Rhetoric of Irony*. Chicago: University of Chicago Press, 1974.
Brownmiller, Susan. *Femininity*. New York: Fawcett Columbine, 1984.
Bryson, Norman. *Vision and Painting*. New Haven: Yale University Press, 1983.
Carscallen, James. "Alice Munro." *Profiles in Canadian Literature* 2. Jeffrey M. Heath, ed., pp. 73–80. Toronto and Charlottetown: Dundurn, 1980.
Caws, Mary Ann. *The Eye in the Text*. Princeton: Princeton University Press, 1981.
———. *Reading Frames in Modern Fiction*. Princeton: Princeton University Press, 1985.
Chesler, Phyllis. *Women and Madness*. New York: Avon Books, 1972.
Coffin, Tristram. *The Female Hero in Folklore and Legend*. New York: The Seabury Press, 1975.
Conron, Brandon. "Munro's Wonderland." *Canadian Literature* 78 (Autumn 1978): 209–12, 114–18, 120–23.

Dahlie, Hallvard. *Alice Munro and Her Works*. Toronto: ECW Press, 1984.

———. "The Fiction of Alice Munro." *Ploughshares* 4, no. 3 (Summer 1978): 56–71.

———. "Unconsummated Relationships: Isolation and Rejection in Alice Munro's Stories." *World Literature Written in English* 11, no. 1 (April 1972): 43–48.

De Mott, Benjamin. "Domestic Stories: *The Moons of Jupiter*." New York Times (March 20, 1983): 1, 26.

Dobbs, Kildare. "New Directions for Alice Munro." *Saturday Night* (July 1974): 28.

Dundes, Alan. *Interpreting Folklore*. Bloomington: Indiana University Press, 1980.

Duplessis, Rachel Blau. "For the Etruscans." *The New Feminist Criticism*, pp. 271–91. New York: Pantheon Books, 1985.

Farrar, Claire R. *Women and Folklore*. Austin: University of Texas Press, 1975.

Fiedler, Leslie. *Cross the Border—Close the Gap*. New York: Stein and Day, 1971.

Fleenor, Juliann, ed. *The Female Gothic*. Montreal: Eden Press, 1983.

French, William. "The Women in Our Literary Life." *Canadian Author and Bookman* 51, no. 3 (Spring 1976): 1, 3, 5.

Frum, Barbara. "Great Dames." *Maclean's* (April 1973): 32, 38.

Frye, Northrop. "Conclusion." Carl Klinck, ed. *Literary History of Canada*. Toronto: University of Toronto Press, rpt. 1967.

Garner, Hugh. *Foreword*. In *Dance of the Happy Shades*, pp. vii–ix. Toronto: Ryerson, 1968.

Gerson, Carole. "Who Do You Think You Are? Review/Interview with Alice Munro." *Room of One's Own* 4, no. 4 (Winter 1979): 2–7.

Gibson, Graeme. *Eleven Canadian Novelists*. (Interviewed by Graeme Gibson.) Toronto: Anansi, 1973.

Gilbert, Sandra and Susan Gubar. *The Madwoman in the Attic: The Woman Writer and the Nineteenth-Century Literary Imagination*. New Haven: Yale University Press, 1979.

Godard, Barbara. "'Heirs of the Living Body': Alice Munro and the Question of a Female Aesthetic." *The Art of Alice Munro: Saying the Unsayable*. Judith Miller, ed., pp. 43–71. Waterloo, Ontario: University of Waterloo Press, 1984.

Gold, Joseph. "Our Feeling Exactly: the Writing of Alice Munro." *The Art of Alice Munro: Saying the Unsayable*. Judith Miller, ed., pp. 1–13. Waterloo, Ontario: University of Waterloo Press, 1984.

Goldberger, Nancy Rule and Jill Mattuck Tarule. *Women's Ways of Knowing, The Development of Self, Voice and Mind*. New York: Basic Books, Inc., 1986.

Gubar, Susan. "'The Blank Page' and the Issues of Female Creativity." *The New Feminist Criticism*. Elaine Showalter, ed., pp. 292–313. New York: Pantheon Books, 1985.

Hancock, Geoff. "An Interview With Alice Munro." *Canadian Fiction Magazine* 43 (1982): 75–114.

———. "Magic Realism, or, the Future of Fiction." *Canadian Fiction Magazine* 24/25 (Spring/Summer 1977): 4–6.

Harvor, Beth. "The Special World of the W.W.'s: Through Female Reality with Alice, Jennifer, Edna, Nadine, Doris and All Those Other Girls." *Saturday Night* (August, 1969): 33–35.

Helwig, David. "Dance of the Happy Shades." *Queen's Quarterly* 77 (Spring 1970): 127–28.

Hoy, Helen. "'Dull, Simple, Amazing and Unfathomable': Paradox and Double Vision in Alice Munro's Fiction." *Studies in Canadian Literature* 5, no. 1 (Spring 1980): 100–15.

Humm, Maggie. "Feminist Literary Criticism in America and England." *Women's Writing*. Moira Monteith, ed., pp. 90–116. Great Britain: Harvester Press, 1986.

Hutcheon, Linda. *The Canadian Postmodern: A Study of Contemporary English-Canadian Fiction*. Toronto: Oxford University Press, 1988.

Irvine, Lorna. "Changing Is the Word I Want." *Probable Fictions: Alice Munro's Narrative Acts*. Louis K. MacKendrick, ed., pp. 99–111. Toronto: ECW Press, 1983.

———. "Hostility and Reconciliation: The Mother in English Canadian Fiction." *The American Review of Canadian Studies* 8, no. 1 (Spring 1978): 56–62.

———. *Sub/Version*. Toronto: ECW Press, 1986.

Johnson, Marigold. "Mud and Blood." *The New Statesman* 26 (October 1973): 618–19.

Jones, Ann Rosalind. "Writing the Body: Towards an Understanding of L'Écriture féminine." *The New Feminist Criticism*. Elaine Showalter, ed., pp. 361–77. New York: Pantheon Books, 1985.

Julian, Marilyn. "Something I've Been Meaning to Tell You." *Tamarack Review* 63 (October 1974): 82–83.

Kareda, Urjo. "Double Vision." *Saturday Night* (November 1982): 63–64.

Knelman, Martin. "The Past, the Present and Alice Munro." *Saturday Night* (November 1979): 16–18, 20, 22.

Kolodny, Annette. "Dancing Through The Minefield." *The New Feminist Criticism*. Elaine Showalter, ed., pp. 144–67. New York: Pantheon Books, 1985.

———. *The Lay of the Land: Metaphor as Experience and History in American Life and Letters*. Chapel Hill: The University of North Carolina Press, 1975.

Kristeva, Julia. *Desire in Language: A Semiotic Approach to Life and Art*. Leon S. Roudiez, ed. New York: Columbia University Press, 1980.

Kroetsch, Robert. *Labyrinths of Voice: Conversations with Robert Kroetsch*. Interviewers Shirley Neuman/Robert Wilson. Edmonton: NeWest Press, 1982.

———. "Prologue." *Mosaic* XIV/2 (Spring 1981): vii.

Laidlaw, Robert. *The McGregors: A Novel of an Ontario Pioneer Family*. Toronto: Macmillan, 1979.

Leacock, Stephen. *Essays and Literary Studies*. London: John Lane, 1917.

Lundberg, Ferdinand and Marynia F. Farnham. *Modern Woman: The Lost Sex*. New York: Harper Bros., 1947.

Macdonald, Rae McCarthy. "A Madman Loose in the World: The Vision of Alice Munro." *Modern Fiction Studies* 22 (Autumn 1976): 365–74.

———. "Structure and Detail in Lives of Girls and Women." *Studies in Canadian Literature* 3 (Summer 1978): 199–210.

MacKendrick, Louis K., ed. *Probable Fictions: Alice Munro's Narrative Acts.* Toronto: ECW Press, 1983.

Martin, W.R. "Alice Munro and James Joyce." *Journal of Canadian Fiction* 2 (1979): 120–26.

———. *Alice Munro—Paradox and Parallel.* Edmonton: University of Alberta Press, 1987.

Metcalf, John. "A Conversation With Alice Munro." *Journal of Canadian Fiction* 1, no. 4 (Fall 1972): 54–62.

Miller, Arthur. *Psychology and Arthur Miller.* Richard I. Evans, interviewer. New York: E.P. Dutton, 1969.

Miller, Judith, ed. *The Art of Alice Munro: Saying the Unsayable.* Waterloo, Ontario: University of Waterloo Press, 1984.

Moers, Ellen. *Literary Women.* London: The Woman's Press, 1963.

Montieth, Moira, ed. *Women's Writing.* Great Britain: The Harvester Press, Ltd., 1986.

Moss, John. "Alice in the Looking Glass: Munro's *Lives of Girls and Women.*" In *Sex and Violence in the Canadian Novel: The Ancestral Present,* pp. 54–68. Toronto: McClelland and Stewart, 1977.

Munro, Alice. Author's Commentary. In *Sixteen By Twelve.* John Metcalf, ed., pp. 125–26. Toronto: McGraw Hill, 1970.

———. "The Colonel's Hash Resettled." In *The Narrative Voice.* John Metcalf, ed., pp. 181–83. Toronto: McGraw-Hill Ryerson, 1972.

———. *Dance of the Happy Shades.* Toronto: McGraw-Hill Ryerson, 1968.

———. "Everything Here is Touchable and Mysterious." *Weekend Magazine* (11 May 1974): 33.

———. "Home, October, 1973. Notes for a Work." Uncollected Short Story Series. *The Alice Munro Papers.* University of Calgary Special Collections.

———. Interviews with Beverly Rasporich, January 1980, February 1981, June 1982, and through correspondence September 1989.

———. *The Irish.* The Newcomers Television Series. Manuscript in *The Alice Munro Papers.* University of Calgary Special Collections.

———. *Lives of Girls and Women.* Toronto: The New American Library of Canada Ltd., 1974.

———. *The Moons of Jupiter.* Toronto: Macmillan of Canada, 1982.

———. *The Progress of Love.* Toronto: McClelland and Stewart, 1986.

———. "Rapunzel, Rapunzel: short story fragments, n.d." and "Rapunzel, Rapunzel, Let Down Thy Gold Hair," n.d. Uncollected Short Story Series. *The Alice Munro Papers.* University of Calgary Special Collections.

———. "Remembering Roger Mortimer: Dickens' *Child's History of England* Remembered." *The Montrealer* (February 1962): 34–37.

———. *Something I've Been Meaning To Tell You.* Toronto: The New American Library of Canada, 1975.

———. "Through the Jade Curtain." In *Chinada: Memoirs of the Gang of Seven.*

Gary Geddes, ed. and preface, pp. 51–55. Montreal: Quadrant, 1982.

———. "What is Real?" in *Making It New.* John Metcalf, ed., pp. 223–26. Toronto: Methuen, 1982.

———. *Who Do You Think You Are?* Scarborough, Ontario: Signet, 1978.

———. "Working For A Living." *Grand Sheet* 1, no. 1 (Autumn 1981): 9–37.

———. "The Yellow Afternoon," short story fragment. Uncollected Short Story Series. *The Alice Munro Papers.* University of Calgary Special Collections.

Noonan, Gerald. "The Structure of Style in Alice Munro's Fiction." *Probable Fictions: Alice Munro's Narrative Acts.* Louis K. MacKendrick, ed., pp. 163–80. Downsview, Ontario: ECW Press, 1983.

Pfaus, B. *Alice Munro.* Ottawa: The Golden Dog Press, 1984.

Pringle, Ian and Enoch Padolsky. "The Irish Heritage of the English in the Ottawa Valley." *English Studies in Canada* VII, no. 3 (Fall 1981): 338–49.

Rasporich, Beverly. "Child-Women and Primitives in the Fiction of Alice Munro." *Atlantis* 1, no. 2 (Spring 1976): 4–14.

Ross, Catherine Sheldrick. "'At Least Part Legend': The Fiction of Alice Munro." *Probable Fictions: Alice Munro's Narrative Acts.* Louis K. MacKenrick, ed., pp. 112–26. Downsview, Ontario: ECW Press, 1983.

Showalter, Elaine. *The Female Malady: Women, Madness, and English Culture, 1830–1980.* New York: Penguin Books, 1985.

———. "Killing the Angel in the House: *The Autonomy of Women Writers.*" *The Antioch Review* 32, no. 3 (June 1973): 339–351.

———. Letter to Joyce Johnson. 8 February 1973, Correspondence Series, *The Alice Munro Papers.* University of Calgary Special Collections.

———. *A Literature of Their Own: British Women Novelists From Bronte to Lessing.* Princeton: Princeton University Press, 1977.

———. ed. *The New Feminist Criticism.* New York: Pantheon Books, 1985.

Snitow, Ann Barr. "The Front Line: Notes on Sex in Novels by Women." *Women, Sex and Sexuality.* Catherine R. Stimpson and Ethel Spector-Person, eds., pp. 158–74. University of Chicago Press, 1980.

Stainsby, Mari. "Alice Munro Talks With Mari Stainsby." *British Columbia Library Quarterly* 35, no. 1 (July 1971): 27–31.

Stewart, Grace. *A New Mythos—The Novel of the Artist as Heroine.* Montreal: Eden Press, 1979.

Stimpson, Catherine R. and Ethel Spector Person, eds. *Women, Sex and Sexuality.* Chicago: The University of Chicago Press, 1980.

Struthers, J.R. (Tim). "Alice Munro and the American South." *The Canadian Novel Here and Now.* John Moss, ed. Toronto: N.C. Press, 1978.

———. "Alice Munro's Fictive Imagination." *The Art of Alice Munro: Saying the Unsayable.* Judith Miller, ed., pp. 103–12. Waterloo, Ontario: University of Waterloo Press, 1984.

———. "Reality and Ordering: The Growth of a Young Artist in *Lives of Girls and Women.*" *Essays on Canadian Writing,* 3 (Fall 1975): 32–46.

———. "Some Highly Subversive Activities: A Brief Polemic and A Checklist of Works on Alice Munro." *Studies in Canadian Literature* 6 (1981): 140–50.

Thacker, Robert. "Alice Munro: An Annotated Bibliography." In *The Annotated Bibliography of Canada's Major Authors* Vol. V. Robert Lecker and Jack David, eds., pp. 354–414. Downsview, Ontario: ECW, 1984.

————. "'Clear Jelly': Alice Munro's Narrative Dialects." *Probable Fictions: Alice Munro's Narrative Arts*. Louis K. Mackendrick, ed. Toronto: ECW Press, 1983.

Théoret, France. "Writing in the Feminine: Voicing Consensus, Practising Difference." *A Mazing Space*. Shirley Neuman and Smaro Kamboureli, eds., pp. 331–36. Edmonton: Longspoon and NeWest Press, 1986.

Thompson, Stith. *The Folktale*. New York: Holt, Rinehart and Winston, 1946.

Tobin, Patricia. *Time and the Novel*. Princeton: Princeton University Press, 1978.

Todd, Janet, ed. *Gender and Literary Voice*. New York: Holmes and Meier, 1980.

————, ed. *Men By Women*. New York: Holmes and Meier, 1981.

Twigg, Alan. *For Openers: Conversations With 24 Canadian Writers*. Madeira Park, B.C.: Harbour Pub., 1981.

Vincent, Sybill Korff. "The Mirror and the Cameo: Margaret Atwood's Comic/Gothic Novel, *Lady Oracle*." Juliann E. Fleenor, ed., pp. 153–63. *The Female Gothic*. Montreal: Eden Press, 1983.

Wallace, Bronwen. "Women's Lives: Alice Munro," in *The Human Elements: Critical Essays*. David Helwig, ed., pp. 52–67. Ottawa: Oberon, 1978.

Welty, Eudora. "Place in Fiction." *The Eye of the Story*. New York: Random House, 1977.

Werner, Hans. "Nothing Phoney." *Canadian Art* 4, no. 3 (Fall 1987): 70–77.

Wiseman, Adele. *Chinada: Memoirs of the Gang of Seven*. Dunvegan, Ontario: Quadrant Editions, 1982.

Woolf, Virginia. *Women and Writing*. Michele Barrett, ed. New York: Harcourt Brace Jovanovich, 1979.

| | | INDEX